It's Only Me

It's Only Me

Pieces from a column

JILL TWEEDIE

Illustrated by POSY SIMMONDS

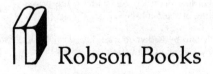 Robson Books

The author and publisher would like to thank the proprietors of the *Guardian* for permission to reproduce material in this book.

FIRST PUBLISHED IN GREAT BRITAIN IN 1980 BY ROBSON BOOKS LTD., 28 POLAND STREET, LONDON W1V 3DB. COPYRIGHT © 1980 JILL TWEEDIE

British Library Cataloguing in Publication Data

Tweedie, Jill
   It's only me.
   1. Women – Social conditions
   I. Title
   300'.8   HQ1154

   ISBN 0-86051-123-5

Printed in Great Britain by Redwood Burn Ltd, Trowbridge, Esher
Phototypesetting by Georgia Origination, Liverpool
Set in Paladium

Contents

For Ilona, to fill in some of the missing years.

Introduction

At one time, I inhabited a fungoid flat overlooking an adventure playground, newly bedecked with climbing frames, ropes, paddling pools, bicycle ramps and rubber tyre swings. And unto this born-again slice of a decaying metropolis came a succession of teenage guerillas who sacrificed all their spare time to the task of hacking down, rooting up, blowing up and burning down every natural and man-made facility. When, finally, this scorched-earth policy had laid waste to the last timber, the last sapling, the penultimate blade of grass, a message appeared overnight upon the one wall left standing. In blood-red letters eight feet high, it claimed responsibility for the mayhem committed. IT'S ONLY ME, it said.

I stared and the earth moved. Could those giant letters, those megalomaniac capitals, hold within their dripping depths an essential key to our times? Some anonymous One out there had felt compelled to brand a huge mark upon each passing eyeball and yet had shied away, at the last squirt of the aerosol can, from putting a name to the ego-trip. What manner of schizophrenia was here revealed? The Jungian Unconscious as opposed to Bourgeois Individualism? The Collective as opposed to the Person? Arsenal as opposed to Spurs? Who knows? Who cares? Nevertheless, I pondered as I leaned upon my rotting sill. The 'me' is all most of us have, all we can expect to know or depend upon or fulfil. 'Me' is the manifold obsession of humankind. And yet, what does this great 'I am' come down to? Only me.

A newspaper columnist, filling a weekly space with opinion and observation, thoughts and emotions, has much the same motive as that anonymous graffitist. You want to tell the world what it can do but who are you, after all, to tell

9

it? You want to communicate what you feel but does anyone else feel the same? A rolling stone at best, you gather some moss because people write and tell you things. You learn that what came fleetingly to your attention has been someone else's lifelong preoccupation. You realize that what you hold to be self-evidently true, others think the wickedest of propagandist lies and what you think a consummate evil, others regard as the lynchpin of civilization as we know it. Sometimes you also find that recording as accurately as possible what you think and feel echoes what others think and feel and have been too busy to crystallize or analyse. Then, bells ring.

Being a woman columnist has its special advantages, not least because you may have got there in the first place because of your sex. Like all women, you have two jobs, one in the outside world and one at home, an uneasy state of affairs. A lot of the time, you hang on by your eyelashes, ceaselessly spinning a hopeful web, like a hyperactive spider, to stretch under life and catch the bits as they fall. Many of us, however successful, have none of the props of successful men: secretaries, company cars, the tacit tolerance of male employers and colleagues for our vagaries, the ability to up roots and go where promotion calls, followed by protective mates, who cope with our children and see to the smooth running of our homes. But this lack, which sometimes seems to sap any hope of efficiency and, occasionally, threatens the job itself, is a plus for a columnist, the very thing that keeps you in close touch with the rest of the world's inhabitants who walk (men and women both) the same tightrope or worse.

Once. I spent eighteen months coping with an alcoholic friend whose husband, understandably, had rejected as past help. I saw then, the unbridgeable gap between what people say is done and what is really done. Under my journalist hat, I interviewed hospitals, doctors, hostels, psychiatrists, policemen, employers and many others officially concerned with the problem of alcoholism. At the end of my research, I could have written a very upbeat piece, full of cheerful and informative details concerning State facilities and the general knowlege, patience and skill of experts in the field.

Under my 'only me', London housewife hat, however, things looked very different. Help, I'm about to be stabbed, I shouted down the phone to the police and oh, they said, unless you have been stabbed, we can't do anything. Please come, I implored a local G.P. and no, he said, I do not want another alcoholic on my list. Make an order for treatment, I begged a local magistrate and no, he said, I shall release the offender with a fine. Keep her in, I besought a local hospital and no, they said, we haven't the room. No employer would give my friend a second chance, no social worker was prepared to acknowledge the problem at all unless the person in question was actually staggering about in front of their noses, singing 'Ah belong to Glasgie'. This example I could multiply a hundred times and thus I know something of the reality beyond the smooth public-relations-to-journalist façade, the quicksands that edge the apparently tended park, the chaos that can so easily engulf anyone who does not permanently reside on the sunny side of the street.

Then, in the late Sixties, a lot of other women who had thought 'it's only me', began to think 'it may be all of us' and the women's movement was born. It was the first cause I did not merely intellectually approve or take on faith, on someone else's behalf, or report as involving others than myself. This time, because I was a woman, the subject as well as the purveyor of the news, I was made acutely aware of journalistic bias in action. The whole concept of straight 'just give me the facts, Ma'am' reportage fell away and revealed, behind its careful smokescreen, ordinary people with peptic ulcers, childhood nightmares, job problems, sexual hang-ups, messy private lives and all the general baggage of emotion and prejudice that every human being lugs around and journalists can so neatly conceal beneath the cool and apparently objective printed word.

I was also forced to realize that many of the greatest thinkers, revolutionaries and democrats of our day or any other—Plato, Milton, Luther, Robespierre, Jesus, Gandhi, Freud, Washington, Lincoln, Moses, Lenin—had managed to overlook the rights and feelings of my half of the human race when they wrote their books, formed their philosophies, fought their battles and changed their worlds. Therefore, all of them, and countless lesser souls, had feet of the thickest Flanders clay, like the academic I had much respected until the moment he extolled Swiss democracy at a 1970 conference, blissfully ignoring the fact that half of that democracy—Swiss women—did not have the vote.

Journalists, on the whole, do little more than reflect their society through a glass and, often, darkly. We are crowd-pleasers, not just because we must please the crowd in order to sell newspapers but because we *are* the crowd, paid upholders of the *status quo*. Where women are concerned, the man in the green eyeshade says 'we did women last week' and 'not paraplegic, menopausal, dyslexic lesbians *again*' and hoots at his wit. Nothing, so far, has persuaded him that the heading 'Women's Page', meant to signify the ghetto interests of the sex that makes woollies and jellies, is sometimes the part of a newspaper most deeply concerned with what really affects people of both sexes and what forms the personal attitudes which underlie national, domestic and foreign policies on everything from industrial relations, crime, economics, education, health and human rights to the awesome issues of nuclear power that may determine the very future of our race.

Many men still feel that 'serious' events must be reported as if they existed in some sealed box, beautifully abstract and thus respectably male, uncontaminated by intimate and inadmissible emotion. Many women, including women journalists, eagerly adopt that masculine view and fight to be free of 'women's subjects', convinced that what happens in Zimbabwe or on the Stock Exchange, in the TUC or at a riot in Southall, is not a woman's subject, has no connection with personal experience and so is, by definition, important. At a conference on management-worker relationships recently, it took four days of fencing before one brave man admitted his resentment at the hard lavatory paper in the workers' loos compared to management soft. Yet that issue (tissue?) summed up more about what was wrong with management-worker relationships than forty foolscap pages of abstract verbiage or statistics.

Living a woman's life, my *ardua* blocked off from the *astra* by such things as lavatory paper (won't the cost force us back to Bronco?...is Spruce Green biodegradable?...should we use newspaper and help the Third World?...why isn't there any when I go?) has taught me that you cannot trust the views of those who supposedly represent us. However apparently concerned, understanding, imaginative or honest they may be, if they need not cope with everyday problems, need not stand at bus-stops or queue at clinics, shop for their food, change nappies, visit their children's schools, wash socks, chat to lonely neighbours, care for elderly parents, have abortions or sit around waiting for kids to reveal their worries, then they only know what is supposed to happen in law courts, in White Papers, in Royal Commissions, in Public Enquiries, in debates, in books, in principle and in theory. They never know what does happen and what does happen is the only thing that counts.

Punch and Duty

'...I don't know which way to turn. We have a row every evening of our lives and each Sunday lunchtime. I'm a sitting duck for his violence and all in front of the child; she's as terrified as I am. The whole street knows about it, they hear me screaming. I've tried calling the police but they only park their cars outside. I've been to the Citizens' Advice Bureau, I've been to doctors, I've been everywhere but no one can make him stop. I haven't the money to leave and nowhere to go. He hits me in the kidneys, he says dreadful things about how I'm mad and all the neighbours know, he spits his food at me. He's stopped hitting me in the face because it showed, now he uses newspapers...'—40-year-old wife and mother

'...Mum and us kids, we spent our lives dreading him coming home. One day, when I was 14, I came home from school and found him hanging in the kitchen. Oh, we were glad.'   —17-year-old girl

PHYSICAL VIOLENCE between husband and wife has a curious ambivalence. More like octovalence, if there were such a word. Once you begin tracing the various strands to the roots you come up against all manner of nasties in the woodshed: inadequacy, fear, alcoholism, ignorance, poverty, and hopelessness, but you also discover warmth, love, laughter, and sex. It is one of the classic 'it all depends' situations where expert outsiders retreat as fast as you can throw questions at them, muttering oblique things about the love-hate relationship and marital interaction. Only one thing is immediately obvious—the vast complexity of each human being and the doubling, trebling and quadrupling of that complexity when joined in holy matrimony with another complex human being.

Traditionally, a great deal of slap-stick humour guffaws its way round the fringes of violence in marriage. Children hoot as Punch beats the daylights out of Judy; the lady behind the door with a rolling pin is as well known a cartoon figure as the appalling Andy Capp; the trick question 'Have you stopped beating your wife?' is always good for a titter and audiences roll in the aisles at the sight of a free-for-all no-holds-barred marital fracas. Presumably if humour is as closely linked with fear as various German analysts would have us believe, we are all dead scared of the matrimonial battleground and release our fears with banana-skin zest whenever we get the chance. A black eye, particularly on a married person, arouses a positive furore of joviality at the office next day—a lot of it with obvious undertones of coyness, almost as if the jokers suspect themselves of asking a far more intimate question than whether the victim bumped into a cupboard door.

And, of course, they are. Any physical contact with another person has its undertow of sexuality and it is not difficult to see that physical violence in marriage has some close ties with a certain rollicking approach to bed—hence the oohs and aahs, hence the hot-blooded ladies who supposedly mourn their husband's dead desires when they no longer beat them, hence the clichéd cameo of the hen-pecked husband whose wife asks huskily, after he's finally thumped her, why he never did that before.

In fact the problem is, initially at least, one of definition. In some marriages one instance of physical violence sends the wife screaming for her lawyer, in others a bi-annual barney is perfectly acceptable and in still others violence is a way of life—one man's violence is another man's how's your father. The standard set depends, in part, on the level of violence the adult experienced in childhood: anyone who has seen a lot of it between parents may well consider a fair portion of bashing or being bashed is quite OK; parents who never touch each other, let alone violently, may raise children consumed with guilt at slamming a door.

I have a totally unscientific theory that the adrenalin released during a fight, whether physical or verbal, creates its own addiction in the body. I know one elderly married couple whose extraordinary behaviour can only be explained thus. But at least these two get a kick, however distorted, out of their battles. In too many cases (the problem is generally admitted to be widespread), such battles are neither funny, sexy, nor in any way life-enhancing. There are women all over this country who live in constant terror of physical assault by brutal husbands, unable to defend themselves through weakness, fear, poverty, children, and the inability to earn any sort of a living for themselves.

Last week a man who had already 'taken a knife to frighten his wife', finally murdered her and killed himself. She had sought help from various officials 'but communications were too slow' and what she must have seen as the inevitable happened. Police, in the words of Scotland Yard, 'are always dealing with domestic disputes, especially in the built-up working-class areas' and although criminal statistics make no distinction between husband/wife and other assault charges brought during the year, a wife cannot get compensation from the Criminal Injuries Board even though she may have left the matrimonial home immediately after the assault. And though the number of divorce petitions filed in 1969 was double that of 1961, cruelty charges had nearly trebled and that does not include other charges in which cruelty was a factor. Of course cruelty can include other acts besides physical violence—anything from taking a motorbike apart on a wife's best carpet to constant verbal abuse, but it seems curious that the cruelty most easily pinned down—via black eyes, bruises, cuts—is no more accessible to the law than the more subtle variations. Scotland Yard itself seems dubious as to the value of calling the police in on a marital heave-ho. 'It depends on the situation,' they say guardedly and, 'It never hurts to seek advice.'

Indeed most people—police, marriage guidance counsellors, probation officers, agony columnists—who come in frequent contact with the problem insist on this conventional guarded approach. The Marriage Guidance Council cite a typical case: 'A woman comes in and complains about severe physical violence. She's very upset indeed and wants to go to court. When her case is due to be heard, she doesn't turn up. Yet later she comes and complains of violence again.'

They explain marital violence in largely psychiatric terms. They talk about the complications behind a violent pattern—the violent partner may be as terrified of his own violence as is his victim, he may need help as badly, and the behaviour of his wife may be subconsciously tailored to draw out his violence, possibly by showing extreme fear herself.

'The middle-class person is brought up to feel everything must be smooth on the surface and, if it is, everything's OK. But this is a false position—everything *isn't* OK. The fact is, you can love and hate the guts of the same person almost at the same time. There is aggression in sexuality anyway, it is present in most close marital relationships. Real feeling spills over into anger, though it may be expressed in verbal rather than physical violence. Besides, the warring couple are not necessarily unhappy and children brought up in a ding-dong atmosphere can be very secure, if the love and care are still there. They learn that love can continue even though hate takes over at times.'

Mrs Peggy Makins, the Evelyn Home letter lady of *Woman* magazine, gets a good deal of correspondence on the subject of violence every week and says her post reflects a general problem.

'These women really don't know what to do. They're desperately unhappy, very frightened, but they're dependent on the man for the support of their children and themselves. I don't think they're thinking much beyond a separation order but they worry, even so, about not getting their separation money. I have the greatest respect for the Marriage Guidance people but they can't actually do very much about a thoroughly violent husband. It's difficult for me to judge how much this is a class problem since I work entirely from letters—all I can say is that it is not confined exclusively to the manual working household. I would think many a respectable bowler-hatted man thumps his wife.'

If in Mrs Makins's opinion, the account of violence in a particular letter seems excessive and dangerous to health, she begs the woman to seek authoritative help. 'Children should not be subjected to this kind of thing, even if it's going to mean them going into care for a while. Sometimes I have a hope that removal itself will give a man pause. I recommend that the woman contact a welfare or probation officer. Social workers are often just the job, they reinforce the woman's confidence and, very bravely, beard the husband and try to bring him to his senses. These men are pretty nasty and their wives live in a kind of terror.' Another expert blames drink. 'The great majority of our cases are really a result of drink and in some the wife is as bad as her husband. But my heart goes out to the woman in her forties, lumbered with five or six children, terrorized by a husband she cannot leave and often worn down to a state of very frail physical health.'

In intractible cases the probation officer may advise a separation order but, even there, difficulties arise. 'We have to point out to the woman that there's no use getting such an order if the parties are going to remain together in the household. There are really only two ways to provide for physical separation. One is that the grieved party, usually the wife, takes steps before the hearing of the case to remove herself from the home. Many women immediately say this is impossible—they have nowhere to go. In extreme cases we have been known to suggest that they bundle the kids into a taxi and deposit themselves all together at the door of the welfare department. The second possibility is that the wife remains at home until the hearing and, if the cruelty order is made, leaves it to the local authority to take steps to evict the husband. The snag is that only a few local authorities will do this. Some take the view that they have no legal right to evict a husband even if the wife does have a separation order.'

Though all the experts disagree, I cannot help feeling that something more could be done to help such women. I also cannot help a suspicion that more is not done because somewhere, deep in the unconscious, men accept what they feel is a natural law—the possibility of violence done to the female by the male—and so there is a vacuum where the law ought to be.

The Marriage Guidance Association does not accept this view. They say any real intervention does more harm than good. They intimate that the problem is too complicated for much action by outsiders. The probation officers, hard-working, dedicated and deeply sympathetic as many of them are, still maintain that neutrality is essential, some violence must be accepted in the 'cultural pattern', an Englishman's home is his castle and couples need to work out their relationships.

There is no doubt that only fools rush in to some kinds of matrimonial disputes and no one could reject the experts' reservations in these cases. But to my mind none of them makes anything like enough distinction between sporadic upsets and the kind of violence that wrecks lives. What validity has any balanced argument when a desperate woman and disturbed children, worn to frazzles after years of recurring violence, are weighed in the scales against the husband and father who causes their distress, no matter how understandable his own problems? In these cases it is not enough to talk about the husband's stress; it is not enough to point out that counselling is available and if a woman doesn't make use of it she doesn't, subconsciously, want it—this, given some circumstances, is arrant nonsense. Nor is it enough to talk about cultural patterns. Violence outside the home is well within some people's cultural patterns (so, for that matter, are drugs) but our society does not tolerate this and police frequently break into Englishmen's castles to arrest men who have assaulted strangers. In holding this opinion I have been told I have middle-class values and that I must try to accept that others do not find marital violence so abhorrent—but if this were true as a principle why don't they ask me to tolerate violence in the streets?

Surely it is time society took over the question of excessive marital violence and announced that this form will not be tolerated either. At the moment, many women are driven to distraction, knowing that wherever they go they will, on the whole, meet with careful attitudes of neutrality, from officialdom right down to the neighbours on their street. Yet why should officials consider it so vital to be neutral? Certainly, the wife may have some hand in inciting the violence of her husband. Certainly some women are ambivalent about it, complaining and retracting that complaint with irritating frequency. But the hard fact remains that it is women, by a vast majority, who get bashed and their children who are terrorized—and everyone admits that parental violence is one of the main causes of juvenile delinquency. Both husbands and wives have problems, but why should only husbands have such a free hand with violent expression of these problems? Why the necessity for neutrality when, though both partners are neurotic and both use verbal abuse, only one uses physical abuse?

The law already puts man and wife asunder for less grievous faults than bodily assault. I see no reason why holy matrimony should continue to provide such a widespread and thoroughly convenient bolt-hole for violent men.

22 February 1971

The War of Words

THE WORD 'POLEMIC' comes from the Greek for 'war' (a Webster is a lovely thing, God wot) and once upon a time it meant aggressive controversy, disputatious discussion. Nowadays a polemic is, on the whole, a much more inward thing; though in theory still controversial and disputatious, in practice it is not because it rarely reaches any audience likely to find it so—it is, for the most part, a rousing sermon to the long-converted. As a commentator said recently about Bernadette Devlin, now lecturing across the United States, 'She has the true gift of polemicist in that she articulates views that her listeners believe they have long held but never quite known how to express.'

Polemics are an integral part of any minority's fight for a place in the sun, since one of the vital ingredients of success is to instil into the minority psyche a confidence in the rightness of its cause, not as easy as it sounds because victims tend to think they deserve their fate. And oppression postulates two other factors: the oppressed are less well educated than their oppressors (at least by the oppressors' definition) and they are also kept in very close contact, either as the oppressors' labour force or as personal servants.

The first factor, lack of education, involves an inability to express emotion in terms of reason and fact, partly because the emotion (the sense of injustice) is too strong to be acceptably compressed and partly because there are very few shared facts. Classical flat geometry is a logically perfect system if you accept the basic postulates; if you don't, the whole system crashes to the ground—what is a fact to the oppressor is nothing of the sort to the oppressed.

And then, of course, at some stage in the history of any liberation movement, comes the realization that to express

21

emotion in terms of reason means using the oppressors' language, their channels of expression and values—whether that be the vote, equal pay or apartheid—and this carries with it the hazards of absorption into the oppressive system. People in power know this: they exhort their victims to be reasonable, to set up a dialogue: a foolproof challenge because the victim, if he accepts, either comes over as an inarticulate hothead or, if he does put his case in a reasonable manner, enters the spider's parlour. After all, if you admit to being reasonable you are forced to take into account other points of view and then, paralysis sets in and any action becomes, from the oppressors' point of view, comfortably remote once again.

The second point, the question of empathy with the oppressor, is an interesting phenomenon. Exactly because of the close contact the oppressed have with their master, the two often meet on purely human terms. Add to that the fact that most victims, trapped themselves, are very aware of the oppressors' self-constructed trap—women liberationists perceive the masculinity trap, homosexuals see the heterosexual trap, blacks highlight white hang-ups—and the pathos of the oppressors' position becomes another block to action. Unfortunately, it does not often work the other way round; power is a most effective blindfold.

Another of the pitfalls in roads to freedom: by the time a member of an oppressed group is in a position (by dint of talent, luck or self-education) to express injustice in terms of reason, he is already in an environment where the opposition is more subtle and he himself suffers less injustice. At this point the movement's grass roots usually refer to him as having sold out and they are usually right.

One solution to this slow de-fusing process is to refuse the path of reason and concentrate upon emotion and its natural medium—polemics. Emotion, compared to reason, is illogical and incommunicable except by action and this kind of action cannot be diluted by the oppressor because it is innocent of 'the other viewpoint'; it bypasses the oppressor's channels and so need not progress at the speed set by the oppressor, who has a vested interest in a snail-like pace. Nor can emotion be sidetracked with anything like the ease of reason, though there are sad examples of emotional side-tracking, particularly in America. The whole destructive 'kill the pigs' movement must be a gladsome thing for the Establishment—better any day that protesters let off steam at the police (and, thereby conveniently antagonize the silent majority) than at precious Them, huddled safely behind their gubernatorial or presidential desks.

So polemics have their place, fighting words designed to crystallize and reinforce feelings of injustice, tailored to by-pass reason and initiate action. And polemics, today, show a distinct cliquishness—their messages are instantly understandable to the victim and anathema to the oppressor. They tend to offer few clues to comprehending a cause that is not yours by inheritance, they smoke with contempt of the outsider, they bang doors in his face. And because polemics do not depend on reason, their conclusions are difficult to disprove; they do not attempt to communicate in the sense of bridging gaps and so the outsider is left without a weapon except, very often, abrupt dismissal of the polemicist on the grounds of insanity.

Thirty-one-year-old Valerie Solanas shot Andy Warhol in New York in 1968 and was sentenced to three years' imprisonment. During that sentence she was removed to a mental hospital where she is to this day. The information about her illness is vague—the guess is a form of schizophrenia. Last week her violently anti-male credo *Scum Manifesto* was published by Olympia Press—it has been out since 1968 in the US but Miss Solanas sold it on the streets of New York for a year before that and its message has been spread by word of mouth ever since: 'Presentation of the rationale and program of action of SCUM (Society for Cutting up Men), which will eliminate—through sabotage—all aspects of society not relevant to women (everything), bring about a complete female take-over, eliminate the male sex and begin to create a swinging, groovy, out-of-sight female world.' No questions, please.

The manifesto is a quintessential form of polemics—reason does not soften one single word, emotion is at white heat throughout. Aggressive, outrageous, frightening, funny, preposterous; it is all these things and more and anyone who drops it like a hot brick, shouting 'The girl is mad!' has reason on his side. Particularly when you consider that the society in which Miss Solanas lives has given its seal to just such a diagnosis.

Nevertheless, it is worth remembering that madness as such does not invalidate the views of the mad: if it did our world would be the poorer for a great deal of literature, philosophy, painting and poetry. Miss Solanas lives permanently within what, for you and me, may be an occasional flash of fury as we notice some particularly blatant or cruel discrimination against women, and so she has value as all have value who live at a pitch of emotion above the norm. It is also worth remembering that her fury (or derangement, if you prefer) is the product of a masculine society, she is a child of a system constructed by men for men—'a highly artificial society enabling him to appropriate the appearance of worth through money, prestige, "high" social class, degrees, professional position and knowledge and by pushing down professionally, economically, socially and educationally.'

Within Miss Solanas's polemic, all men and a goodly number of women are outsiders, pushed out willy-nilly by her extremism and contempt for their humanity (she bypasses the 'other point of view' with a vengeance). Oddly enough, this month brings another book, to be published by Cassell, which is also a polemic, though this time more subtle and on the side of the silent majority (aren't the silent majority getting very noisy?). And this time I still feel the faint bruising as that door slams in my face for a change. Miss Elizabeth Manners is headmistress of Felixstowe College for Girls and her book *The Vulnerable Generation* is a plea to an older generation to stand firm in their ideals against what she regards as a sex-ridden trash-orientated society out to corrupt and exploit teenagers. Thus far, well and good.

But the polemicism, the door banging, starts with the preface and continues throughout the book—Miss Manners makes it clear that anyone so intransigent as to criticize any opinion of hers stands condemned as a trendy who reaches 'for the vitriol at the very mention of the standards which I should like to see upheld and for whom *decent* is a pejorative word'. She also, and cunningly, points out 'I am not a professional writer, still less am I a professional psychologist, sociologist or educationist. I do not claim to be expert in anything at all...' By doing this she invokes the 'too clever by half' syndrome in her non-expert readers.

And the door continues to bang shut after every sweeping generalization—'I am supremely uninterested in their opinions...I am resigned to being ridiculed...I shall almost certainly be attacked by the progressives for saying this and no doubt they will produce facts and figures to prove me wrong...I do not care a button.' Indeed to winkle Miss Manners out on any point, however debatable, is like trying to extract a limpet from its shell—every time the mollusc peeps out it hisses the equivalent of yah boo, sucks and snaps shut again, nipping your fingers painfully.

Miss Manners: Why *should* those of us who happen to think that there is still room in the world for truth, gentleness and consideration, for responsibility, for service and, above all, for love, be treated as simple-minded fools, living in a romantic dream?

Me: Oh but, Miss Manners, honestly I don't...

Miss Manners: These writers and critics, these manipulators of the mass media, try to justify their preoccupation with the sexy and sordid by saying that this is 'real life'...

Me: No, no, you've got me wrong, I never meant...Bang. Ouch.

Miss Manners, methinks thou dost protest too much—but then, of course, that is what polemics are about. Infernal rubbish or holy truth, depending on which way the door bangs.

All demonstrations are fleshed-out polemics, happenings that have more to do with reinforcing solidarity within the ranks than luring spectators from pavement or box—conversions will come later, as fall-out comes.

And so it was with the Women's Lib demo on Saturday. I went, unreasoningly fearful that me and my friend Ivy would be alone stomping down Regent Street, running the sneering gauntlet of Saturday shoppers. But there they were at Hyde Park Corner, all the lovely sisters, giggling and shivering and bawdy and prim and I turned and turned again, gloating at the numbers before and behind, my motley frost-defying sex.

Because sex is all we really had in common. Odd to think, in the middle of Oxford Circus, that inside our overcoats, under our mufflers, coiled within our sweaters and vests is the same intricate reproductive system—fallopian tubes, uteri, vaginas and breasts—and that that is why we're here, on 6 March 1971, in the snow. When, since the beginning of time, have men ever marched because they shared a particular sexual apparatus? Ludicrous, shameful, ridiculous, perish the thought.

Goodness knows our outsides were various enough. Long and short and thin and fat, quiet middle-aged ladies in careful make-up, bare-faced girls with voices loud as crows, maoists, liberals, socialists, lesbians, students, professionals, manual workers, spinsters, wives, widows, mothers. One, two, three, four, we want a bloody damn sight more. Biology isn't destiny. Equal pay *now*. Bed or wed, are you free to choose? I'm not just a delectable screwing machine. Capitalism breeds sexploitation. *Freedom*. There were even women so politically committed that the very sight of Downing Street submerged '24-hour Nurseries' with 'Tories Out' and 'Kill the Bill'.

And when we arrived at Trafalgar Square the demo arranged itself into a symbol so apt as to seem planned. One girl at the mike, four girl photographers and a solid phalanx of great, grey, brawny men blocking the view of the women. Get out, shrieked the women, get away, get back and the men, genuinely startled, got back. Communicators themselves, they communicated the women's case—men, men, men, grouped at the foot of a soaring phallus with Nelson, a man, at the top.

'Look at you all,' said a girl to a male photographer. 'If that doesn't tell you something about equal job opportunities, I don't know what will.'

The photographer looked as superior as a man can in a howling blizzard. 'I'd like to see *you* going into a shower room full of naked men after a Cup Final,' he said. 'I'd like to see *you* going into a room full of naked models,' she said. 'Try and stop me,' he said. 'Try and stop *me*,' she said.

In the crowd a tiny 'Gay is Good' placard vied gamely with a huge Women's Lib banner. 'Here, it's *our* demonstration,' said Women's Lib testily. 'It's against oppression, isn't it?' snapped Gay Lib. 'I was chucked out of my job last week because I'm gay. We're more oppressed than what you are, any day.' Women's Lib raised her eyebrows in ladylike fashion and turned back to the platform.

A middle-aged woman in fur has been lured from a bus stop to join the march. 'I'm a graphic designer and what do I read in a trade magazine last week? Some man complaining about how difficult it is to get a job at 45. Huh, I've had difficulties getting jobs all my life—the moment they hear your voice on the telephone they don't want to know.'

Another woman, skin flushed with Panstik, had a hand-scrawled notice pinned to the front of her tweed coat. 'I've come all the way from Sheffield, I can't afford the fare but I must do something for the single woman. We don't get paid nearly as much as men but still we've got to find rooms, pay the electricity, feed ourselves. It's not fair, it's just not fair.' Behind the pebble lenses, her huge eyes watered.

Then the speeches were over, vast congratulatory relief filled the square. The demonstration had happened (miracle) and it had happened well (greater miracle). Girls stood in groups, stamping and chatting.

'There was only one thing. The weather. The trade unions had such a marvellous day and we had to go and get *this*.'

'Well, love, what did you expect? God is a man.'

8 March 1971

Two into One Won't Go

'SHOW ME YOUR FRIENDS and I'll show you who you are,' goes the saying, but if you happen to be married, amendment is immediately necessary: I'll show you who you half-heartedly are, who you sometimes are, who you can just about bear to be.

Friendships *à deux* are, to me, outward signs of the dilution, the homogenization of the personality that seems a sad prerequisite of every happy marriage—the original saying holds true only when applied to one person choosing his own friends one by one, a process in which all of us define ourselves and the outer perimeters of our characters from that moment when, at 7 or 8 years old, we turn our attention from our parents to Johnny next door.

And then we fall in love and marry. Even Romeo and Juliet, had they staggered past the courting stage, would presumably have felt a need for the occasional friend in their glass-house world. But when husband or wife produces the best friend from school or university, the truth stabs home for the first time: one-and-one works but what about one-and-two, or, God help us, two-and-two? The situation is fraught with variables and only one thing is sure; in friendship the constant presence of a third party subtly alters the original relationship, watering it down in the thin blue liquid of compromise. Human friendship may, perhaps, be compared to a beam of light. If that beam focuses only on one person the light is strong and pure. If it has later to encompass two or more it must widen and, of necessity, become weaker. Heaven knows, it is rare and precious enough that one person, liking another, has that liking reciprocated. How much more rare that two people should like two other people exactly as much: husband X warming to husband and wife Y, wife X deeply fond of wife and husband Y, wife Y snug as a bug with husband and wife X, husband Y full of bonhomie with husband and wife X. Such a level of perfection is unlikely and so, being the gregarious creatures we are, we are forced to shift our chairs back, discuss the goings-on of the local vicar rather than the concept of religion, the relative merits of Volvos and Fords rather than the ethics of car-owning.

All of which, on first observation, might seem anything from perfectly harmless to positively worthy; better an evening passed in company, without acrimony because no controversial subject is broached, than an evening with two people locked in earnest discussion, the third in a coma of boredom and the fourth infuriated into an incipient rash. And yet this dilution of conversation and of atmosphere demands the dilution of the various personalities involved. We are impelled to choose our friends from our own negative virtues for their negative virtues—'let's have Gordon, neither of us mind him' rather than 'how about Rose, I think she's great even if you can't stand her'. Settle for the safe, invite the uncontroversial, wine and dine the generalizers, go on holidays with the couple so colourless you hardly know they're there.

I do not believe that you can really know any other human being except on a one-to-one basis. Only the breaking of that barrier of embarrassment that falls between any two people isolated together constitutes the defining of identity for those two people. (You can only define your own identity by using others as walls: there you are so, therefore, here am I.) But it is just this kind of direct communication with anyone but the husband/wife that marriage tends to rule out. It is OK to define yourself through your partner but woe betide anything rather more extravagant, however asexual.

So these days I have become a fierce and embattled advocate of a comparatively unsociable philosophy: the formation and retention of friends to the exclusion of their various spouses (spice?) if that liking is not mutual, even if in so doing that tacit assumption of marriage is questioned: whatever we do, wherever we go, we do and go together. This implies a certain ruthlessness in social life. Suppose I meet a woman whom I find extremely interesting and wish to see more of her. Two days later I invite her and her husband (as yet an unknown quantity) to dinner. She becomes even more interesting but he talks almost exclusively about apple tree pruning, fascinating if you like apple tree pruning, asphyxiating if you don't. Is there any real reason why I should not, in future, ask her to come to dinner alone? And why should she be forced by my request (as inevitably she will) into some complicated heart-searching about loyalty to her husband? Surely one of the proofs of his real identity as a person is exactly that some people will not warm to him or his interests.

After all, who wants to leave (or admit that their spouses leave) so faint an impression on others that we can be present anywhere almost without being noticed, like a canary twittering aimlessly in a cage? And any married person who, in my thoroughly biased and dogmatic opinion, refuses to accept invitations from new friends on the grounds of presumed insult to the left-out mate is voicing, not loyalty, but 'love me, love my dog'. *Dog?*

29 March 1971

Party Jesus

LAST WEEK, A YOUNG MAN came up to me at a gathering and began to talk. He had a long and gentle face framed by long, straight, thin, blond hair and he informed me that his name was Jesus Christ.

I was surprised, mainly I suppose because he looked so very much like Sunday-school posters of Himself, feeding the birds, patting the lambs or simply sitting covered with children like an apple tree in blossom. 'You may be taken aback to hear me say this,' he said understandingly. 'Not at all,' I assured him politely. 'Well, some are, some aren't,' he said 'The fact is that I am Jesus in a late incarnation.' I said yes, I had not imagined he was Jesus in his first incarnation, on account of his youthful appearance.

Finding that I was, on the whole, unrocked by his revelations, he began to tell me of his wanderings, both Biblical and twentieth century. I was most interested and there was no doubt at all that his knowledge of Jesus's original peregrinations was accurate enough to be worthy of far more conventional ecclesiastics. He peppered his accounts with a lot of such human details as how the side on one of his sandals split during the 40 days and 40 nights in the wilderness, giving him such extremely painful blisters that he hardly heard the Devil offering him power over the world. 'Of such small mercies is the Kingdom of Heaven made,' he said gratefully.

Ater an hour of what one might call an outline of his references, Jesus launched into his real purpose in talking to me—that his mission, as always, was to persuade such flotsam as fell across his path to go forth and love their fellow men, refuse hate, forswear war and at all times suppress the wicked ego.

Later, he took some small home-made biscuits out of his

jeans pocket, gave them to me as a priest gives the communion wafer and took his leave, smiling in the sweetest manner and gracefully blessing my person. There seems to me no particular point in investigating his claims, one way or another. Certainly, if Jesus did make a comeback in the flesh I see no reason to suppose his approach would differ greatly from that of my fair-haired friend, nor would I expect him to exhort me on different grounds. I was particularly taken with his words on suppressing the ego—though I freely admit I am no theologian, as a mere black sheep in the flock I interpret the negative approach to the ego as very purely Christian.

And the paradox is evident. Those with little or no ego (or identity, if you wish) are likely, almost by definition, to end thinking of themselves not as Joe Smith but as Napoleon, Florence Nightingale, St Teresa of the Flowers or, of course, Jesus—depending to some extent on sex. Thus they become people labelled in our society as nuts, loonies, round-the-twisters; to be pitied if obviously harmless, to be locked away if possibly threatening. Yet their madness arises, at least in part, from the shrunken ego considered so desirable by Christians.

If my party Jesus ended on a psychiatrist's couch, presumably that psychiatrist would do what he could to build up the 'damaged' ego, on the current theory that we can only love others if we love ourselves. A theory straight from the Bible, of course, but diluted constantly, it seems to me, from childhood on in the name of Christianity.

What quantity of ego is too much ego, what too little? My party friend had lost his ego, his sense of identity, entirely. Is he mad or is he Jesus?

29 March 1971

Want Ads

PEOPLE WHO NEED PEOPLE, warbles Barbra Streisand, are the luckiest people in the world. She warbles, if I may say so, with her semantics on the blink. It is not lucky to need people if you live by yourself in a Manxian lighthouse, a cottage on Egg or even a bed-sit in Balham—to be lucky you need people *there*, locked in your hungry arms or, at the very least, sitting across from you saying what terrible weather we're having for June. Need, alone, does not produce people, especially if you've just arrived home after 30 years in rubber or you're a widow with small children or you're plain and miserably shy and all the men in the office are queueing up for gold watches.

The proof of this pudding is in a mass of magazines, usually in the columns marked personal. There they all are, the people who need people, lines and lines of tiny cries, inch after inch of impacted curriculum vitae, each one a gently bleeding lonely heart looking for same. But these bleeding hearts are thoroughly efficient, once roused. They carefully place their ads where they're most likely to find—not the one and only Mr/Mrs/Miss Right but the broadest spectrum possible—and by far the most popular publications are those brisk, no-nonsense weeklies devoted entirely to advertising, whether it be caravans, pianos or people. Indeed, at times it is difficult to distinguish between the ads for caravans, pianos and people: the approach tends to be equally practical, wide-ranging and oddly impersonal.

Why, one asks oneself, has Box 304 been driven into print when all she wants of life is 'a gentleman, non-smoker'? Are we to suppose that Count Dracula would do, provided he gave up his Balkan Sobranies? Is she honestly trying to tell us that every live male on her present horizon does nothing but flick ash all over her twin-set and pearls? Can this marriage work, based solely on a mutual repugnance for fags? And Box 304 merely echoes an all-over theme—few advertisers demand anything of their future mates that a particularly bright dog could not provide, given that he was 'of genuine and loyal character, uncomplicated, healthy, with clean habits and no ties' and not snappy and irritable like some terriers I know.

Most advertisers seem equally at a loss for any positive assets of their own to offer the opposite sex. Does 'Young Lady (London N.)' have no traits more riveting than the fact that she is generally on the telephone' and 'not very keen on dancing'? Can 'Divorcee, Hampshire' expect Cupid's dart because she uses 'all modern aids to beauty'? Will men flock to 'Typist, 32' because she is 'clean'? God knows, it isn't easy to stand out from the crowd but you'd think a girl could come up with more to her credit than 32 years of dedicated washing. Better, perhaps, not even to try, like 'Bachelor, 40s, nothing much to offer' or 'Businessman, not attractive, balding'. At least they sound quite endearingly hopeless.

When it comes to height, however, few concessions are made. Understandable, perhaps, that 'Gentleman, 5ft' feels impelled to state his case—it would be undermining for him, to say the least, waiting there under the clock at Victoria for someone like me, swaying towards him with all 5ft 10ins like the Leaning Tower of Pisa. But is it essential to 'Officer, 6ft' that his one true love be 5ft 6ins? Why should I be so cruelly excluded from his 'good manners, own hair, slim build'? Does he realise what untapped passions he may bypass, applying such rigid measurements?

But then, passion is very low on the lists of needs and wants, the permissive society has tainted no one here. In five closely-packed pages of ads in one newspaper only half a dozen touch on sex in any way other than that enigmatic adjective 'broadminded'. One 'Lady, and Oriental' goes so far as to say she is 'passionate looking' but is that far enough? *I only ever said I looked passionate, Mr B, so kindly take your hands off my cheong sam.* Ref. X.P.X. describes herself as 'very generous in love', the naughty thing; Box 1102 hints at fireworks with her 'Latin temperament'; a person of 'Cont'l birth' mentions that her curves are in the right places and 'Waitress, Penge' makes so bold as to say she has 'good figure, with a good bust and excellent limbs'—enough to send any gentleman mad with lust. In fact the gentlemen, God bless 'em, are more modest and restrained: not a single one is cad enough to stir the female blood with anything more potent than 'manly'.

Obviously they are all sensible enough to realize that, in a happy marriage, a bit of the other is as nothing compared to a bit in the bank. Advertisements, on the whole, sound more like income tax returns than attempts to lure kindred souls. The men hasten to mention that they are 'owner-drivers, own freehold home a minute from the sea, earn well over £2,000 and have no problem with mortgage'. Some are not above flashing their wealth about—a property developer (33) talks at length of his 'very large income, own house and another in Spain', which luxury he hopes to share with interested parties. I am driven to suspect him of being 4ft., of unclean habits, with endemic halitosis and untoward behaviour at full moon—how otherwise to account for the dearth of ladies in his life?

Even the ladies seem, quite frequently, to earn 'more than £3,000 p.a.'; a goodly sum for anyone with no apparent talents other than 'a modern outlook'. A few positively beg for trouble. One widow mentions a capital of £10,000 and own house—has she given up all hope of being loved for herself alone? And is she prepared to share Mrs Durand Deacon's fate, flushed down the plughole by a fortune-hunter with nothing to mark her passing but some false fingernails and an empty Box No.?

And then, of course, there are 'shared interests'. the best foundation (after money) for any partnership. Here it becomes immediately evident that Britain's theatre managers, with their whining complaints about empty houses, are misleading the public, since every single advertiser is obsessively concerned with 'going to the theatre'. Shaftesbury Avenue must be black with them, arm in arm, off to their favourite pastime; trains from Norfolk, nr. Sidcup, Essex sub. and Middx must be crowded with frenzied playgoers. Come to think of it, this phenomenal interest

35

doubtless accounts for such long-running plays as *The Mousetrap*. Night after night it is obviously packed with slim built, bespectacled, frly tall owner/drivers escorting ladies (41), prev. married, no obj. glasses, clapping like mad and giving each other speaking looks or sidelong glances, depending on whether they are 'broadminded' or 'very refined'.

Concert-going is another marked obsession and whole orchestras are waiting to be formed from among the mate-hunters 'versed in musical instruments' and 'talented upon the piano'. The Arts are another popular, though vague, interest, tailing off into more mundane pleasures like 'the occasional drink and meal out with Cont'l cuisine' and something referred to, even more vaguely, as 'motoring about'—the next time you get stuck behind one such on a motorway do try to be a little more restrained with the hooter, it could spoil a blossoming friendship. A high proportion mention 'interest in animals and outdoor' (do they mean big game in Kenya or Flopsy, their tame white bunny in the backyard?) and a few men say they speak several languages, which adds a racy *je ne sais quoi*. Only a small minority mention religion: C of Es bracket it with Gram. ed.: RCs say, carefully 'not practising' (nice to have a lie-in on Sundays, after all); Jews tend to say 'of the same faith' and one 'Jewish Gentleman' manages to combine two general points by saying he wishes to meet 'woman of any religion over 5ft 2in'. Some leave things fairly open—'must be A Believer' and one or two demand the opposite: 'must not be a churchgoer of any kind'. *No, Miss A (Lancs) and what's more, no praying beside the bed either if you please.* Tall Indians and Cultured West Africans maintain a discreet silence upon the subject and only one man in several hundreds mentions political beliefs, but he goes overboard, throwing aside 'looks, status, nationality' with reckless abandon in favour of any woman, 18-35, 'with very strong Communist views' and, naturally enough, mentions nothing as bourgeois as marriage.

My heart goes out to him, doomed as he is to failure here in the heartland of Britain, light years away from the dreaded Women's Lib. These female advertisers are *real* women—'feminine type, excellent cook, home-loving, very domesticated, no obj. one child'. Some admit shamefacedly to careers they will drop like hot cakes, given the first faint strains of the Wedding March and even the bolder spirits, 'strong personality, independent' stress their horror of wearing the trousers. 'I hold down a well paid exacting job but in spite of this I have managed to retain my femininity.' Well played, Gladys.

A majority have already been through the marriage mill and lived to tell the tale: 'husband so wrapped up in his work that he failed to appreciate what a charming and attractive wife he had and by the time he woke up, it was too late'; 'feel the need for a good man's company since an unhappy marriage to a man well below my standards'. Some women have seen better days but hope still springs eternal. 'I married money and my husband's wealth was bottomless' (but he takes to drink and she splits). 'I married against my parents' wishes and disaster overtook my marriage' (my heart belongs to Daddy). 'My husband pursued a succession of women' or, even worse, 'my husband walked off with never a word.' Men, too, have suffered, poor dears: 'I had the unfortunate experience of only meeting affair seekers and this is not what I want.' Goodness no, I should hope not. I'll bet he met up with Waitress, Penge, flaunting her good bust and wrapping her excellent limbs about his person, the trollop. Still, they all rally bravely enough, get themselves kitted up in 'smart clothes' and face the marital fray again as 'divorcee, ip' (everyone here is an Innocent Party—how will they manage with the new divorce law and its refusal to apportion blame?).

The *New Statesmen* personal ads, on the other hand, follow a beautifully logical order of human endeavour. Starting from the top and working down we find suggestions for joining clubs, that panacea for all lonely people. 'Thoughtful Socialists belong to the Fabian Society'; 'Fraternal Group offers new thinking, new contacts, helpfulness'; 'Encounter Group for the enterprising but responsible'. Should these prove too overwhelming, we proceed to individual sessions with s.a.e. Box 867, we are ready to come out into the open and demand our N.S. birthright—'intelligent left-wing man'; 'Graduate, arts-orientated' and 'woman with concern for education'. Should response be thin on the ground, the next batch of ads for Marriage Bureaux ('educated people specially catered for') is obviously guaranteed to succeed, since the next line of offers for the happy couple is 'Durex, latest Continental, Japanese and American brands'. And the last in the column of ads tell a terse tale of tragedy or success, depending on the way you look at it. 'Pregnancy Testing, Fee £3.'

Finally, for any leprous, acne'd and still unattached sex fiend who has followed the story so far, we come to the bottom of the barrel in the search for a mate—the dissolute Oz, the wanton IT, the navy-blue Ink, the key-hole Private Eye. Here, ads offer neither decency, health, cleanliness, loyalty nor any other recognizable human virtue, including matrimony. Couples of many sexes bump together like moths in the scorching flame of unnatural desires ('25-year-old sadomasochistic social worker wants to meet an interesting sort of woman for a mutually painful relationship'): shack up briefly in appalling pads ('no strings attached') and celebrate their two-week anniversary (elastic bands) by flagellating off into the Moroccan sunset in a ghastly sort of van.

It takes all sorts, the tender trap.

21 June 1971

Lists Lists

MAKING LISTS is almost as essential to my life as breathing; in fact, I sometimes wonder how I manage, day after day, actually to breathe without reference to a list starting 'breathe'. Whenever I feel faintly distraught, whenever those bands tighten round my skull like the poor lady in the ad., I do not take tranquillizers or long walks or have a nice lie down. I merely sit and make a list and as the items go down, one under the other, in that heart-warming, productivity-enhancing way items have, the tension in my muscles begins to evaporate and a holy peace sets in. All those tiny thoughts, darting in and out of my grey matter like minnows in a coral reef, get emptied out on to paper and once again my head is a lovely void, echoingly empty as a Chinese gong. To such as I, the kind of brain that can contain even one hour's minutiae without exploding is for ever a foreign object.

Lists have another vital purpose: they are the only evidence that contradicts the near overwhelming impression that time passes in a turmoil of activity, signifying nothing. When I arrive home hung, drawn and quartered by eight hours of running around in circles, I can take out my ballpoint pen (red, for ticks), tick off that morning's list of Things to Do and a forward movement, however slight, is suddenly made manifest. On really bad days I am forced to reverse this procedure by first doing things, then writing down what they are and then ticking them. This method has much to recommend it because, by its very nature, nothing can be left depressingly unticked. It also eliminates that nasty habit lists have of proliferating like hydra heads as you hack your way through: 'Monday. Phone doctor' (tick). 'Collect prescription doctor, make appointment oculist' (tick). 'Prescription to chemist, oculist's phone out of order, chemist

39

closed, transfer all items Tuesday' (tick tick tick). I have known lists that start with one item on Monday and pyramid out by Friday to 18 items all concerning the first, like Asian flu in print.

Occasionally lists take on a life of their own and become a form of action in themselves. Overcome at twice-yearly intervals by the nagging fear that I am always out eating other people's food and drinking other people's drink I put aside an entire evening to compose a list of guests for a future rave-up. Under my efficient pen the list swells quickly from 20 to 80 names, all neatly divided into sexes and each one argued and fought over in a highly convincing way. Then, of course, it becomes necessary to list 'Drinks' and 'Suggestions for Food' and, at last, quite worn out with high living, I tuck the completed lists away for another six months and reel off to bed in the small hours, stomach groaning with listed food, eyes red with listed booze. I sometimes have a mild hang-over in the morning.

Often, obsessive list-makers of my ilk tend to list things that could hardly be forgotten—a supreme effort to exorcise even those items clinging most tenaciously to the rafters of the brain. I have a list-mongering friend who starts each new day with the item 'Get up' and at 8.30 a.m. the first tick gleams triumphantly beside it. The day in my own diary set aside for the birth of my son starts 'Ask the milkman extra pint' and carries, somewhere in the thicket of self-commands, the short but compelling note 'Have baby'. Diaries serve, too, to retain rather more permanent lists designed as optimistic blueprints for the whole 12 months ahead. One such lists my physical shrinkings and swellings (waist, upper thigh, bottom) and I also keep a kind of annual Things to Do on an altogether higher echelon than the daily list. These items are the trimmings, the activities other people always manage, the things I might manage if I ever miraculously produced the Ultimate List, ultimately ticked. Such lists say, against all odds, 'Get old maps framed', 'Make patchwork quilt' and 'Sort books into categories', but it is a vintage year that sees even two ticked off. It takes too much out of me to keep abreast of such relatively modest demands as 'Fix lavatory seat' and 'Unblock sink'.

At this very moment, all across England, the really dedicated list-makers are composing their *oeuvres d'été*, the Great Holiday Lists. I have always held that I should be able to leave my house at the drop of a hat with everything vital contained within the plastic limits of a sponge bag. So far, no one has asked me to go anywhere further than Battersea at the drop of a hat and a good thing, too, because my sponge bag is an unfinished symphony, its list foundering on such knotty problems as 'if entero-vioform, why not aspirins, indigestion tablets, hay fever sprays, calomine, insect bite soother? If safety pins, why not needles, thread, scissors, nail files, elastic? If brush, why not comb? Is my journey really necessary?'

Then, of course, there is my one perennial list: those rare beings picked out to be on the receiving end of my Christmas cards. Perhaps rare is hardly the word because the very fact of having made such an efficient list inexorably milks away the impetus actually to buy and stamp and post Christmas cards. Thus no one, I regret to say, has received a card from me for the past three or four years but they are quite welcome to inspect my list at any time. It's the thought that counts.

But perhaps the most traumatic mile-stone for list-makers, the Red Letter Day of the list-making world, is that time, once every two or three years, when a new address book requires the old listings to be transferred. Puissant as a god I survey name after name and the moving pen writes, the power of life and death in its commanding nib. A student met on a beach in Yugoslavia hits the dust, a certain Cooper, A.J., Clapham, follows him, the pen wavers and Yolande Goldworthy (dressmaker, NW3) survives by the skin of her teeth till the next great cull.

Though lists have their practical side they are also a hitherto neglected aspect of the Arts. My own are more your crafts—straightforward, concise, admirably comprehensible—but other people's, ah, what poetry, what revelations are here! Yesterday a friend laid at my feet her own offering, a few humble lines written in haste yet full of the tears and mystery of great art. 'Reddy-rust coloured binding, very wide. Make table. Do ice-skating. Stop drinking for three weeks. Stop eating for three weeks. Lab

41

exam. Write again Warner Bros.' All the hopes and fears, the highest aspirations of mankind are there and I am not ashamed to admit that the words 'write again Warner Bros' brought the hot tears scalding down my rugged cheeks.

Nor am I alone in my view of Lists as Art. On the lighter side, Cole Porter was a great list-maker and summons up all the bitter-sweet traits of a loved one with those memorable items 'you're the top, you're the Coliseum, you're the top, you're the Louvre Museum, you're a melody from a symphony by Strauss' (actually, Strauss never wrote any symphonies but never mind, list-makers' licence), 'you're the National Gallery, you're Garbo's salary, you're Mickey Mouse.' And George Jean Nathan, writing about his friend H.L. Mencken, tells of how Mencken 'could counter everyone's catalogue of ailments with a lengthy list of his own' and prints one such from a typical Mencken letter: '(a) a burn on the tongue (healing); (b) a pimple inside the jaw; (c) a sour stomach; (d) pain in the prostate; (e) burning in the gospel pipe; (f) a cut finger; (g) a small pimple inside the nose; (h) a razor cut, smarting, and (i) tired eyes.' Rabelais, perhaps the most famous list-maker of all literary figures, uses his lists to turn slim volumes into unpickupable tomes, lists that run across six pages, lists that spring from the inner, untrammelled exuberance of the born list-maker.

'There (Gargantua) played at Flushes, at Primero, at Grand Slam, at Little Slam, at Trumps, at Prick and Spare Not, at Hundred-Up, at Penny-points, at Old Maid, at Cheat, at Ten-and-pass, at Thirty-one' and so on for another 204 likely and unlikely games until we all fall asleep exhausted, along with Gargantua.

Terser and to the point was a list a friend of mine came upon in the Royal Naval Stores. It started 'Pots, china, gold fluted, Admirals, for the use of'. And who will ever forget Sir Michael Redgrave's television recitation in *Beachcomber* of the much under-rated and deeply moving monologue entitled 'A List of Huntingdonshire Cabmen'? Constant Lambert, conductor and composer, was another to be bowled over by list fever. He composed the only known symphony based entirely on an auctioneer's list:

'1st Movement. Lento Lugubre—allegro marcato. Lot 18.

Mahogany stained coal purdonium, ditto commode, dog bed, small deal table, grained box of sundry tools, two pieces of deal board' ending at 'quantity of wallpaper (a.f.)'. The Maestro himself comments on the dramatic and forceful fugato at the words 'dog bed' and if that does not put lists up there with the Fine Arts, I don't know what will.

And then there is Sei Shonagan, that lovely little lady-in-waiting at the Court of a Japanese Emperor. How pleasant to think that nearly 1,000 years ago she sat (or, more likely, knelt) behind a bamboo blind and composed some of the most exquisite lists ever printed—now reprinted in Penguin Classics as *The Pillow Book of Sei Shonagan*. Sei lists everything that flitted across her lively mind over some ten years, from 'Depressing Things,' 'Different Ways of Speaking,' 'Times when one should be on one's guard' to 'Things that gain by being Painted' and 'Things One is in a Hurry to See or to Hear':

'When a woman has just had a child, one is in a hurry to find out whether it is a boy or girl. If she is a lady of quality, one is obviously most curious; but, even if she is a servant or someone else of humble station, one still wants to know.

'Early in the morning on the first day of the period of official appointments one is eager to hear whether a certain acquaintance will receive his governorship.

'A letter from the man one loves.'

I must go now. I feel a list coming on.

30 August 1971

43

The Blue Belles of Brighton

THE SHORT-ORDER COOK on the Brighton train emerges from his
sweat box with yet another plate of eggs, bacon, sausages and
tomatoes. He eyes the hungry queue and disappearing again,
his voice floats back. 'Last week, with Labour, it was just
cups of tea. This week it's full breakfasts and pots of coffee.'

Huge BBC vans pack the parking lot at the Rank
Conference Hall on the Brighton front. I pick up my press
badge at the information caravan outside, adorned with
posters of the tanned and rosy Heath, his now substantial
second chin nothing but an air-brushed blur. The Securicor
men at the gates in their strange Star Trek caps nod me
carefully through, satisfied with my false colours, unable to
penetrate my plastic Conservative card to the mad bomber
within. No mere floating voter may enter here, this beanfeast
(like the other) is reserved only for the staunchest of the
Party, the Bluest of Blue, delegates hand-picked from the
grassroots of England. Pity though—why not a public gallery
where the man-in-the-street might see Labour and
Conservative at full strength, naked and unashamed,
undiluted for public consumption by their leaders,
unhampered by the need to appeal to any but their Own?

Inside, the hall is vast and oblong, the faithful pack in on
three sides and around the gallery above. On the fourth side
the platform floats like a pale blue quilted cloud in the
floodlights. Below is the speakers' rostrum, flanked by tables
marked 'Press' and 'Verbatim Note-Takers'. The press lolls,
reading newspapers, the Plana-typists commune with their
earphones, the faithful are hushed, intent on every word. As
I enter the speaker's voice booms out from loudspeakers
everywhere. It is a Mr Hugh Simmonds (South Bucks). Mr
Simmonds looks, from my eyrie in the gallery, for all the

world like Christopher Robin saying, loudly and firmly, his prayers. 'There is nothing wrong with inherited wealth. It has done this country a great deal of good in the past.'

The current debate is on economics and taxation; not so obviously emotional as, say, yesterday's stirring debate on hanging but actually touching the very heartstrings of Conservatism. Mr Simmonds is embarked upon an impassioned defence of 'that iniquitous word floating about, "unearned income." ' He maintains, against no opposition, that it is not unearned because if people choose to put their capital at risk, then surely they are earning every penny they get from taking that risk. I think of the risks these brave men take—investing with extraordinary courage in land or in housing for investment and a frisson runs through me. Selfless gamblers one and all. What soul so dead that it cannot appreciate such courage? Mr Simmonds ends his speech with a fine flourish: 'It is,' he says, 'the duty and the function of the Conservative Party to look to the well-being of the industrialist, the entrepreneur, the men of enterprise and adventure—in short, the men of excellence.' In even shorter, Mr Simmonds, the men of greed. Oops, pardon me, sorry I'm sure.

I look shiftily around me but the faithful are unperturbed, they applaud Mr Simmonds, the man of excellence, roundly. The lady beside me in the twin-set and pearls sets her diamond rings aflash with the vigour of her approval. I am momentarily stunned by this sudden cold blast from the shires. The figures of my childhood, the Scrooges, the Wicked Landlords, the Grinders of the Faces of the Poor, the Jasper Jodpurs of many a moral tale, long watered-down by adulthood, spring suddenly to life again. Good heavens, so it's true after all? It wasn't just my obsessive imagination? They really do believe in Capitalism, they really do worship the Golden Calf? You'd never know, would you, seeing the Heathcos. on television, in print, in person? The leaders give quite a convincing impression of being much of a muchness with Labour, really. A touch of liberalism here, a soupçon of heart there, humane as the next man. But here, down here in the sturdy grassroots, things are altogether tougher. Here we see what the blue rosette really means to its aficionados: a deep and touching concern for Number One.

Speaker after speaker feed the faithful with the phrases they love to hear: 'Those much-maligned men, our friends the speculators' (clap, clap); 'as if employer is somebody who is a profiteer and has something to be *ashamed* of' (cheer, cheer). There are indignant attacks on the capital gains tax, on estate duty, on the sufferings of men who, after toiling all their lives, are faced with having to pay £12½ millions in death duty, and are therefore forced, much against their patriotic souls, to live in barbarous Switzerland. Verily, verily I say unto you, the heart bleeds for such victims.

The ladies, a majority at the conference, are visibly moved by these iniquities. Everywhere throughout the hall their immaculately coiffed heads nod agreement under the famous Tory turbans. Ample bosoms (agleam with sequins or modestly moulded in tweed) heave with wifely outrage at the deprivations of their menfolk, menfolk willing to lay down their lives amassing wealth for their country and their Queen. They are, on the whole, a handsome lot, well-boned in face and corset. Mrs Unity Lister, chairwoman of today's proceedings, is handsome too, presiding over her queendom like a *grande dame* of the theatre or *Vogue's* Mrs Exeter at her gracious best. Shiny white hair lifts softly off noble brow, a royal smile permanently lifts the corners of the coral mouth, she is Harrods personified and deeply admired by all the other ladies. It is not hard to see that such women, regarding their comely features each day in the gilt mirrors of the stockbroker belt, keeping their regular hair-dressing appointments, enduring their regular facials, have a vested interest in money, in conservation, in preservation, in the *status quo*. Change of any kind can do those English Rose complexions no good at all.

And these ladies represent, in their living breathing selves, all that the Conservatives stand for. They do not need help because everything in their garden is already lovely. They ask quite simply for non-interference, they want no rocking of their neatly-painted boats. One speaker, talking of small businessmen, sums up their ethos nicely: 'These small enterprises do not look to the Government for active help, but they ask not to be hindered.' Labour asks Labour leaders

46

for change, for a better life. Toryism asks Tory leaders merely to make sure the good life goes on.

The unemployed are spectres at this feast, uninvited guests, unasked intruders. Not once is there any applause for statutory expressions of concern, not one expression of concern remains unqualified. 'Of course,' goes the refrain, 'we must concern ourselves with the problem' and, quick as a flash, come the ifs and the buts.

'Had you realized that out of every 100 people in the country who are anxious, able and willing to be employed and desirous of being employed...no fewer than 96 people find that they are able to do this without any difficulty whatsoever?'

'Is it not depressing that out of nearly one million people unemployed there seem to be very few indeed who are able to look beyond the simple method of getting a job? There are massive opportunities for people who will stand up and get on with providing some income and some employment for themselves in terms of being self-employed.'

So there we have it. Not only are the unemployed responsible for the straits they find themselves in (the Right Hon. Anthony Barber himself says 'the simple fact is that workers have priced themselves and their fellows out of a job'), but they are also quite capable of finding employment if they were not the work-shy shirkers we all know they are. The Good Life, Tory-style, is just round every Sunderland street corner. Every man his own entrepreneur.

Down in the bar the bonhomie is louder and lashed with whisky. Jim Prior is there, Minister for Agriculture, his ruddy face a cartoon of a cartoon of his Leader. Young clean-cut Tory dames—aware, it seems of the well-shaped sides whereon their bread is buttered. Snatches of conversation cut through the amplified voices of the speakers in the hall:

'We've only got two buses now, to our village, but we don't want more. They'd only bring Americans and the wrong sort of people.'

'Very stimulating debate, I thought. I think it will teach us all a lot about, well, politics.'

'At the last Board meeting I tried to interest them in some of those changes but they're so *conservative*, really.'

'I've no objection to these students' unions giving a few quid to Bangla Desh but they're not supposed to, you know, it's against the rules. As for giving to Black Power, well...'

'We ought to put up a banner "Has Macclesfield been forgotten?" When can you mention it; under the Irish problem?'

'Oh yes, she's very powerful. Well, she's really a man, anyway.'

'I'm all for less taxation myself. I've got a divorce coming up.'

The voice of the speaker is piped even unto the ladies' lavatory. Women comb their hair and apply lipstick in rapt silence, afraid to miss a word of the Chancellor's views on tax restructuring. If these ladies burned their bras, the party would collapse. One wears a badge on her uplift: 'I've made up my mind, don't confuse me with facts.' Another bears an 'I trust Ted' under her chin. Outside, in the bright sea glare, a crowd of old age pensioners stand and stare, expressionless. 'Ted' say their placards, 'our shopping basket is getting lighter. Pensioners want £8 now.' The Old Pump House does a fine lunch, I hear.

In the afternoon, fed and well watered, the heat in the hall rises. Truncated little faces dot the front tier of the platform like heads in the Sooty Show. There's lovely Madame Thatcher and—ooh—Ted himself, glowing with health, grey hair perfectly groomed (you can do such wonderful things with Steel). There's John Davies, face like shrunken chammy and Robert Carr, skin papery as a Chinese Mandarin. Here comes Maudling, lumbering like a bear and Julian Amery with hooded eyes and Lord Home, fragile as dry bones. Seated, they stare across our heads with expressions of the deepest concern, strained (perhaps) with the awful effort to stay awake. Two ladies behind me nod off, and wake again, chins spiked by marquisite brooches. Two people sleep poker-straight upon the platform.

The debate on Northern Ireland limps by, distinguished only by the dearth of speakers with anything but Home County accents. A suggestion that the Southern Irish be given passports and treated like any other aliens brings the audience momentarily to clapping life. A lady assures us that she is proud to be an Ulsterwoman, in purest Knightsbridge. The spark set alight this morning by taxation has faded and cannot, it seems, be rekindled by faraway places or even by education, the next debate. One man arouses everyone with jokes and becomes, immediately, the favourite son. He dismisses the school milk question with a merry quip: 'Last week, in this hall, we heard about the return of rickets to our children. This lunch-time, a Brighton shopkeeper bemoaned to me that the Socialists were spending a great deal more money last week on all manner of goods than the Tories are this week—and you can make what you like of that.'

And he ends by confirming his burning ambition: to kiss Mrs Thatcher. Another speaker backs him up: 'My experience is that many of the children did not want that milk in the first place. I also deplore the recent Milk Marketing Board advertisements which seemed to imply that some crime had been committed.'

At last the day is over, once again the bars fill and the faithful file out for an evening of business and pleasure. Photographers, doubled up most of the day in front of the rostrum, straighten out with glad groans. Outside, in the first faint dark, the pensioners still stand, quiet as cattle at sunset.

18 October 1971

The Politics of Hate

HUMAN BEINGS ARE interminably exhorted to love one another by persons as diverse as mothers and monarchs, Headmasters and hippies, Popes and pop singers. Love thy neighbour, love thine enemy, make love not war, you made me love you. Love, it appears, is a many-splendoured thing all right, nice work if you can get it but not an emotion presumed indigenous to man, not in any way guaranteed part of his make-up if left *au naturel*, unhounded.

Yet we are all born with a longing to love. Small children are endlessly loving, and I have never observed anything about my fellow men that justified so blanket a pessimism. Since the command to love is so repetitious a part of most religions I sometimes see it as just another of the ways in which man (wearing his masochistic God hat) sells himself and his brothers short. And I am constantly amazed at the way in which religious people loudly applaud their peers, not for loving other people but for the emphasis they put on 'doing for God', what most ordinary people do equally well out of instinctual love for man. Indeed, it has crossed my mind, in the dark of the night, that the whole carefully structured religious edifice was specifically formed not to help the ordinary person become good but the bad person to become ordinary—how else to explain the general blindness to man's goodness, the accent upon his badness, the amount of rejoicing in the scriptures on account of sinners and prodigal sons rather than your run-of-the-mill nicey?

Man is a gregarious animal. He needs close contacts with his own species to survive and, when he does not have them, he suffers and, perhaps, goes mad. Man loves so easily, so naturally, that he is a great deal more likely to put himself at risk through love than through love's opposite, hate—the poets talk frequently of dying for love, of hearts breaking for love but there is little enough about hate, other than the bibliography of madness. In fact, man loves so well that he often finds himself unable to hate even those who threaten and oppress him.

So alien is hate to him, so little is he able to staunch his loving heart that he has invented 'principles' to hate instead of people. Lord Longford's favoured precept 'love the sinner, hate the sin' is an example of this attitude—it is as if his Lordship thinks (and perhaps he does) that sin exists on its own, a nasty sort of cheesecloth hanging over our heads, descending at times to make us sin but basically nothing at all to do with us. In fact, of course, there is no such thing as a principle *in vacuo*; a principle is created by men and acted upon by men and it is sophistry to argue that you hate the principle and not the man.

Love makes cowards of us all. One of the most familiar sights nowadays is the spectacle of two men on television going at each other hammer and tongs, accusing each other of all manner of political crimes and public nuisance. But what do we see as the theme music rises, as the credits roll? These same two men smiling and nodding at each other and if the television programmes of my experience are any criterion what they are saying is: 'Hope I didn't come on too strong there, old man, didn't mean to be rude or anything, quite agree with your point and, anyway, how about a drink?' And I am left on the edge of my chair as their beaming faces fade, left seething and steaming and despairing because men like that are never going to change anything, in Ulster or the Clydeside, for the poor, the unemployed, the immigrant or anyone in dire need because they love each other too much to hate enough. The same scene takes place daily in the House of Commons: men flay each other in public, on the floor and toast each other later, in private, in the bar, listing the admirable qualities of their erstwhile opponent.

All of which may sound reasonable enough, even praiseworthy and yet, at times, I wonder if it does not lie at the root of why change takes so long, why injustice hangs round our necks like a millstone, why violence takes to the streets—forced out there by the implacable chumminess within.

Many an angry man, seething with hatred (back in his own home town) for the inequalities and poverty he sees around him, fights his way through to a position of some power and, once there, is overtaken by a softening of the heart. He meets, in person, the faces behind the policies he hates and what does he do but like them, warm to them? He may fan his anger for a while, tell himself that the man nodding kindly to him in the corridor is, by his beliefs and actions, directly contributing to the injustices he left behind but slowly, inevitably, the embers burn out, the face of the enemy blurs into the features of a personal friend and, all passion spent, he joins the Power Love-In.

It happens to us all to a lesser degree. How often have I mentioned to a friend how much I abhor so-and-so's statements and actions, only to have the friend reply, 'Oh, but so-and-so's really very nice, you'd like him if you met him.' Then what recourse do I have, knowing my own weakness, but never to meet him so that I can continue to abhor his actions, unseduced by his personal charm, fine war record and kindness to dogs? It happens when a friend voices opinions I find harsh, dangerous, unfeeling. I may protest but my need to love and be loved cracks my voice into a placating gentleness, even into laughter, and I am betrayed, I betray, through insufficient anger. I have even suppressed my outrage at everything from anti-semitism to women's inequalities on points of etiquette: after all, he *is* my host, she *is* so much older than me, he's so nice in other ways, she *is* my mother-in-law. Another friend, wiser than I, once advised me not to use logic in arguing with someone whose views I deplored. 'What we need to do,' he said, 'is to make views like racialism seem as ill-behaved and loutish as using four-letter words in a Victorian front parlour. Don't try to convince, just sweep up your skirts and ask the person to leave the room because you are not amused.'

Recently a black man wrote to me about his feelings for white people. He said: 'I hate them for making me hate them'—so much against the grain goes hate. In fact, so far as I have observed, the main problem for organized black people is not hating white men but loving them. They gather together, not to plot their downfall but to try, through a sort of group-therapy, to expunge, at least for a while, this paralysing love. It can be no coincidence that in many protest groups the insults most feared have not to do with hate but with love (you nigger-lover, you whitey-lover, you pig-lover). The biblical command 'love thine enemy' is carrying coals to Newcastle: the problem for the oppressed is much more likely to be learning sufficient hatred to get out from under.

To understand all is to forgive all and to change nothing at all.

1 November 1971

A Little Rough Stuff

I WAS BROUGHT UP in the diffuse but all-embracing belief that inside every male was a seething volcano of sex, a churning stream of lava kept under control only by dint of iron discipline on the man's part and extreme caution on mine. No one actually said so but all their attitudes screamed it. I was adjured to be 'careful' when I was with a man, I must never be guilty of 'leading him on'. I mustn't even flirt or I might get 'more than I bargained for'. As the Victorians prepared their daughters for marriage as lambs for the slaughter, so I was conditioned into accepting that my body was not my natural possession, a cosy kind of blanket that wrapped me round, but an indecent sexual object whose indiscreet use might, quite rightly, inflame men to dreadful deeds.

Breasts, they hinted, were not for the feeding of infants but dynamite directed against the sorely-tried male and to show them in any quantity was to risk driving decent men mad. Legs, uncovered beyond a certain point (and the certain point, in Victorian times, was the ankle), stopped being convenient walking aids and became twin red rags to the neighbourhood bulls. Shoulders, neck, hair, eyes, nose, lips: all had no normal functions that did not also carry the added weight of being designed to flare men's nostrils and start that inner volcano on its way to eruption.

The implication was always that men could not help themselves, that sexually they were at all times very nearly out of control and so it was my duty, as a woman, to cover myself and lower my eyes if I wanted to stay out of trouble, though exactly what trouble they never bothered to explain. The boys I grew up with absorbed this social propaganda eagerly and, as a result, were often brainwashed into total sexual irresponsibility, drunken engine drivers in charge of runaway trains with every one colluding to blame the drink.

Understandably, they matured with few restraints, leaping upon women in cars, thrusting themselves from all manner of dark corners and, when the protest came, switching quickly over to the drunken engine driver: 'What can I do, it's bigger than both of us, you are too beautiful, I can't help myself, you drive me wild.' The wretched girl, half flattered, half frightened, accepts the man's morality, knowing that society will take his side, not hers. After all, isn't she wearing false eyelashes, swooping neckline, soaring skirt? If unbridled passions are aroused, isn't it her fault? Isn't she, in fact, asking for it?

The next step back there in the dark corner—pant pant, grope grope—is rationalisation: Man's apparently inalienable right to believe that women who push them back and say no are actually, fundamentally, pulling them forward and saying yes. And here is revealed a dreadful tangle of emotions, an inextricable Gordian knot, a circle so vicious that its roots may well have vanished for good. Women, we are frequently told, are generally masochistic—it would be surprising, given their generations of submissive conditioning, if they were not, fantasies and all. And women, we are also frequently told, do not know their own minds until they are coerced. And this belief allied to the myth of uncontrollable male sexuality and the convention that a woman's body is there not for herself but for men, leads straight along the primrose path to rape.

Straw Dogs, Sam Peckinpah's bloodiest contribution to sadism, illustrates all these points to sickening perfection. A young wife is raped by two village louts and Mr Peckinpah obviously believes she deserves everything she gets. After all, the shameless hussy has a) slept with one of the men before her marriage, b) wears no bra, c) pulls up her skirt to examine a ladder in her tights and, worst of all d) appears to be keener, if anything, on sex than her husband. Heavens to Betsy, the girl's begging for it. On cue, in come the village rapists, she struggles, she gets belted, threatened with a gun and down she goes in the familiar foggy foggy dew. Ah, but wait now for the *coup de grace*, ladies and gentlemen. All is not lost. Our heroine is a woman like other women, despite her aching jaw and dislodged teeth. Soon, sweetly soon, her little arms steal round her rapist's neck and boom ta-ra boom, she's loving every minute of it.

At this point in the film a long sigh escapes the men in the audience and they lean back, triumphant. Didn't they always say? Didn't they always know in their bones? The ladies, God bless 'em, like nothing so much as a clout across the earholes to add spice to the act of love. Mild-mannered men (till now) curse their own gentleness and vow to be different in the future. Later in the film a teenage girl walks the village idiot out on a moonlit night, seduces him into kissing her and, by her accidental death, triggers off the last twenty minutes of mayhem and bloody murder. The message comes over crystal clear: flaunt yourself, however unconsciously, and you'll get your come-uppance, if you'll excuse the language, because rape is always the woman's fault. As the middle-aged manager of the cinema commented to me afterwards: 'If a gentleman makes a personal approach of this sort to a woman, most of the time she likes it.'

And, of course, women think so too—none more than the respectable middle-aged housewife. *Straw Dogs* and, in particular, that rape scene, was discussed on a Granada television programme by a panel of Gallup Poll-picked men and women and all of them blamed the rape unanimously on the girl. One apple-cheeked lady, smiling brightly, pointed out that, after all, the girl had slept with one of the men before her marriage so what else but rape could she expect?

Unsurprisingly, given these feelings, the incidence of rape goes up in this country every year. In Washington, capital of rape (one woman every 15 minutes) official advice to females is to submit, advice echoed by a male friend of mine last week who pointed out with some asperity that there would be no violence in rape if women didn't struggle.

Unfortunately for such optimists violence, in many cases, appears to be the *sine qua non* of the act; many women are beaten up, mutilated and killed *after* being raped. And, in direct contradiction to the paternal advice not to struggle, is the widely-held opinion that a woman really determined to resist rape will always succeed. 'Rape,'says one of Britain's best-known pathologists, 'is impossible without consent. The consent may be through fear or may be fatalistic after a struggle, but the fact is that a normal man cannot rape a normal woman who struggles unless he has assistance or knocks her out.' This, I regret to say, is one of the most scarlet of red herrings, another careful nail in the old coffin. It's all the woman's fault.

Apart from the fact that fear *is* coercion, it has escaped this expert's attention that many men, particularly in American prisons, are raped by their fellow men, for all their superior strength. But then, rape being a uniquely male crime it is obviously up to men to defend it, justify it and otherwise wash it out of existence. Certainly the idea of a man being raped by other men is rather more shocking, an event higher on the list of traumas. If T.E. Lawrence had been a lady would experts have spent quite so much obsessive time tracing his subsequent behaviour back to a possible Turkish rape?

As far as I am concerned, rape is quite simply definable as any coercion, particularly the use or threatened use of physical strength, that makes a woman submit to intercourse against her will. That woman may be a vestal virgin or Salome of the Seven Veils—raped she is if she didn't want it.

But, of course, it is deeply ingrained in us that only a virgin can truly be raped: as the old saw puts it so endearingly, a slice from a cut cake is never missed. And this adage, whether official or not, lies at the root of the working of our rape laws. Ludovic Kennedy, avenging angel of Timothy Evans, falls into exactly this trap when he took up the cudgels for a man given a ten-year sentence for rape. The man was accused, among other charges, of forcing a girl hitch-hiker to practise fellatio upon him and Mr Kennedy's triumphant haul, the 'most dramatic piece of evidence' upon which he felt the case should be reopened was that the accused man's solicitors received two obscene photographs anonymously, after his conviction. The photographs showed the girl, naked except for suspender belt and stockings, with a man's penis in her mouth and the pictures were accompanied by a letter that said, among other things, 'She's always doing this to men.'

The moral is obvious. Any girl who would sink so low as to practise what society in general considers a sexual perversion has no right to that society's help when she is forced to do the same thing to a total stranger. It follows, therefore, that if you can prove a woman promiscuous, give evidence that she has intercourse with the men she chooses, she has stepped outside the pale and is fair game for any man.

In fact, the way British law and British prejudice stands at the moment, a woman's only redress in the law courts is her rape by a perfect stranger. A survey of sex offenders in England shows that most are unmarried and most had left school at 14. Only 11 percent were known to have had any form of higher education, the largest single group were labourers, many had been drinking when they committed offences and there was a higher percentage of men with deformities or disfigurements in the group. From these figures one writer recently and predictably concluded that 'without being facetious they could be said to have been the men who by their violence gave rape a bad name'. In other words, rape between acquaintances cannot happen, just as rape in marriage has no legal existence.

We know, of course, that it does. Incest, for example, is often a synonym for rape and a high percentage of all our grandmothers, at least, were raped on their wedding night and from then on through endless nights of marital struggle, apparently because few men ever thought it possible (because of the masculine moral edict imposed on women) that their wives could actually accept sex willingly. There must be thousands of households across the country where rape will be committed tonight, carefully camouflaged in the sacraments of marriage. Men drunk; men obstinate; men indignant will have intercourse with reluctant wives because they want to, because it is their right, because they have such overriding needs, because they are stronger.

A girl (how many girls?) was raped last month by more than eighty Pakistani soldiers and went out of her mind. How many men can truly say they see no connection, however small, between this extreme event and their own occasional behaviour?

3 January 1972

Marrying Manville

LILY OF THE VALLEY fills the room and in its wake comes Mrs Anita Roddy-Eden Manville from Atlanta, Georgia, who has very blonde hair and very red lips and is very vivacious. A living breathing chip off old America, not blueberry pie or the Fourth of July, but diamonds are a girl's best friend and there ain't nothin' like a dame and the dance hall ladies in every Western you ever saw. No wonder Mrs Manville worries increasingly about the way her country is going.

'In my heyday, every girl in America had this dream of marrying a millionaire. But today, what interest do they have in material things? They'd rather find a pad in Greenwich Village. It's sad. It's a terrible problem now in the US, these runaways from good families. A girl was murdered a little while ago, she was living with a Negro janitor. Her family had all the money in the world, and she threw it away to get killed in a basement.'

Mrs Anita Manville didn't throw it all away. Back in 1952, in her prime, she married millionaire Tommy 'Marrying' Manville, a gnome-like gentleman who had already entered and escaped the bonds of matrimony eight times with the consummate skill of a Houdini, and who was to take on another two wives after Anita. Those were the days, my friend, the grand old days when nobody who was anybody had less than a fistful of spouses, when sometimes it must have seemed that half the world was the other half's ex. Those were the God Bless America days when a marriage lasted as long as it took to fly to Reno, when the sound of *Here comes the bride* was the prelude to a lifetime of dedicated litigation and when 'alimony' was a word a woman could pronounce with honest passion.

In an effort to recapture those golden moments, Mrs

Manville Number Nine has written a book called *The Lives and Wives of Tommy Manville*, out in February from W.H. Allen. In doing so, she has proved beyond a doubt that today's youth is made of pretty poor stuff compared with youth in America over the past few decades. Look at Mrs Manville. She took on, without blenching, the most-married man of her time (anyone's time for that matter) because he was mad, he was exciting, he could make a girl feel she was the only one. Money had nothing to do with it.

'When you asked him about his previous life he'd say "Sweetie, that was the Twenties, that was the Thirties, that was different. You're the one for me, this time it's for keeps." And you have to remember that he was a widower when I met him. I was the only woman who married him after a wife had died.'

Mrs Manville the ninth feels very close to a number of the other Manville wives. Sometimes, she says, she has trouble remembering her own name. Is she Florence or Lois or Avonne or Marcelle? Bonnie or Billie or Sonnie? Georgina or Patricia or Anita? There's only one she knows she isn't, the only non-blonde, last wife Christina who will inherit half of the Manville estate. Christina, says Anita, belittled the other women who had loved Tommy and, because he didn't like children, gave up her daughter to marry him. Once, pushed, as she says, beyond human endurance, Anita asked her why the hell she didn't go back to Buchenwald, Kraut. Maybe there are a few lampshades you haven't finished.

Tommy Manville was not, it appears, the most generous of millionaires. Tight as the bark on a tree is the way Anita describes him. Nevertheless he paid dearly enough for his matrimonial hobby: the combined total of time taken by his fifth, sixth and seventh marriages amounted to less than two months and eighteen days, and the three wives got paid off to the tune of 70,500 dollars. The last of these marriages endured all of seven hours, and the lady settled for 18,000 dollars for her time and trouble. Ten Manville wives at least, says Anita, were fine, good, compassionate women. And Tommy? As columnist Louis Sobel points out: 'He may have been a playboy but he was no philanderer...let's face it, he married the girls, every one of them.'

'In those days,' says Anita, 'marriage was important where today it is unimportant. I'm a horrible prude myself, always have been, isn't that silly?' Others were prudes then, too, not like now. After being divorced by Mr Manville, Anita married actor John Sutton and paid out thousands of dollars when a blackmailer threatened to reveal that her divorce was illegal. But John Sutton found out. 'I confessed everything to him. John took the only honourable way out. In his direct British fashion he filed immediately for an annulment. He would not live with another man's wife.' Marvellous, isn't it, how Mr Sutton managed to hang on to his morals, in spite of two previous marriages. Anita admires him for that.

But then, life with Tommy Manville might well have been designed to make a woman admire almost anyone else for anything else. The Manville house, where Tommy took his brides, was named Bon Repos but not a lot of repos went on there. Once safely within, Tommy hurled abuse at his wives, locked them out of the house, called the ever-willing police to settle their hash, howled at their bills, was constantly drunk, extremely disorderly, once shot Anita in the foot and always, with meticulous care, informed the newpapers of his every move. Publicity, says Anita, was his god and indeed he appears to have chosen his wives entirely on their copy value, warming briefly to them if they got his name in print, cooling off if they flagged in the pursuit of linage. The Second World War upset Tommy no end, hogging the headlines as it did, pushing his name off the front pages, selfishly taking over.

Tommy Manville died in 1967 and his lunatic Disneyland died with him. Since then Anita has been fully occupied in fighting his will (she expects 350,000 dollars since she claims she is the last legal wife).

'I'm in court all the time and now I have to fight my way in through the sympathisers for Angela Davis. The blacks never had it so good, in my opinion. We have black senators, mayors, governors but nobody notices all this. They're in every place in life. I'm a Southerner and I've had to face the enmity of the North. They say "Oh, you're from *Georgia*" as if we're out beating slaves every day. I'm tired of it. The blacks didn't burn any Southern cities, you notice. It was the

North got burnt, not the South. That's because we've always treated the blacks right. Last week I went to the movies here and a man put on a Ku-Klux-Klan hood. "Hooray for our side," I shouted.'

Mrs Manville has had a tough time in the courts, too. 'In America we have the best judges money can buy. The women judges are flaming lesbians and one of them, I have a file on her going back years. She came up through the criminal courts and brought all the dirt with her. She hates women with a purple passion. I followed the Chicago Seven Trial, oh yes. I thought the judge leaned over backwards to be fair, though some of the press made him look incompetent. He was not. Good thing I'm not a judge. I'd have hanged them all the first day.'

In between litigations, Anita Manville has almost completed a book on the life and times of *Papa Doc* Duvalier of Haiti, a particular favourite of hers. 'I want to show his other side, the dedicated man I met 20 years ago who gave a quarter of his life to his people as a doctor. No one else will print this. He did a damn good job fighting off revolutions, and if anyone got shot they called him a murderer.

'I've seen more poverty in New York City than in Haiti. There's a New York child in hospital every day with rat bites and that doesn't happen there. They may only have little calico dresses, but they're not bitter. When Jean-Claude took over, Baby Doc I call him, there was no bloodshed and no fighting. The people loved Duvalier and so they accepted his son. The Ton Ton Macoute? I know the head of that, he's *divine*. Graham Greene sat on his behind at the hotel, drinking up a storm. He was shown every courtesy and he goes away and writes a book like that. But, of course, there's nothing like being a blonde in Haiti, it's much better than being Graham Greene.'

And Mrs Manville is presently much exercised about the treatment of Howard Hughes by the press. She has, she says, known him all her life and was working on a book about him for five years until he asked her to stop and she did. You owe a person that much. 'Anyone who retreats from the world gets an unkind press. Look what happened to King Ludwig of Bavaria, they said he was insane, but he was not. When the doctor came to take him away he said, "I don't think I will live under restraint"—and he killed the bloody doctor and himself. When I visited his palace in Witgenstein I kept thinking that in the next room I'd see Howard Hughes. I have very strong ESP. The funny thing is, you see pictures of Ludwig and Howard side by side and they're absolute twins.

'They used to call him the Tommy Manville of the West Coast—he said to me once, "I don't marry them, Anita," and I said, "I know you don't kid, but you sleep with them." You know the last words he said to me, that tall, gorgeous man in his sneakers? The very last words? He looked at Captain Bligh, my English bulldog and he said "Very fine dog, very fine dog." And with that he disappeared into the night. That man didn't inherit anything like what Tommy inherited, but look what he did with his money. Tommy was an idiot, he threw it away. Charlie Chaplin came right out with it the other day, he said "The most important thing in the world is money" and we've known that in the US for a long time. Mind you, I don't feel that way, myself.' Money doesn't mean anything to her and that was what made Tommy Manville determined to marry her.

'Women have always had freedom to get what they want, if you're strong you can always get what you want. Women's Lib, huh. I'd like to knock that Gloria Steinem (high priestess of American Women's Lib) on her arse. If we were on a television show together there'd be a fist fight. She deserves it if anyone does. The best Pharaoh Egypt ever had was a woman, Queen Hatshepsut. She wore a false beard in order to consolidate the country. And Marie Denise, Papa Doc's daughter, is one of the most intelligent women in the world.'

Manville wives, says Anita Manville, were not gold-diggers. She and others of them gave Tommy *back* money, very often.

'Sonnie, for instance, deserved a lot more than she got. Though she was married for only seven hours and got 18,000 dollars, Tommy humiliated her. And Billie wouldn't take a penny, she loved him with all her heart.' Mrs Manville records in her book that, 'Billie had been childishly happy and thrilled as she displayed her gifts from Tommy. "He gave me a 135 carat aquamarine" she cried in delight. "And 5,000 dollars in war bonds and so many furs—a mink, a silver fox coat and a jacket of fox also." '

It was, you see, a cleaner world in those days in America. Greenbacks at the end of every rainbow and a millionaire for every girl who played her cards right and believed in the American dream. Today, what do we have? Commies taking over, niggers in power, women burning their bras and, above all, a truly appalling indifference to the sancitity of marriage. Not to say a distinct feeling against the sale of fox furs. Fings ain't what they used to be, but Mrs Anita Roddy-Eden Manville remains undaunted.

'There'll never be another Manville but I met a marvellous millionaire last week. He's awfully nice—I hope he's more generous.'

New readers start here.

17 January 1972

Man's Best Friend

'WHAT,' THEY SAID, 'are you going to do with yourself now?'

'I dunno,' I said (Actress? Novelist? Explorer?).

'Don't know was made to know,' they said. 'Take a secretarial course.'

So I did, slinking into the college doors in dark glasses in case any of my old school friends recognized me and said but I thought you were going to be an actress, a novelist, an explorer. Once inside, to my shame I quite enjoyed myself. There was something very relaxing about sitting in a line in front of blank-key typewriters, pounding out a salvo of quick brown foxes and to this day I have a sneaking fondness for high tinny typewriters that zap out industry for all the world to hear. I fancied myself at shorthand too; all those pretty loops and swoops were satisfyingly creative and stepping up speeds from day to day without sacrificing anything of the delicate tracery posed a small but definite challenge. How beautiful a page of shorthand looks—who would dream that banalities underlie the imagery, that translation reveals no fragile haiku but the ponderous phrasings of a yours of the fifth ult.

I passed out of college with a diploma for 130 words a minute, fast enough to take down court proceedings. There was a drawback, though. Once armed with this diploma, they seemed to think that the next logical step was to get a secretarial job (I knew there was a catch somewhere). For some weeks I hung about the parental home, peering sideways at sits. vac., hoping for the magic ad that would say 'Wanted: secretary to actress, novelist, explorer'—already the ceiling of my expectations had dropped several notches; no longer could I hope to be something myself, only to help someone else be something.

As Mr Richard Sharples said in the House of Commons a while ago 'the vast majority of women are in jobs which are an extension of their traditional domestic rôle...a vast majority of women want jobs in these areas.' Well, I didn't but there I was, already on the treadmill in spite of the fact that as yet I had had no more to do with the traditional domestic rôle than breaking the odd dish, washing up. Does secretarial work prepare you for the domestic rôle or the domestic rôle prepare you for secretarial work?

In the end, actresses *et al.* being disappointingly thin on the ground, my first job was in the typing pool of a large London advertising agency and I loathed every single minute of it. The moment I entered the offices every morning at 9 a.m. I ceased to exist as an individual and became a movable machine with female secondary sexual characteristics. Notebook at the ready, I scurried from executive's office to executive's office like small change chuntering from department to department in an old-fashioned store. Mostly, the men looked up with blank eyes, told me to sit down (straight back, sharp pencil) and dictated letters squeezing out each word with all the reluctance of a furred-up kettle. Huge voltages of energy were left untapped, to be expended on immensely close and deeply boring examination of my nails. A few men looked up with another sort of blankness in their eyes and, noting the outer perimeters of the machine, made the heavy sort of overtures men permit themselves to make to serving girls. Back in the pool, the typing that had been near-perfect at college began to degenerate fast. Letters went out blotched with tears of humiliation and fury. Three weeks later, so did I.

In those days, people used to brainwash girls like me by saying that secretarial skills were an open sesame—*per qwertyuiop ad astra*. These days, they say the same. In between I have learned one general lesson. If you want to do anything else at all but secretarial work, don't do (or admit you can do) secretarial work or you'll end up—abracadabra—a secretary. And what, you may ask (leaving aside ingrained prejudice), is so bad about that? One quarter of the female work force is in clerical work of some kind and you could say they are on to a cushier deal than their sisters in factory work, for a start: better surroundings, better pay and plenty of time for looking at nails. But all is not gold that glisters and here, particularly, a little surface scratching is in order.

First, always suspect any job men willingly vacate for women. Until the end of the nineteenth century all secretaries were men but when the first woman was sent out with the first typewriter there were no sexual skirmishes at the barricades, no entrenched men shouting of invasion, no questions in the House. Second, contemplate the following quotes and ask yourself to whom they refer.

'She is an endlessly helpful and understanding individual ...she will help him through a troublesome day and guide him through difficult times...she respects him, is proud of his successes and tries to help him avoid failures...fits into the framework of his personality and adapts herself accordingly...never tries to mould him to her ways...gives him all the help she can when things go wrong and keeps her own feelings under control.'

A Victorian tract on the wifely virtues? (What wife would stand being talked to thus today?) A ladies' mag feature on a Royal Nanny? A training manual on Guide Dogs for the Blind? Wrong, of course. This is a list of the key qualities expected of that independent, swinging, emancipated girl-about-town—Miss Secretary, 1972. Expected in particular by Lance Secretan, boss of Manpower Ltd., self-billed as among the 'foremost supplier of secretarial help in the British Isles' and author of a new Pan guide-book to slavery called *How to be an Effective Secretary*. And how to be an effective secretary is to develop the kind of lonely self-abnegating sacrificial instincts usually possessed only by the early saints on their way to martyrdom. All very handy for the bosses, of course, and indeed the book is quite clearly written with the best interests of the boss in mind. 'You will,' says Mr Secretan at one point, with holy pomposity, 'create irreparable damage if you just drop a letter of resignation on his desk.' To whom, one asks oneself, to whom?

The interesting point about many books written for secretaries is that it is hard to imagine them addressed to women in any other job or, for that matter, men. Helen

Gurley Brown's notorious tract *Sex and the Office* appears to be a guidebook to prostitution via the typewriter and, what's more, prostitution physical *and* mental. Mrs Brown outlines the sexy wheeze of a secretarial friend, a girl obviously destined to go far, in one direction at least.

'...she walked over to the door, locked it, took off her blouse and bra and started to work *al fresco*. She had been happily in this dishabille or *no* habille for some time when the door burst open and a co-worker, male persuasion, burst in. (*Any* girl can make a mistake and take the lock *off* when she thinks she's putting it *on*. . .') And 'You shouldn't think twice about embracing any cause dear to your boss. . . I became a Republican to impress my boss...'

The most junior male employee straight out of college would never stand for the prim admonishments to be found in Mr Secretan's book and I cannot imagine a factory girl taking to his interference in such matters as clothes, looks, friends and gossip. Worse, any secretary who actually followed Mr Secretan's advice would undoubtedly find herself (a) loathed by everyone in her office and (b) working harder and harder for this privilege.

'Competition is exciting; why not compete with yourself and see how you can improve your performance? If you usually can type ten letters in an hour, set yourself a new standard of twelve and you will soon find that not only is this your new production level but it will give you much greater pride.'

Nor is she likely to get what appears to be the only perk of the secretarial life—the boss in marriage. Mr Secretan says the ideal secretary 'should be fresh and smart and certainly fashionable but not flamboyant, bizarre or attempting to win the contest as the office beauty'. And, he adds, 'pay more attention to making up your mind than to making up your face' in an obvious attempt to keep the wretched girl bound for ever to her boss by the plainness of her features.

Mr Secretan also assumes that a good secretary's whole life will revolve around her job, which wouldn't matter too much except that her job, in his definition, sounds rather more like a description of a tunnel than a human being with a personality and needs of her own. A secretary 'is the means by which, and through whom, her executive initiates, handles and completes a project' and in order to achieve this feat of midwifery, she must fortify herself 'for a productive day at the office...get a good eight hours' sleep each night, have a balanced diet and take regular exercise.'

Nor, of course, must she ever talk about her own life or feelings. As Mr Secretan points out, 'a work study showed that on an average morning a group of girls in a busy office mentioned their problems on six different occasions. Each time, they lost anywhere from a few minutes to ten or fifteen minutes of working time.' Fie, fie, girls. Just because your bosses are gathered in a clump discussing the latest rugger game or the amount of whisky they drank last night is no reason for you to think you have any reciprocal rights. Worse, she is not even encouraged to make friends in this office where she spends eight hours of every day.

'Do not...let socializing interfere with your work. Often it is not good practice to become close friends with one's colleagues...be discreet in selecting your friends and in confining your friendships to non-business hours.' And if the wretched girl is bound on friendship, well, '...while you may become friendly with your female companions you should use discretion when socializing with men from your organization.' One can see Mr Secretan's point, of course. Women can gossip together without doing any real harm, just like servants. But gossip to *men* and who knows what may emerge to damage your boss and *then* where would he be?

Some people might see *How to be an Effective Secretary* as a useful handbook—and there are, of course, chapters on the usual secretarial aids, 'Layout and presentation of Work'. 'The Secretary and Meetings' and that old, your favourite and mine, 'Filing'. Some might see it as a joke. I, personally, find it faintly obscene, based as it is on a conception of a category of human beings needing no other aim in life but a sort of blind one-way devotion to another. A nurse's work could be defined roughly in the same way but she devotes herself to people, not one person, and those people are in great need—nobody ends up in hospital bed demanding her ministrations to further their own personal ambitions. Others in vocational jobs help people, often selflessly, who cannot help themselves, either mentally or physically. But to whom is a secretary devoting herself so selflessly, with all the dedication of a nun for her God? Most often, to a man in his job for the money it brings him, the status it confers, the creative satisfaction it bestows or the expense account that pads out the whole. *He* may come in late, be bad-tempered and hung-over ('if he is abrupt, be tactful; if he is moody, be cheerful') go out at eleven for a drink, stay out till 3.30 for lunch, come back dined and very wined, pinch his secretary's bottom, quarrel with a colleague and quit at 4.30 for his country cottage, leaving her to pour oil on the waters. *He* may rely on her for most of his success and he will reap the praise and the rewards at the end. She has no such opportunities. She is expected, in fact, to do most of the work of a wife (including, at times, sexual favours) without the status or financial security that being a wife usually entails.

Mr Lance Secretan (earning a good living from all these subservient egos) appears unprepared to allow his secretaries even enough ego to presume she would like to learn about a job for her own satisfaction. 'Spend,' he says, 'every minute that you can watching, listening and reading everything that is relevant *to your executive's job*.' (My italics.) As one man said: 'The way to distinguish the secretary from the shorthand typist is through her relative ability and interest in anticipating *the executive's needs*.' And '. . .the secretary can no longer look at her function merely as routine but must look at it now as an integrated and essential *extension of her executive's responsibilities*.'

He comments, too, 'always remember that during working hours your time is paid for by the company for whom you work. It is dishonest to use it for private purposes' and then adds, in an abrupt volte-face, 'but it may be necessary for you to deal with certain of your executive's personal matters. . .it is frequently helpful to them to have a reminder of personal appointments, important dates, anniversaries, etc.' What's sauce for the goose is, obviously, not sauce for the gander, however junior his position may actually be.

There are intelligent, educated and creative women throughout this country who look to their typewriters to fly

70

them, like magic carpets, to the top. Of course, this can happen and, sometimes, does. Unfortunately, when the opportunity for promotion finally comes, the unfortunate girl very often finds that her secretarial interim has exacted a lifelong penalty. As someone commented to me recently of a woman producer in a television company: 'She's got lots of talent and very good ideas but she just can't seem to push them through. She was a secretary, you see, and she got too used to catering for other people's needs.'

Mrs Marjorie Hurst, head of the vast chain of thigh-fixated Brook Street Bureaus, says she is an ardent advocate of women's rights. Why, then, cannot she and others like her, push for transforming secretarial work into a formal apprenticeship system in which an ambitious girl may, in return for her skills, learn her executive's job and within an agreed time, take on the job herself or another within the company. Those girls who have no wish to advance may simply sit and file their nails and good luck to them.

13 March 1972

71

Storming Sessions

BACK IN THE AGE OF INNOCENCE, oh my children, anyone with enough bread, a hall and a head for administration could put on a conference. In those days, once the theme was set ('Communications in a Shrinking World', 'Prison—Rehabilitation or Revenge?') the format followed a deeply predictable pattern. A chairman was selected and speakers were invited: Professor This and Lord That, Television Personality Rock Whosit, Bishop Thingummy and Mr Whatsisname MP. The events were usually divided into sections: one plenary session followed by a half-hour on 'Whither film?', an hour on 'Management—Uses and Abuses', an afternoon on 'Training Schemes—Are They Enough?'. Posters and advertisements went out, the audience came in. All was neatly arranged: a platform, chairs, microphones, flowers here and there, glasses of water, notepads, pens. Ladies and Gentlemen. Great honour to welcome. Well known to you all. Benefit of his wisdom. Rhubarb rhubarb rhubarb. At the end the organizers could either conclude that the conference was a success (packed audience listened attentively and clapped in the right places) or a failure (sparse audience snored).

Days of wine and roses, speaking conference-wise, and days no longer with us barring Mothers' Union get-togethers in Nether Wallop or IBM courses in Computer Programming attended exclusively by computer programmers. Nowadays, staging any sort of conference is an occupation almost as hazardous as a civil rights march in Belfast and I doubt if Lloyd's would care to underwrite the chances of successful completion. The more all-embracing and social the theme, the worse the odds.

It was all of three years ago that I lost my own conference

innocence and the events of that momentous occasion have been repeated many times since, to the point of howling monotony. Invited suddenly to take part in 'a discussion', I found myself being fenced off from the common herd and edged behind a table with an odd assortment of others. The table was at one end of the hall, the audience sat below us in a semi-circle, nothing extraordinary here. A respectful hush descended, we were introduced and each of us made a short statement of our beliefs, opinions, prejudices. The audience clapped respectfully, if not warmly. Then our chairwoman, a lady of headmistressy mien, graciously opened the discussion to the floor. There, it staggered on for a while. People bobbed up and down, saying for what it's worth and from where I sit and were rewarded with bright headmistressy smiles from our table. And then, somewhere in the back of the hall, the voice of doom was heard. 'What,' it said, 'are we all doing here?' Faces turned towards him, a few sshhings could be heard, the chairwoman coughed and said she thought that was a *most* interesting question. The voice boomed inexorably on. 'What,' it said 'do you think you're all doing up there?' And from the darkness a great accusing finger swung up and pointed at us, on the platform. For me, at least, it was a moment of horrible truth. In my head there was a great rattle and various pieces of the jigsaw fell into place. What *were* we doing up here?

Before I had time to ponder this most interesting question a person almost at my feet shot up and fired the next and pithier salvo. 'All I want to say is. This is all I want to say. I've never heard such a load of effing rubbish in all my effing life.' Exhausted he fell back and a quivering woman took his place. 'Effing bourgeoisie,' she commented, 'sitting up there, telling me what you think. What do I care what you think? I'm a working class woman and I'll tell *you* something.' She did.

And so we were off on the Big Dipper I have since come to know so well and, at times, to love. In a tidal wave of four-letter words the age of the ordered conference drowned before my eyes; a familiar structure collapsed and, for me at least, has never been satisfactorily put together again. Over the next years I watched conference after conference bite the dust, some in a holocaust of physical action that made my own little hassle look like a Sunday School tea. Fights often developed after the first wave of shoutings, small knots of bodies heaving and swaying as the chairman talked gamely on. Next, bands of battle-dressed people of both or either sex rush the platform, take over the mikes and spend the next hour or so bawling their utter contempt for everything. Behind them, only minutes later, appear the familiar placards of Gay Liberation. Gay may be Good. It is certainly Omnipresent.

After them it's a free-for-all, a huge and aggressive confusion of everyone who's ever had a yen for a mike and an audience, from lady poets who make sweet moans for as long as they can before being bodily removed to Jesus freaks who declaim that if we knew Jesus as they know Jesus, oh oh oh what a man. The crowds are often enriched with other ingredients: IRA supporters, Women's Liberation, Maoists, and Trotskyites, Black Panthers and Birth Controllers, Anti-Apartheiders and Anti-Polluters and, occasionally, Young Conservatives in aggressively conservative suits. Altogether, a centennial of Central Casting. In the end the mikes die of over-strain and the crowds stream off, hoarse-voiced, steaming gently like horses after a steeplechase, exchanging addresses, expressing admiration and mutual support or aggression and mutual antipathy. The melancholy faces dotted here and there are the people who actually came to actually hear the actual speakers, benighted fools that they are.

But now the supplies of adrenalin are running low and things have arrived at an impasse. Conference organisers have become haunted people, their faces drawn, their eyes shifty. Some make determined efforts to counteract the likelihood of invasion; they issue brightly nervous invitations to various 'trouble making' groups in the hope that official inclusion will avert disaster. Chairmen, kibbutzed by shouting hordes, bare their teeth in terrible smiles and offer their microphones with many a shout, 'Do join us, it's a free country, say what you have to say'. They have lived to regret even this and some may be seen wandering to this day in the wings of deserted conference halls, bewildered defrocked figures mumbling the sad jargon of a byegone age. 'I don't see where all this *gets* us,' and 'They shout but what do they *say*?'

With hindsight, the break-up was inevitable. Conferences have for too many years been unforgivably static, unbelievably insensitive. If you must hold a discussion on the spread of authoritarianism it is, perhaps, a trifle unimaginative to set up the discussion on authoritarian lines. Nor is it surprising that those people who feel they suffer most from authoritarianism should choose to point this out noisily, physically if need be. And the once accepted gap between 'experts' and 'the masses' has closed in many people's minds: they are understandably reluctant to sit down there and listen to others up there pontificating upon what they see as petrified theories, irrelevant to their own way of life, often responsible for blocking their own activities and producing the phenomena they hate, whether it be prisons, pollution or high-rise flats. They want, at the very least, to argue back, man to man. They do not wish to crouch at the feet of a master.

Democracy in action, you might say (well, try shouting). But what kinds of format are likely to replace the old? So far, no one has come up with sure-fire answers. Too much organization is out but too little is simply chaos, a cacophony of voices signifying nothing. Pop festivals, situations some would imagine were the very essence of fluidity, have come under attack for their financing. People now at the Bardney Festival have spent days plotting to get in without paying, to them a matter of principle on the grounds that festivals should be free, that the organizers should raise the funds from—well, here they tend to become less coherent but a mutter is heard of record royalties and concessions and film rights. Nor do other underground organizers fare much better. *Time Out*'s own media conference at the Roundhouse a few months ago cracked up in a hurricane of invading women, intent on having a say in an all-male world. What is becoming clear is that the conference, if structured, must embody the theme to be discussed, must reflect in that structure the basic principles of the audience or the group that called it into being.

The women's movement has probably done as much soul-searching as any on this problem. Rebelling against a masculine structure, it is particularly important to them, when they come together, that they do not reproduce this system, this hierarchy. One current solution is to start with a theme-setting general discussion and then disperse into small talk-ins, groups who carry that broad theme into the particular. *Time Out*, perhaps as a polite way of rapping the knuckles of their own countrywomen, gave a complimentary report of the Paris Women's Conference last week.

'Most striking was the form of the meeting, which combined the experience of the small group with the needs of a large meeting. Each area of discussion was conducted by a group of women. Squatting on the stage or on the floor of the hall, passing microphones between them, they gave accounts of their own experiences...the microphones were open to all, anyone who wanted to contribute simply went to join the group: the fluidity and dynamism of the conference was a public expression of the feminist forms of democratic discipline.'

And there you have it, the great aim of the neo-conference, the medium is the message all over again. Gynaecologists, stockbrokers, establishment groups of all kinds may go on expressing their rigidity and elitism by their platforms and their speakers and their gavel-banging chairmen but if your thing is grass-roots, man, you better be down there, squatting on your haunches, head no higher than anyone else's.

29 May 1972

The Shankill and the Falls

ALL, SO FAR, A BIT of a nervous giggle: the security flight from London, the airport baggage inspection. The road cuts through magnificent hills and down there is Belfast, spreadeagled and smoking in the valley. Then we are in the Protestant Shankill Road and the giggles stop. Hardboard (Business As Usual) seals off the blank fronts of every third shop—later a Belfast man says sourly if you break your glasses here and go to an optician, he won't put new glass in, he'll board them up. Here and there between the long lines of terraced houses a burnt-out gap like a missing tooth. On the walls, great dripping letters: 'Ulster Is Not For Sale' and 'God Save the Queen' (The Who? The *Queen*?). Barbed wire curls along warehouse walls, brown paper criss-crosses surviving glass, a row of familiar double-decker buses top a bank of sandbags and camouflage nets. And a British soldier squats, sleepy-eyed, by a wall, rifle on shoulder.

At the Europa Hotel—one long corner boarded up from the last parked car explosion—a man in a shed peers into my handbag and frisks the men. The staff have the twitches after a row of bomb threats: one chambermaid survived five with equanimity, heard of the sixth at home one night and collapsed. And the day after I left their jumpiness was justified. I sit in the coffee shop and stare uneasily first at the huge plate glass window in front of me, then, at the parked cars outside. In Belfast you learn to give a wide berth to parked cars. And as I sit, four armoured troop carriers whizz across the street, hung about with soldiers and guns. There is some sort of trouble, people gather, I move closer to the plate glass, invincible as any amateur in the face of sudden death.

The soldiers walk about, shouting orders, the street is sealed off. An empty parked car, I am, told, down aways. You don't want to go down the Falls Road alone, the hall porter tells me, best not. I do, of course, and again trouble. A high-rise council flat, commonplace as any in London except for the soldiers crouched by glass balconies, guns poking viciously through the sides. What's going on? A passer-by shrugs: looking for that chap that escaped today. Down two blocks the children are flooding out from school. I have only been here an hour, so far.

In the afternoon I am driven up the Catholic Falls Road ('Up the IRA', 'Civil Rights or Civil War'), bumping carefully over the slow-down ramps. Taxis are everywhere, two bob into town because the buses have been burned. We come into Andersonstown, a suburban Catholic estate, neat little council houses edging neat little roads. Well, what *were* neat little roads. Now they are covered with broken glass and bricks, left-overs from yesterday's encounter between the Saracen armoured cars and the local kids. We stop at one house like any other and are welcomed into the sitting-room. Vivid patterned carpet, vivid patterned wallpaper, a cocktail cabinet gleaming with silver, a large television in the corner, a Tchernikoff green Chinese girl on one wall, a small boy lying on the Ercol sofa.

'He's not been too good,' says the lady of the house. 'The doctor's coming. Coffee?'

The tiny room is blue with smoke and bulging with men, all are members of the Provisonal IRA. There must be hundreds of such rooms all across Ulster, crammed with just such men, Protestant and Catholic, unemployed and talking obsessively, endlessly, exchanging the gossip of the times.

'Ah was it *your* brother shot? Seven pints of blood was it? He got one through the pelvis, one through the shoulder, they say he'll never walk again. Why shoot him lying on the ground? And they talk about peace.'

'Three fellows down the road, taken up to the barracks, beaten senseless. Well, they'd had two fellows shot in that regiment, two nights ago.'

'The Saracens came in last night, bayonets tied on, cassettes shouting out, 3 a.m. it was. Eileen's roses was all budding, they pulled up every one. Get those effing lights out, they shout. Eileen says do you mind, I've got a sick child in here. We heard glass breaking, went over the road, soldiers pouring in everywhere. When I got up the top of the stairs there were three soldiers standing at the kids' beds, rifles pointing at them, where's your Mamma, where's your Dadda. Margaret's front door was lying against the stairs. You can't forget these things. I remember Archie—one of the best. When the soldiers got through with him he was no better than an ijut.'

The men slap big hands on their knees to emphasize each point, their eyes flash from one face to another. The small boy on the sofa is sick on the counterpane, his mother carries him out of the room, turning as she goes to say why don't they declare martial law, it'd be more honest. More coffee, more fags.

'All this peace thing going on now, what does it mean? People just sign these petitions, nobody states what kind of peace. They say, those women, they got 95 per cent of the people here but they never came to this street or the next that I know of. The priests force them to sign, their collection boxes have dropped because the money's going to the IRA, not the Church. Mrs over the road, she said she'd signed five times, sign early and sign often, that's what she says. There are kids come out and sign for the whole family and no sinner in the house but a bed-ridden grannie. The women don't realize what they're doing. Hang up your guns and be butchered in your beds, that's what they're doing.'

'One of the women who took the petition, her husband had a heart attack when he saw her on television, coughed up a pool of blood right on the floor. Look Mrs, he says, will you shut up about Mr Whitewash and look after me.'

The child is carried back and dumped on the sofa. Another child comes in and turns on the television. The men raise their voices over 'Miss Helen and Romper Room' (the name now used for the IRA punishment cells).

'I'll tell you what I hate. I hate to see a man of God getting up in the pulpit and putting a curse on his own community. Priests say everyone throwing a stone is a Communist but they didn't say that when the youth defended their churches. Where will they be when the UDF come in? Well, the hierarchy of the Church will never go against the Establishment—two weeks after Conway met Whitelaw he was preaching anti-IRA. It's turning the youth against the

Catholic Church. That Father, with his colour telly and his three bottles of whiskey a day, he goes up to the wife of a Provo, gives her a whole long lecture, breath reeking, and then says her husband's lying up at Victoria Hospital, shot.'

A cloth-capped man pokes his head round the door and says did you hear, 75 internees have just been returned. Turf Lodge, I hear.

'Big bucking deal. Tortured and everything and then they let them out. Big bucking deal. I'll tell you what, though. The crime rate's never been lower since the IRA took over. The drug rings we've smashed, yet we send statements to the papers and do they print it? That woman tarred and feathered, she'd broken up a home, got the daughter on drugs, pumped them into her. . .' I ask what drugs. The men turn and look at me as if I were insane.

'. . .time was, if you was tarred and feathered by the IRA, you packed your bags and off. Now what happens? The British press put them on a pedestal, they build these people up, yet the IRA never punished anyone who didn't deserve it. That woman's back now, putting young girls on the game, away back into the business. And I happen to know that girl they said was pregnant, she was never pregnant at all. All I know, there's more people joining the Provisionals every day. The English aren't interested, we know that. They think the violence is all on our side. My sister writes from England, you'd think nothing was going on with you. We had a gun battle here last night.'

Head round the door again. They're picking up ex-internees again, did you hear? Another head: there's two Saracens up the road. The men say 'excuse us, please' and pour out the back door. Children start running, dogs bark. The boy on the sofa is sick again, Miss Helen on television says, 'Now gather round, kiddies,' there is a rattle on the front windows and we all jump. The girl with me, Protestant member of the Alliance Party, says her mother has never, in all her life, been in a Catholic home. She wouldn't believe it could be like this, she says, looking at the shining floor, the lintless carpet.

The next day, a Protestant woman from the Shankill Road repeats to me almost all the Falls Road stories: this time the man turned into an ijut is beaten up by Catholic louts, the man shot in the pelvis ('he'll never walk again') is shot by the IRA, I can't say enough for the British Army, gentlemen they are, every one. A friend says she'd commit murder if the Queen was degraded in front of her but if the British Army are such gentlemen, why do they leave those Cats in Derry, barricaded in, they don't pay *rent or rates*. Her voice cracks with emotion. But then, everyone is emotional here; as they begin their long interchangeable recitations of bombings and maimings and friends gunned down they start to tremble. I know for a *fact*, they say over and over, I know for a *fact* and they sway backwards and forwards on the edges of their chairs and shake their fingers and shake. The myths (the facts?) come down like plastic foam over a fire and harden into an impenetrable shell, today's stories turn into folklore as you listen, the outsider.

And, of course, outsiders are no good to them. They launch into explanations, a few minutes pass and they turn to confront each other again. Every now and then pure humanity, pure shared experience breaks through: two women, Catholic and Protestant, both with a son, a husband shot, come towards each other and hold on to each other's arms. I know Mrs Docherty, you've lost someone, too. I know, Mrs Campbell. A second ticks away, they stare into each other's faces, their hands grip, unspoken words hang in the air. And then: but Mrs Docherty, you will admit, when our boys came up to the top of the road that time, it was *your* boys waiting, with bottles and stones. Ah no, I can't think that Mrs Campbell, not *our* boys, not *my* boy. He's a good boy, always stayed at home, never got mixed up in that kind of thing. No, Mrs Docherty, yes, Mrs Campbell, I happen to know for a *fact*...

Like a bad marriage, a marriage torn from the beginning with quarrels, adrenalin now has poisoned them all with the sickly injections of love and hate. They chant their grievances against their partners but when the front door slams and the partner walks in, their eyes light up, the addiction is fed, they are locked once more in each other's unyielding arms. When I left London for Belfast, I thought I knew something of the problems of Northern Ireland. When I left Belfast for London, I knew I knew nothing.

12 June 1972

Melancholy Baby

IN THE BLIND AND DIZZY YEARS of late adolescence, I was hardly aware that children existed at all. As for babies, they simply made up the contents of passing prams or small bundles in other people's arms. When I became pregnant for the first time I sat and wondered what babies wore, other than nappies of course—whatever it was, it didn't seem to come under the category of clothes. Perhaps one simply wound them up in woolly scarves and hoped for the best.

I was a long way from home at the time, with no friends yet married, never mind pregnant, so when the baby was eventually born I was shattered to realise that, under cover of the drama of birth, a squatter had moved permanently in and, what's more, a squatter who most unreasonably demanded to be fed every four hours. Overcome, I succumbed to a bad case of the post-partum blues and wandered miserably about my flat in an old dressing-gown, eyeing the baby as if he were an unexploded bomb and, if he cried, joining in. Until this moment I had never even been responsible for a budgerigar and here I was now, expected to take on a whole human life. Waaah.

I can't be sure that this early experience accounts for my deep belief that the uterus of a woman does not necessarily fit her for the long-term care of children any more than the you-know-what of a man, but it certainly helped. Maternity was not, for me, doing what came naturally. It took me four months to think of my child as anything else than 'the baby' and it was only in the day-by-day tending of him that love began to grow, as it would presumably grow in a man in the same position. Motherhood is a learned process and only ten years later, with the birth of my youngest son, did I feel immediately the love and tenderness they said I should have felt way back then.

But some of the old ambivalence remains and I have mixed feelings about children to this day. Part of it arises, I suppose, from a child's split nature—children can be awe-inspiringly horrible; manipulative, aggressive, rude, and unfeeling to a point where I often think that, if armed, they would make up the most terrifying fighting force the world has ever seen. Little faces blank with the ignorance of suffering, little eyes alert with interest as you bleed to death. But children can also rise to heights unreachable by adults: they will forgive awful suffering at the hands of those they love, they will offer their whole selves to you with a trust uncontemplatable by grown-ups, they are touching and endearing and vulnerable to a point of constant alarm to those who love them.

And the other part arises from the fact that I would rather be a father to a child than a mother. Here he comes, that God-like figure, a treat for two hours rather than a burden for twenty-four, a symbol of fun and games rather than a permanent routine. His job to play about on the floor, mine to see to a myriad niggling needs: the dentist, the doctor, the time-to-go-to-bed-rows, the fitting of shoes, the washing of clothes, the eat-up-your-spinaches, the must-wash-your-hairs, the no-you're-too-young-to-do-thats. No one wants to be thanked all the time but when no one thanks you because they cannot know what they have been spared through your forethought, a certain (doubtless immature) resentment can be felt.

Part of the experience of bringing up children (left sternly unmentioned by Dr Spock) is boredom. My boredom threshold is low at the best of times but I have spent more time being slowly and excruciatingly bored by children than any other section of the human race. How long, oh Lord, must I watch my youngest do (badly) the vanishing egg trick by my bed at six in the morning? How often must I hear him sing (off-key) little Billie had a ten-foot willie? How democratic, I ask myself, can I afford to be without actually gibbering.

Because that is the heart of the problem. If you believe, as I do in theory, in an active democracy in the home, the jostling for an adult foothold becomes, at times, near intolerable. I find myself envying relations who bring up their children on

83

authoritarian lines—how nice to have the double advantage of a) thinking you're right in this policy and it is best for the child and b) thereby bringing up quiet, polite children who impress other adults and leave you alone.

If a child of mine begins a low, unmelodic hum that burns through the brain, I try to leave remonstration until the last possible moment, until the moment when I feel that if the hummer were not my child but another adult I would nevertheless be forced to say, politely, I wonder if you could see your way to stopping that hum. An authoritarian parent would say almost immediately, with wondrous simplicity, stop that bloody humming. And an authoritarian parent would save himself a great deal of anguish. The trouble is that children, given an inch, take thousands of miles—they have no real concept of democracy except insofar as it operates for themselves. It is in the democratic household that children regularly comment to their parents, 'you're so *stupid*,' It is in democratic households that the fruits of two hours' cooking are laid in front of the children and pushed away with insane giggles and appalling comments. Personally, I shout several four-letter words and whisk the dish away forever and see respect dawn in their eyes. But why? It doesn't at all fit in with my theories, I'll tell you that.

The crunch for democracy in a capitalist society comes with money. My children have a Rockefellerian attitude —they want an ice cream, they want a comic, they want, they want, they want and what is an adult to do? I can't pretend with any conviction that 5p is too vast a sum to part with. I can't expect abject gratitude. I don't want to lecture them constantly about how hard money is to come by.

Sometimes, faced with photographs of starving children, bruised and maimed in war, I look at my own sleek well-fed demanding infant and unnameable emotions assault me. No, of *course* I don't expect him to be grateful.

Yes I do.

26 June 1972

Witnessing Jehovah

TWO BLACK LADIES got their feet in my door last week and asked me what I thought about the Creator. From thence, by devious routes (like me saying what did black ladies think the Creator had ever done for black ladies) we got on to a discussion about women's rights and, breathing heavily, they pushed the latest issue of *Awake* into my hands. *Awake*, in case any reader lives in some unthinkably remote eyrie, is the magazine put out by the Jehovah's Witnesses. 'What,' asks the front cover, 'about Women's Liberation?' and illustrates its theme with a drawing of an ineffably unliberated woman wearing an iron curtain sort of suit and a trapped sort of expression, as well, it turns out, she might.

The first article, 'What is Women's Liberation Saying?' is a competent enough job of reporting the main aims of the movement, from equal pay and abortion on demand to child-care centres and equal division of household duties between husband and wife. So far, so good. But a downward spiral starts with the next piece, 'Is there any truth in what they say?', a lovely 'on the one hand, on the other' exercise in which any admission of the truth of discrimination is instantly counterbalanced by awful warnings about what equality could bring—women fighting in the trenches, digging coal in the mines and, horror of horrors, shovelling manure with a farmer husband. Then, with a sharp rap on the knuckles for women who pose nude (thus encouraging men to be sexist), we are whisked on to the next piece, 'Each designed for a role'.

Here it is revealed that where a woman excels is in her rôle as a mother, and this is backed up by a quote from a woman who writes, 'It is my fondest desire to be feminine, which is my natural rôle in life, and to encourage my spouse to be more masculine, according to his nature.' Why any woman should have to *encourage* her wretched spouse to behave according to his nature is not discussed but then, *Awake* is not overly concerned with the niceties of logic, bless its proselytizing little heart. Sternly it is brought to our attention that really happy women, admired, respected and cared for by good husbands, would not dream of wanting to be liberated from such hedonism and the writer adds, more in pity than in anger, that 'when a woman has a husband, father or brother who does not understand her rôle and her needs and who does not treat her right, then she can indeed be unhappy. Very often these are the women seeking liberation'.

Well, it's so true, girls. Take my brother. He just had no interest at all in my rôle or my needs. He kept climbing up trees and shouting cowardy cowardy custard at me down there and not appreciating the burnt pastry I was occasionally forced to make. With a history of deprivation like that, who can wonder at my attachment to women's lib?

But the real iron fist in the velvet glove comes smashing down in the last article of the trilogy, 'How should men treat women?'. Kindly and with infinite condescension the writer explains, 'the woman certainly is in no way inferior to the man in the quality of love', and then goes on to point out that men have, whether they like it or not, been given heavier responsibilities by God. The Adam and Eve legend, crux of women's lib attacks on religious myths, is cunningly turned on its elbow:

'The woman rebelled first, then the man—Gen. 3: 1-6. From this some have concluded that if it were not for women we should be in the Garden of Eden. But . . .'says *Awake*, springing gallantly to the defence of womankind, 'man was created first and made the family head with the greater responsibility. As the captain of his ship, he should have steered a straight course even in troubled seas. But that first man, Adam, failed as a family head. Since he had the greater responsibility, he had the greater guilt.'

There, you see? It wasn't our faults at all. Goodness me, how could it be? You can't honestly blame subnormal human beings for their little peccadilloes, now can you? From then on, a thick smokescreen of quotes hangs over the argument.

Ephesians 5:23 says, 'A husband is head of his wife as the Christ also is head of the congregation', and the writer in *Awake* adds, in what appears to be genuine bewilderment, 'if there were no head in a family, what would happen? There could be constant bickering and disagreement over decisions, with no one making the final one. But it is necessary for the welfare of the family to have someone authorised to make final decisions and God has assigned that rôle to the husband'. Well, bully for God—or rather, for male Jehovah's Witnesses.

Oddly enough, an unregenerate sort of reader called Mrs Simmonds wrote to me the next day enclosing a copy of *Awake*. She comments, 'I think the generally sly tone of it is very unpleasant. But for the Uncle Tom, I'm all right Jack type of woman it must make palatable reading.'

Mrs Simmonds, I fear your father, husband, brother did not treat you right, either.

26 June 1972

Otters' Hell

THE SUN BEATS DOWN on Dorset—green meadows spread under blue skies and, in the pleat of a hill, one grey church steeple. A perfect summer's day and what more traditional a way to pass a perfect summer's day than watching, say, an otter being torn to pieces? As Father did, as Grandfather did, as all the Grands have done since King John was young.

Under the bridge the stream runs clear and calm. A moorhen flicks about among the waterweeds, a duck and her five ducklings scud along, leaving tiny wakes. And here they come, the otter hunters, plodding downstream, hounds writhing amiably through the reeds, men and women trudging behind. As they come the ducks scatter, the moorhen flaps in panic, the air splits with the honk of a hunting horn. Merrie England incarnate.

But the idyll is rather spoilt by the appearance of a raggle-taggle trail of long-haired yobos in patched jeans—so very different from the forest-green suits of the elderly huntswomen, the white breeches and forest-green jackets of the distinguished huntsmen. They move slowly, with diginity. The yobos move fast, with none. They run ahead of the hunt to the bridge and out of each tattered pocket comes an aerosol can. The sides of the river bank are carefully sprayed and a strong, pleasant smell of lemon nips the nose. The hunters come to a halt, stand watching these activities, turn from the stream and walk slowly up on to the bridge. Us here, Them there. Only the hounds, their nostrils blocked with Bob Martin's Anti-Mate, lope cheerily between the two groups, all sense of smell momentarily over-powered.

The yobos—young teachers, students, from all walks of life as they say—are members of various groups, from the Hunt Saboteurs Association through the Dorset CROW

(Campaign for the Relief of Wildlife) to reformist members of the RSPCA and the League Against Cruel Sport. There are many such groups throughout the country, some purely local, some local branches of larger bodies, most of them concerned with a wide variety of conservation issues. They are united today, as they unite here and there, weekend after weekend, under the banner of ending bloodsports—whether it be fox, otter, stag or the new hare coursing. The big organizations lobby Parliament. Meanwhile, back at the ranch, they aim to save the life of one particular animal on one particular day—they believe in direct action and direct action is what they often get.

Well, you do, if you insist on challenging what is looked upon in some circles as a genetic inheritance: the right of an Englishmen (with money, of course) to spend his leisure pursuing and killing wild animals—who belong to no one in law—in the most athletic and picturesque manner possible. Mr Francis Bennion, currently occupied with preparing his case against Peter Hain at the Old Bailey on 24 July for curtailing an Englishman's freedom to enjoy cricket, has made no secret of the fact that, if he wins, he intends to turn his attention to these hunt saboteurs for 'conspiring to disrupt lawful events'. Such lawful events as otter and fox hunting have been 'sports' for well over three hundred years and, for their supporters, that is an argument in itself. They have other reasons too, of course. That hunting is the natural and humane way to stabilize a healthy animal population. That animals don't feel as we do. That animals *do* feel as we do—and so enjoy a good hunt. But because hunters are doing something they enjoy and that enjoyment is approved by the law, arguments on their part are hardly necessary.

Things are very different for the protesters. To begin with, they are often countrymen themselves, and that means living cheek by jowl with neighbours in a way townspeople have forgotten. In Dorset, for instance, something like five landowners share the county and tenant farmers are not in the best possible position to deny their landlord the right to hunt across the land. Farm workers, too, living in tied cottages, are unlikely to protest on matters of principle. The local magistrates, doctors, heads of police—all are probably members or followers of the local hunt and protesting tradesmen may find their outlets drying up. Some members of CROW have already suffered a degree of harassment: anonymous phone calls in the night, strangers making inquiries about their credit standing and their political views.

The overall pattern is, of course, feudal, and the main emotion underlying feudalism is the arbitrary belief in treating well those who serve you well and badly those who do not conform. And this feudalism extends to animals, too. The country landowner thinks himself a country and animal lover *par excellence*, and shows his contempt for hunt protesters by calling them townees, ignorant of country life. At times, this may be true, but by no means necessarily. Many a young townsman (and countryman) these days knows more about the actual facts of animal life than the older countryman, who tends to base his knowledge on old wives' tales and, anyway, believes such knowledge can only be bred in the bone. 'Books,' snorted one huntsman, faced with a protester, 'he says he's learned about otters from books.' I suspect that animals, domestic or wild, are to many countrymen possessions, where townspeople tend to think that animals have a right to exist independently of the wishes of human beings. The two views do not look like meeting yet awhile.

So, direct action. These protesters have a certain tolerant affection for the otter hunters. 'They're not bad old codgers,' said one. 'Just relics of the nineteenth century, dinosaurs with no reasons for doing what they do except that they have always done it. And, anyway, they're a dying breed.' In the 1920s there were 30-odd otter hunts in this country, now the numbers have dwindled to seven but then, otters are dwindling too, it seems. That the otter hunters feel the same tolerance for the protesters is not so evident. Today, a general effort is made to ignore their very existence, but an underlying irritation is evident in the flushed cheeks and distant eyes of the huntsmen. Come out for a peaceful day's hunt and what happens? Yer pestered by interlopers and yer hounds are put off the scent. A fine thing when yer can't kill an otter because you've got a young person of doubtful appearance and worse pedigree breathing down yer neck.

Back at the bridge the groups close in. The only young huntsman (all the rest are elderly) is a blood, a Flashman in the flesh, blonde, high-coloured and handsome. He carries a plaited whip and he raises it as he draws near to one of the youths who carries an aerosol can.

'I catch you spraying that in my hounds' eyes and you'll get a taste of this.'

'I don't spray it into hounds' eyes and, anyway, it's harmless.'

'Harmless, is it? How'd you like me to spray it into your eyes?'

The youth says go ahead and gives the huntsman his spray. It is held six inches from the youth's eyes and sprayed directly in. The youth blinks, the huntsman drops the can, laughs and swaggers off. Honest-to-God swaggers. A hunt follower in a tweed hat comes close to the group and stretches out his neck, face working.

'I shot five Germans in the last war and each of them was a better man than you.' The group gaze at him. Another follower comes up.

'I fought in two world wars but I'd have let Hitler in if I'd known about you. Teach you all a lesson.'

The group gape and snigger in a thoroughly ill-bred and unGerman way. How can they, callow youths that they are, understand the deep feelings of a man who fought the murderer of six million Jews to preserve his own right to kill otters?

One such callow youth, undaunted, decides to talk to an awe-inspiring otter lady, a huge St. Trinian's schoolgirl in her green uniform, wielding her six-foot otter stave. He asks her what the notches are for (they scar three quarters of the stick) and she replies, eyes fixed on a point beyond his face, that they mark the otters she has killed. And the crosses, he asks? Those are for two otters killed on one hunt. She adds, brightly, that this does not happen very often. Doggedly, the youth continues. Are otters pests? No, says the lady. Well, do they taste good when you cook them? The lady's eyes, glazed over with warm amusement. My dear boy, you don't *eat* otters. Oh ho ho ho *no*. Really? says the youth in his thick way. They're not pests and they can't be eaten. What do you

91

kill them for, then please? The lady's smile sets as she gazes with consuming interest at the horizon. Beside her the Major—a fine specimen of an Englishman with curling moustache and a florid complexion—gazes at her. They are not related but they could be twins, two C. Aubrey Smiths, incredibly noble, with faces made for the quelling of natives or felling lions at a glance. They don't make 'em like that any more.

The youth shuffles off. Poor old cows, says his mate with the tenderest affection. The hunt breaks up for lunch and the protesters adjourn to a pub. But they leave a girl on guard by their cars—the poor old cows have been known to deflate tyres and put sugar in the petrol tanks of absent antis, in defence of their rights.

After lunch, the harassment begins again. Over the fields beside the meandering stream plod the hounds, the whippers-in, the huntsmen and the protesters. At every stop, the youths engage the huntsmen in conversation. Sometimes there is no answer, the eyeballs glaze, the smiles freeze. Sometimes fury breaks through, bursting tiny veins in the varicosed cheeks, shaking the whipping arm.

'The trouble with you people—yer none of yer *work* for a living. Otherwise yer wouldn't have the time to come down here and pester us.'

'How come *you're* here then,' says a protester, a tired edge to his voice. 'If *you* had any work to do, you wouldn't spend your time killing otters.'

Impasse. Clenched jaws. Twitching muscles. Anthropologists tell us that over-crowding makes human beings aggressive, but they have not researched a much stranger and more common phenomenon—give a human being 500 acres to himself and his aggression towards interlopers makes an overcrowded townsman look like the original Caspar Milquetoast.

The hunt moves off again, continuing purely as a ritual now. Lemon fills the countryside and the hounds wouldn't know an otter from a rusty bucket. But they break a duckling's neck efficiently enough. A protester picks up the hot, soft body and holds it out to a passing huntswoman.

'Your trophy for today,' he says, stroking the soft dappled feathers.

'Poor little thing,' she says brightly. 'Make a nice duck and green peas for someone tonight.'

They despise each other.

On July 19, at Dorchester Magistrate's Court, four hunt saboteurs (three of them CROW members and, for what it's worth, vegetarians) are coming up for trial on a charge of disturbing the peace at a March fox hunt where fighting broke out. What makes this case unusual, indeed unique, is that four huntsmen (the Joint Hunt Master, the Hunt Secretary and two followers) are also charged. The eyes of many bloodsport fors and antis will be on this case, and Francis Bennion will doubtless pick up a few valuable tips, too.

'Fox hunters?' says a CROW member. 'Oh, they're much worse. Young Tory businessmen on the make. And it's much more dangerous for us. They use the horses, you see, to isolate us and they can whip you or kick you from the saddle. And they take children along, too. A kid came out from a cornfield where they got the fox, she had the brush, and blood all down her dress. I went up to her and asked how old she was. Eleven, she said. Then her mother came up. Get away from my daughter, you pervert, she said.'

What is otter hunting? 'A hunt consists of a pack of hounds, a gang of men and women, many armed with long steel-tipped poles, together with a terrier or two. They usually meet two or three times a week from April to October. Many hunts last two to four hours. In its efforts to escape, the otter will often swim under water, but this is of no avail, for the sportsmen and women line the river bank to look for the tell-tale bubbles coming up from the otter—eventually the otter will be caught. This frequently happens when it clambers out of the river too tired to swim further. Whether it be on land or in the river, the kill is not quick for the otter has a thick coat and desperately fights for its life against the pack of dogs. The huntsman tries to retrieve the otter as soon as possible after the kill so that its head, feet and tail may be cut off and given as trophies to guests and hunt members. Finally the remains are cut up and flung to the hungry hounds.' (From a pamphlet by the League Against Cruel Sports).

'The otter may become extinct in Britain. There has been a dramatic fall in the otter population of Britain over the last seven years or so. While it may be difficult to do much about some factors affecting the decline, it is clear that hunting, which serves no useful purpose, should be stopped immediately.' (The international wildlife magazine *Animals.*)

3 July 1972

Period Piece

THERE ARE THREE HUMAN conditions that have been labelled, through the centuries, unclean, untouchable. The leper with his eaten face and warning bell; the low-caste Indian, cleaner of the sewers of Bombay; the woman menstruating.

Male-run societies all over the world, from the dawn of history to the present day, have barred such women from the life of the community. At their approach, crops wither, cattle and sheep and goats abort and die, clear water becomes polluted, cakes in the oven fall, rain doesn't. At times, their very presence in the village is a threat and they must be sequestered in huts outside, away from the beds of their menfolk, whose stomachs they would cause to burst. The Christian and Judaic religions have been at least as stringent—once, a menstruating woman was forbidden to attend religious service and any woman so eager to visit her god that she broke the taboo served a penance of seven years.

So when I began menstruating and my mother said oh dear and then, hastily, isn't that nice, now you know you can have babies, I was not overly impressed. Indeed, I was downright horrified. The onset contradicts so deeply any other pattern evident in life that it tends to be a thoroughly unwelcome upheaval for the majority of eleven- and twelve-year-old girls. Until then blood has always been feared, the result of accident or illness, the usual accompaniment to pain, the terrible red signal of doctors and death. Now *this* blood, newly flowing, is called natural, the proof of womanhood. Click click goes the little computing brain and out shoots the answer, based on previous programming. Nasty. Frightening.

Until then, Nature or God has been praised as efficient, practical, infinitely adroit and tidy. Now it becomes clear that one aspect, at least, is extremely inefficient, impractical, clumsy and anything but tidy: something that affects a female around 450 times in her life (and useless for many years) could surely have been planned more carefully. Until then, too, most girls have thought themselves as healthy and strong as their brothers. Now, insinuations of weakness paralyse the growing muscles. They must stand by as others splash in sea or swimming pool, a mother urges on them an elderly caution: best not to have a bath, best not to overtire yourself, best to take a note to school and avoid gym today. Why? Because, dear girl, you are *unwell*.

Nor, until then, have most girls thought themselves anything but children. Now the blood comes and the shadow of adulthood touches their years for the first time; and an adulthood confined, apparently, to the bearing of children, an intimation of sex as a burden, wearisome and messy. A glaring contrast to their brothers' first hints of sex. Boys are familiar with their genitals from the beginning—there it all is, displayed quite openly outside the body, capable of being handled and producing pleasurable sensations. Girls know next to nothing of that hidden channel in themselves until it makes its presence known by bleeding as a wound bleeds, mysterious and disturbing, heralded, often as not, by headaches and waves of cramps in the night.

And though Mother may show some satisfaction, in private, that her daughter is normal and growing up, all the real signs a child can interpret from past experience signal shame, secretiveness, an event to be coped with behind closed doors, like family quarrels or excretion. Few parents celebrate the menses by announcing it, loud and proud to assembled friends. Few, if any, congratulate the child, throw a party, buy a present, send a card. The message comes through clearly enough. Menstruation is a shame.

Until the age of 11, my brother and I were wholly undivided, two skinny grubby kids climbing trees, confiding jokes, quarrelling and rude and friendly, a twin knot of unity against the intrusion of the adult world, scoffing and scuffling and picking our noses and hooting like loons in corners. And overnight, the change. Across the beach he came running, come on, come on, dragging me over the hot sands to the water's edge and then I had to say, digging my heels in, not hooting not screeching, no I can't. And watch his eyes glazing, his skin reddening. Oh, he said, oh I see, and turned away and left me. The barrier had fallen between us and never again did it entirely lift.

Him for the fun and the freedom and the pleasure. Me for the boredom and burden and the dull aches. I looked over the blue sea and howled with frustration and outrage, knowing what he had not yet understood, that not everything was for the best in the best of all possible worlds, that God could be mean, too. Now I was in the conspiratorial harem, initiate of that ubiquitous underwear drawer where the women of the house kept oddshaped packages. Yet, searching through my favourite books, I could find no mention of the thing that had happened to me. No heroine from Pamela through Jane Eyre to Mad-Cap Moll of the Fifth had ever menstruated and I didn't *want* a baby.

Later, of course, resignation sets in but the burden remains and subtly alters, month by month, life's pattern. No man can guess how many apparently irrational decisions, how many sudden changes of behaviour are due not to the basically irrational and changeable nature of woman, not to the fickle moon nor even pre-menstrual tension but to the plain, practical fact of four or five days' bleeding. I have sat with boyfriends in theatres and cinemas, at dinners and parties, laughing and enjoying it all and then—oh Lord, oh no, oh yes—the ominous pull at the abdomen, the inexorable dampness. And irrationally, illogically, on an apparent whim, I demand to be taken home because I'm bored, because I'm tired, and want to be alone, because lies and lies and more lies, because (God forbid I should ever admit) I need a sanitary towel.

Nor can I, for four days in every month, act on impulse, say yes, why don't we all go on after the party, go midnight swimming, run down to Brighton and see Roger, stay up all night and see the dawn. Why? Because I haven't got a spare sanitary towel is why, because I'm still undisciplined and the shops are shut and I am unprepared. How can I trek across the Sahara, hitchhike to Samarkand just like that? How, for heaven's sake, do you ask for what you need in German, in

Italian? If you merely point at a promising-looking parcel you end up in your hotel room with baby's plastic pants, size 1.

There's the constant fear of accidents, the arrangement of the wardrobe so that, today, you don't wear the white slacks, the pale green linen, the shortest mini-skirt. How long have I sat firmly on chairs across the world, sweating with fear that my rising will reveal the unrevealable? How many times must a man have thought me victim of chronic bladder trouble as I dash yet again for the ladies.

Once, working as a temp in an office, I gained in one short evening the evil reputation of a lady drunk. Going into a bar with three men, after work, I sat with a gin and then, shall we go, they said and yes, I nodded. I rose, I turned to look at myself in the mirror and sank like a shot swan, back into my seat again. What else to do but demand another drink? And another and another. The men became uneasy, my eyes unfocused, eventually each one departed and I sat there, adamantly drinking, rigid and wretched, alone till the bar closed and the last customer was out of the door. Then, handbag clutched in back in a curious way, I tottered out and was sick in the ladies. Next day, in the office, they'd locked the portable bar.

I was even afraid to accept invitations to stay during that time of the month, afraid of sleeping in a snow-white bed and waking to shame, to the indelible signs of my presence. Hot and embarrassed I would scrub away, the sheet humped over the basin, the mattress revealing my misjudgments to the world.

All very well, I often feel, for those sporty fresh-air sex handbook writers to tell us we must not feel shame about sex, how we must love our own bodies. By the time I had my first experience of actual sex I had already logged up seven years of menstruation as my only other sex-linked experience and they tell me I shouldn't be inhibited? Ashamed? Constrained? A man with sisters has had all of that time, too, to build up an impression of feminine secrets, of the smells and stains that emanate from women. He may compliment us on our shining hair and bright eyes, the pure sweet smoothness of our skins, our dainty ways, our delicacies. But all the time he knows and we know that down there, blood may be silently seeping. Unclean. Untouchable.

Once married or embarked on sex, things change for the better. That monthly letting becomes, if not less annoying, at least occasionally welcome for its proof of infertility. Later, the flow is loved for its disappearance, for its announcement *in absentia* of greater things to come, though you could call it out of the frying pan into the fire. And with the first baby comes an equally welcome release, at least for me, from pre-menstrual cramps, from the swollen raw-nerve feeling that presages, for some women, the flow. But come a child, two children, three and the womb is not satisfied. The periods go on and on and on, an atavistic, antiquated reminder of what? Today, when men may land on the moon and aim their cameras at Venus, I am still below, feet planted heavily on earth, living evidence of some mad plan to populate this planet out of existence, my mindless womb bleeding hopelessly, hopefully—a lunatic and megalomanic organ, dumb, deaf and blind.

Yet perhaps, in the Seventies, the end of such waste is in sight. Perhaps my daughters will, quickly and neatly, extract each 28 days the evidence of profligacy. It could, of course, stop now if women, all women, were suited to the Pill and took it 350 days a year but the penalty for interfering with inefficient nature is still there—that many extra days in which to incur thrombosis, depression, weight, headaches, frigidity and even sudden death. Shall my grand-daughter be freed from even these penalties by some dedicated researcher or scientist? It seems perfectly possible. How long before it seems necessary to others but women?

7 *August* 1972

Just Very Good Fiends

NOW, AT LAST, the rooms are empty—silence reverberates like a touched gong. The childish voices that have effed and blinded all summer from the adventure playground have now switched to the school playground. John and Mary are back at school, all's right with the world and my copy of Illich's *Deschooling Society* is up in the loft where the pigeons go to the bathroom.

Who, I ask myself wearily, gains from this six or eight week stretch each summer? Teachers? Most of them have to take holiday jobs to pay the rent. Parents? A father's ordinary working life continues, varied only by the fact that he can't get anywhere near the television set until the Epilogue. The working mother spends most of her job time imagining the kids flinging themselves under cars or over policemen. The housewife mother shops and cooks eight times more often and works eighty times harder and (because advertising does its job supremely well) worries that hers are the only children in the western world not spending their entire summer wandering along golden beaches, knee-deep in water ski-ing, motor boating, shrimping and big dipping. The children? A vast majority hang around lamp posts stirring up the summer dust, cuffing each other stupid or sitting sag-jawed in front of the box. That most of them still maintain they prefer holidays to school is less an accolade for holidays than a fearsome comment on school.

But be all that as it may, these holidays I tried. My God, I tried. First findings: in order to give children a good holiday you start by tearing up every guide on how to give your children a good holiday. I freely admit the possibility that my children and my children's friends may be severely retarded, deeply disturbed and highly unlike your children, but mine are turned on by none of the suggestions as to their holiday activities listed by industrious folk with the kind of kids I never met. My sort of child does not, voluntarily, wish to know about 'Spitalfields in the Eighteenth Century'. Unless propelled by a swift kick they do not proceed towards the Science Museum for an exhibition on the discovery of oxygen. Their grimaces are too awful to describe when I suggest (from *Time Out* yet) a lecture on 'You and Your Analytical Chemist '. They remain as dead at the mention of slides on the history of ballet, youth in China as depicted on Ming vases, the bee—its life cycle and community organization.

I did try, though. Twice I tried with museums. Once we went to the Natural History and once to the British, me pushing and them moving their legs backwards and forwards. Four things interested them—the blue whale, the dinosaurs, the mummies and an old dried-up corpse under glass. After that they said they were tired, their backs ached, their heads ached, their feet ached, their hair ached. An octogenarian just after a major operation has more energy than children of nine, ten, eleven, twelve, fifteen and sixteen.

Emerging, I asked hopefully what they had liked best about the museums. Being searched when we went in, they replied as one child. The conversation from then on concerned, not the interesting habits of blue whales, but how you could conceal a bomb in a Coke tin, a camera, your denim hat, the sides of your jeans. Look mummy if I was going to bomb the Natural History museum I'd...Mummy you're not *listening*. If you put a bomb in the litter bin *there* and you were *there*, would you be dead? Or would your arms blow off or your legs or what? You know that dinosaur we saw, I said. Well, that dinosaur has a very special sort off tail that... They turn blank midwich-cuckoo eyes at me. Dinosaur, they say. What dinosaur?

I went on trying, I made lists of sporting events, skating rinks, swimming pools. I scanned fly-posted walls for pop concerts like a dirty old man looking for graffiti. I got out maps and traced the snakes and ladders of bus routes and underground lines. I spent hours on the telephone not getting times of performances and not making provisional bookings.

I stood in theatre queues for hours to get tickets.

Typical of the results of my efforts: an hour booking tickets for *Jesus Christ, Superstar* three weeks ahead at enormous cost. The day arrived. I remind them that tonight's the night. *Tonight*, they say in shocked voices. But tonight it's *Dracula, Prince of Darkness* on *television*. In a parental pet, I swish out of the house and swish back again an hour later, tickets resold and my wallet pinched from my handbag. This event immediately generates great interest and until the film the rooms buzz with action as each child takes turns at trying to pinch wallets from the pockets of other children pretending to be me. Once again the fringe event becomes the star turn.

About now, temper and energy beginning to fray, I try to conjure up my own childhood feelings again. Surely I was altogether different: more sensitive, curious, imaginative, receptive, civilized? Into my mind floats the disconcerting memory of Aunt Lilian, huge benign ex-headmistress, who descended each holiday from the fastness of Norfolk to drag my brother and me round the educational sights of London. I see again our frightful behind-her-back faces, I hear again the whines, the moans, the giggles. Can I have a drink, an ice cream, go to the loo, go home.

I remember, too, little Jennie-Louise, peer and neighbour. Jennie-Louise would send round careful notes inviting us to her Pollock's Victorian Theatre show. Our mother would accept on our behalf. We would go. Jennie-Louise had small chairs in rows and we sat in rows and watched Jennie-Louise's flappy bits of paper and listened to Jennie-Louise's flappy voice and saw all the mothers smiling and clapping. We hated Jennie-Louise and my brother, driven mad by boredom, sat on her Pollock's Victorian Theatre. What, said my mother, is the matter with children today?

Slowly I relearnt what children really like or, failing what they really like, how you can force them to like what there is. You can use the *Guinness Book of Records* technique: that is not a dry old insect, that is the Biggest Grasshopper in England. This is not a boring piece of paper, this is the Oldest Piece of Paper in London. That is not a Greek scarab, that is the Smallest Greek Scarab in the Whole World. Exaggeration, superlatives, lies if you like, can kindle a light in the blankest pair of eyes. Another technique is deliberate misinformation. That, you say, is a Blue Whale. A large notice proclaims it to be a Dolphin. A short time lag and then the sneers come thick and fast. That's not a blue whale, that's a dolphin, hee hee, ho ho, you got that *wrong*.

Next, I learnt that anything anyone tells you is unsuitable for children is the only thing suitable for them. Detecting a quaver in the voice of the Roundhouse booking clerk at the thought of children at the Voodoo Dancers of Bahia, I knew I was on the right track. They sat riveted throughout the evening and talked the rest of the night about the goat that would have had its throat slit, the hen that would have dripped blood all over the man if only they'd seen it really, in Brazil.

In fact, drama in strong doses is what makes my children's days. A dull car journey forces out my story of how a lorry with sheet glass sticking out of the back decapitated a passing motorbike rider and how his motorbike still holding his headless body, looped round in front of the lorry driver, who promptly crashed too. Attention is total, boredom ceases on the spot. Where did his head come off? What did they do with it? Did the blood spout up to here or here? What did the lorry driver think when he saw it? Did he crash badly? Did he die too? Did his head come off? Soon we were at our destination, as merry and gay a family as ever you saw.

This is the list of events that made my children's holidays and will be remembered for years ahead. Readers with delicate stomachs stop reading here.

An alsatian, who came slowly towards us, began frothing at the mouth, turned slowly around and around and fell stiffly on its back, legs straight up in the air. The RSPCA van arrived, the dog was put in the back and driven away. I spent the rest of the afternoon turning slowly around and around frothing at the mouth and falling down with my legs stiffly in the air. They captured me and stuffed me on the sofa. Highly recommended, *Guardian*

Some boys are seen from our window, in darkness, battering at the adventure playground house. They break in. A flickering flame is seen in the black interior—they are trying to set fire to a chair. An excited babble breaks out among the childish audience. From the trees comes a policeman, running. The teenagers dash off. One is trapped. After that, nothing happens for a long time but the audience remains to the bitter end, cheering and encoring. Will run and run and run, *Sun*

Fishing boats come in and I comment on their picturesque lines. The children remain unstirred until they see three large skates flapping dismally at the bottom of a plastic hamper. The water is clouded with blood. The children stare until the last gut has been ripped out and thrown to the seagulls. Not to be missed, *Daily Mail*

A boring swimming hole and a cloudy day transformed by the fact that a woman's body was found drowned only two days ago, right under where they are swimming. Entertainment for all the family, *Evening Standard*

A long rainy trip down the river to Kew. Irritability and yawns break out. A child returns from the bar with a Coke and announces joyously that the barmaid is drunk. They all rush off and rush back again, intermittently, to report. She's going like this, she's reeling about, she's chucking the bottles out of the window, she's going to be *sick*. The audience laughed and laughed, *Daily Telegraph*

A fight breaks out at Speaker's Corner. Two old drunks weave about buffeting each other and cursing. The children's heads peer under their arms and gaze up, fascinated, at their distorted faces. One old man collapses, an ambulance is called, he's heaped on a stretcher and trundled away. Mustn't be missed, *Sunday Times*

Just before school starts the children turn their flower-like faces towards me, smiles wreathing their dewy faces, Mummy, they say, that was the *best* holiday we ever *had*. Their little mouths fasten on my throat. Mummy is it *here* that Dracula bites? Is it *here* he'd get the most blood?

16 September 1974

Without a City Wall

THERE IS A GREEN HILL far away, without a city wall. This green hill was once black and at 9.15 a.m. on 21 October 1966 it moved. 144 people, 116 of them children, died under it. Aberfan.

Joan Miller, lecturer at Cardiff, has written a book, *Aberfan*, about the 'aftermath of the tragedy': the ways it affected all the people of the village, bereaved or not, and welded them through much anguish into a closer and more concerned community, concerned for itself and for others. Aberfan's red and white floral cross, for instance, is now a familiar tribute wherever tragedy strikes children, from Germany to the Transvaal and the Ynysowen male voice choir, born out of a spontaneous burst of song to celebrate the removal of the monstrous tip, now sings free for any organization concerned with those in need. There are silver linings to even that murderous black cloud.

Among other things, the book started me thinking again about the value of the church. In this disaster, like all others, the thin veneer of everyday routine cracked open and the vulnerable interior was exposed, floodlit for all the world to see and shudder, like a wounded body in an operating theatre. Faced with this, faced with Aberfan, an atheist like myself sees very clearly the advantages of the church, not as the Bride of God dispensing his word and his worship, but as a social institution that has stood for near 2,000 years exactly because nothing else provides what it provides, even shorn of all religious content.

Long ago, I rejected the idea of a personal God, a life after death and all the trappings of a comforting mythology as many have done before me and more do alongside me today. Logically enough, I rejected the church as an institution too.

Whatever the church itself may claim, it seems most people now are unbelievers except in the vaguest cross-my-fingers and christen-my-baby way. A recent survey conducted by the British Council of Churches reveals that the Soviet Union has a higher percentage of regular church-goers than Britain. Yet reading of Aberfan I began to think that perhaps I had thrown the baby out with the bathwater.

As far as can be gathered, the people of Aberfan are a cross-section of the rest of us; some believers, many agnostics, some unbelievers. But when the coal thundered down the mountain, it was the church that came into its own. Not because everyone suddenly decided to placate a vengeful God who had taken little children because of their wicked bingo-playing mothers, their Sunday morning lie-a-bed fathers—as the church's message might well have been 100 years ago. Not because latent belief flowered once again in grief. Not even because, as far as can be ascertained, God dispensed any heaven-sent comfort to his flock. It was simpler than that. The church offered certain concrete practical advantages that no other organization or individual could provide.

The first advantage is that, like Everest, it was there. Familiar buildings already used for meetings, centres for the dissemination of information, the combating of destructive rumours. A week after the disaster, it was a Baptist Minister, himself a bereaved parent, who had the facilities to call together and form the Parents' and Residents' Association, invaluable in representing the community's needs.

Then, when extremes of human emotion are reached, most people do not want to think. Above all, they do not want to think. They want to be cradled in some ancient womb where whatever must take place, takes place; where the fearful actions may be veiled in movements and words as familiar and worn as old stone steps, where they may simply appear like puppets and let the strings pull the numbed limbs about into appropriate gestures. The Humanists and other secular organizations have forms of service for funerals but active thought is needed. Someone must pick out the favourite sayings, poems, music of the deceased. Someone must arrange it all into a harmonious whole. Someone must think.

In the church, even the minister need not think.

To take part in a ritual that is comparatively new goes against the very grain of bereavement. Death pulls the dead away and pushes the living back into the past; emotionally, at least, they become as little children. No accident that an undertaker dresses in the fashion of a century ago—high wing collar, gloves, top hat. The need to be reminded, however unconsciously, that this grief (or even joy) has happened to your parents and your parents' parents is, in itself, a comfort and a salve for bitterness and particularly vital today, when death is so little a part of our daily lives. It is difficult to see how new ceremonies, raw as fresh-hacked wood, constructed for you but not for your father, can fill this need. The gabbling of the Lord's Prayer (or the turning of a Tibetan prayer wheel, for that matter) is as much a defence against reality as anything else and its value is exactly in that. The mind cannot cope immediately with emotion, it needs an interim filled with sound so that it may lie mercifully dormant for a day or so.

It is sad for the unbeliever that these traditional comforts must be rejected in the name of a Christian virtue, honesty or, if accepted, flawed with splinters of guilt and confusion. The clergy are often caught up in the confusion too. Here and there, they refuse to christen the children of non-church goers, which I find understandable enough, if rather quixotic.

Non-church-goers complain, after funerals, that the minister at the crematorium conducted the service without feeling, impersonally. No wonder, since he doesn't know them from Adam and yet it seems unfair that because society has evolved no satisfying alternative to religion, an increasingly secular society must either give up the age-old table d'hôte or feel hypocrites.

Another of the Church's advantages emerges quite clearly in the grief of Aberfan. There, on that day in 1966, were people direly in need of comfort, needing above all to talk and talk about the dead. And there were also hundreds of others ready to help: social workers, psychiatrists, academics, every one of them only too willing to descend like a second avalanche upon the bereft village. But the people of Aberfan rejected them. And who can blame them? Who, wretched and torn, wants someone recording the tears as they fall, the outbursts that explode from uncontrollable emotions? Who wants to suspect that their own private grief will eventually form some study, some overall survey, some thesis labelled 'The Grief Reactions of Ten Aberfan Mothers?' However trained, however compassionate, social workers and sociologists are felt to have another end in view than merely comfort and, in all fairness, they do. Involved, energetic, immensely kind today, tomorrow they will retreat into the groves of academe and write a book on you.

The clergy, on the other hand, are insulated figures. They have taken a vow of confidence and the beginning and end of their task in that situation is to comfort. Whether, as men, they are good or not so good, skilled or awkward, clever or stupid, hardly matters. Their job is to act like bullet-proof vests into which sorrow, bewilderment, anger will bury itself and never penetrate to the outside world. In fact, as Joan Miller makes clear, social workers did a great deal for the people of Aberfan but in a way they were forced to be wolves in sheeps' clothing.

Aberfan's general wariness of social workers is shared by others, too. A friend of mine, in prison, was visited by a social worker of great dedication and good intent. My friend felt, after a while, that they had become friends rather than person-in-need versus person-doing-good. Later, she discovered her letters in the social workers' dossier on her. 'I wrote those letters to *her* from *me*,' she said miserably. 'I felt terrible when I saw them in the file. I thought we were *friends*.' As an atheist, no padded minister was available to her and so cynicism set in.

There are other aspects of the religious life that are badly needed by the secular. Like the coming together that Sunday services involve, like the cathartic of confession and the discipline of meditation. Where else but in church can people of all sorts, rich and poor, good and bad, young and old, meet every week to share a ritual together and get to know each other? Where else are you expected to get down on your knees and think about your behaviour, your actions as they affect yourself and others? Where else is the rich man's outlet—a listening psychiatrist—available gratis to all and sundry but in the Catholic confessional? Mumbling at a priest through a grille may seem to some (and often to me) the height of futility, particularly since most of the sins to be confessed seem, to the secular mind, among the best things life has to offer. But because the Church gets the contents of the confession wrong does not invalidate the act.

From an atheist point of view, the problem is quite simply explained. Man invented God and the trappings of religion in order to satisfy some of the deepest human needs. The central dogma is now no longer acceptable but the trappings are still vital. Our children, rejecting and confused, are being swept up into myriad new and, often exploitative movements, becoming zombies under the control of fanatical fellows of dubious origin and more dubious purpose or taking, pathetically, to astrology, a tattered witchcraft or a hopeful worship of neo-Grecian gods. Some would say the answer is in some great new Christian crusade for these lost souls. I believe the answer is in a gathering together under the old familiar rituals, the beautiful language, the necessary disciplines without the dogma and a body of people dedicated solely to others.

Our Humanity, which art here, hallowed be thy name. Thy kingdom come, thy will be done, on earth. We hope this day for our daily bread and let us help each other to forgive ourselves our trespasses and those who trespass against us. Let us not lead each other into temptation and let us deliver each other from evil. For a true Humanity is the kingdom, the power and the glory, for ever and ever, Amen.

14 October 1974

Woman Slaughter

COLIN MIDDLETON MURRY, son of John Middleton Murry, has just published his childhood memoirs. The book is called *One Hand Clapping*, which title comes, you may remember, from one of those deeply profound or possibly highly shallow Zen questions. Master to pupil: 'What is the sound of one hand clapping?' Pupil: 'I don't know.' Master slaps his face.

I presume, from reading this book, that Mr MM's title sprang mainly from his experience of the black doom-laden figure that dominated most of his youth, a stepmother of the wickedest variety called Betty, who slapped, kicked, and cursed her way through a terrorized family without even asking them pointless questions as an excuse. At one point, referring to the awful Betty's raging, Mr MM says, 'I lack any scale of normal human experience upon which to draw for reference. Only once did I ever come across anything that seemed in any way remotely like it and that was a court case report in the *News of the World* in which the defendant, goaded ultimately beyond the limits of human endurance, had snatched up a hammer and battered his terrible tormentor into the ultimate silence.'

This statement raises several interesting if chilling points. First, Betty was a woman whereas most of the really appalling autocrats of family life have been men—Mr MM himself had an eminently respectable grandfather (in the eyes of his society) who kept his family atremble with Law, Order and many a swift kick up the Khyber. Second, Colin's father, the elder MM, in spite of all Betty's provocations, mysteriously remained with his wedded virago for many years and apparently was only ever once goaded enough to say to his son, 'she's mad, quite mad'. Third, of course, is the

110

surprise verging on incredulity that the reader feels at MM's long-suffering because he is a man and she is a woman. The other way round would be accepted with sympathy but little surprise. And lastly, had MM suddenly shed his cloak of inexplicable meekness and done exactly what the unknown *News of the World* defendant did, he would surely have been advised by his legal eagles to plead provocation, would probably have succeeded in having murder reduced to manslaughter (or womanslaughter, to be accurate) and emerged a free man under a suspended sentence.

Women, other than the freakish Betty and her even more active sister-under-the-skin Lizzie Borden, are not in domestic life much given to violence of a physical sort. Mrs Erin Pizzey and the female residents of homes for battered wives could testify that many women endure years of continual violence from their husbands with what appears to be extraordinary yet quite accepted restraint, bolstered, often, by a pathetic belief that Beast will some time, somehow, change to Beauty overnight.

I remember talking to two women at Erin Pizzey's Chiswick haven, one of whom had been shot in the neck by her husband and, in hospital, had refused to charge him on the grounds that he would then certainly kill her. The other woman, a pretty fragile blonde, had been locked up with her young daughter in a room by her husband for a year and subjected to bouts of revolting cruelty and degradation. Both appeared more bewildered than embittered by their experiences. Now, thanks to Mrs Pizzey's dauntless crusade, the lives of battered wives seem to have taken a turn for the better. Society has begun to accept the once *outré* suggestion that holy matrimony does not necessarily sanctify black eyes and broken ribs, that husbands do not automatically assume the right, at the altar, to beat the living daylights out of wives. But when carrying battering to its logical conclusion, homicide (and its diversionary frill, provocation), women are still at a crippling disadvantage.

A report from Los Angeles underlines this legal disadvantage. Two women were raped. After the rape, one woman killed her attacker an hour later and was found guilty of second-degree murder (a five-year sentence). The other waited a whole day before killing and has been indicted for first-degree murder. Presumably the defence, as in this country, depends on murder taking place 'in hot blood'. In other words, you kill the offending person on the spot, in which case—if provocation is accepted—you spiral rapidly downwards from murder to manslaughter and probable acquittal. But woe betide you if you let any time at all lapse between the provocation and the killing because that, by legal definition, is your actual heinous first-class murder. The fact that a woman is unlikely to be physically or mentally able to kill an attacker on the spot is too bad for her, an aberration conveniently overlooked by legal dogma.

In an interim report on homicide and provocation produced by Bedford College, University of London, legal provocation is defined thus: (a) was the killer provoked into losing his self-control? and (b) would a reasonable man have reacted to the same provocation in the same way as the killer did? Even the pronouns overlook the female. The report adds: 'The only other matter which the law insists upon is that reaction to provocative conduct must be *in the heat of the moment*. Time to cool off loses to the killer his right to claim that he was legally provoked.' (My italics.) The example cited is that of a man whose victim (his erstwhile mistress) had gone to their former home to remove her furniture, including the bed.

It is that phrase 'in the heat of the moment' that most tells against women and it comes, therefore, as no surprise to learn that male offenders formed 94 per cent of both sexes who *successfully* pleaded provocation. The key to this is that the majority of women are simply unable, in the most literal sense, to express any murderous impulses they may feel 'in the heat of the moment'.

First, women are likely to have been conditioned from childhood to suppress feelings of anger, to displace them or even not to recognize them until too late (too late meaning, in this case, when the plea of provocation would no longer stand). Then there are often children standing about weeping with terror and though we are led to believe that they are obscured from a father's sight by a red haze, a woman is seldom so single-minded. She tends, no matter what scenes of mayhem may be distracting her attention, to worry about what will happen if their parents chop each other to bits in front of them.

And then there is the crux of the matter—physical strength. Most women, correctly or otherwise, assume their strength to be less than a man's (and if you assume it, so it is). Certainly most husbands are bigger and taller than most wives. Physical attack or retaliation for attack is likely only to reap the storm and even if she could manage to get in a well-aimed swipe she is usually too plain terrified of the consequences to do so. Her blood may be at boiling point but without the muscular strength to act immediately the 'heat of the moment' will perforce pass her by.

Small wonder, then, that women killers traditionally elicit little sympathy. What man on what jury, well accustomed to a good old free-for-all in the pub on Saturdays, can identify with the silent devious bitch who scatters strychnine on the stew, stabs a man already unconscious through drink, or plots to pay other men to kill her spouse? Hot blood? No way. These are the unforgiveable, truly malicious afore-thoughts of the physically weak.

The other stroke against her, once she is in a court of law, is the psychological attitude of a preponderantly male jury who must decide what 'a reasonable *man* (my italics again) might expect his own reactions to the given provocation would be'. There is, as yet, no woman on that Clapham omnibus. As one lawyer put it to me: 'Seventy to 80 per cent of all murders are domestic and juries tend to sympathize with the chap, especially if there is a history of quarrels.' Indeed, so much is this the case that provocation, as a plea, seems a quite blatant technical balancing device worked out by both defence and prosecution in the judge's chambers to allow the jury to ease its conscience by finding the defendant guilty of manslaughter and not of murder. The argument is that murder is difficult to prove, juries reluctant to convict and provocation at least gets some form of conviction.

Another difficulty for women in homicide cases is that, since in almost all successful provocation pleas the victim is the wife, she is six feet under and hardly in a position to defend herself. As the Bedford report says: 'Victims of all other crimes have at least the added invariable distinction of

113

being potentially the chief witness for the prosecution. The murder victim's demise effectively removes the physical object to which any such judgment can attach.'

Not only effectively removes but also allows the defendant full rein for his plea of provocation to a jury who sometimes seem to believe every wife (once murdered) necessarily a nag, a slut or a whore. Reading newpaper trial reports over the past few years I am forced to the odd conclusion that our society believes any woman who 'taunts' her husband with his impotency or her rich and varied sex life has, in the opinion of 'reasonable' men, committed such a heinous crime that murder is its only logical punishment. Two cases of successful provocation pleas in the Bedford report were those of women who persistently nagged their husbands'.

Other cases are legion. One man said his wife taunted him with her lover's sexual prowess and kept talking of leaving him and the children. She was strangled and he was given an 18-month suspended sentence for manslaughter. Another man had what he called a nagging, bingo-obsessed wife' who taunted him with impotence. He got four years and was released after three and a half months. Another had a wife said to have been suffering from depression. To begin with, he blamed her murder on an intruder and later said his wife might have been having an affair with another man'. The defence pleaded that his difficulties with his wife had put his job in jeopardy and 'something must have snapped in his mind'. He got five years for manslaughter, though Sir Carl Aarvold, to his credit, refused to accept a verdict of 'murder with provocation' by an eager jury.

An entire village got together to plead leniency for a man who killed his wife because she refused to return to him. 'She seemed,' it was reported, 'completely indifferent to what he said and it was then that the spring snapped.' That ubiquitous snapping spring got him nine months, suspended for a year. And, even more curiously, a mother begged leniency for the killer of her 16-year-old daughter, whom he had battered to death. The killer pleaded provocation and the judge, after commenting that he had to ensure 'human life is not made too cheap', sentenced the quick-tempered lad to three years' detention.

The point about all these cases and many more is that there remains a nasty fear that justice has neither been seen nor been done and that what is sauce for the gander is no use at all to the goose, quick or dead. Even more important, is provocation a plea that a civilized country should continue to allow? Doesn't its very presence admit the inadmissible—that murder is sometimes excusable, a suitable retribution for such crimes as nagging, taunting, desertion? I am not for a moment pretending that women cannot behave in a way calculated to arouse murderous impulses in the bosom of any reasonable man but surely there is a paradox in the idea that a reasonable man can commit murder? What, for instance, could a 16-year-old girl have done or said that makes her death by battering understandable to reasonable men?

The whole question of provocation reaches its nadir of inadmissibility in cases of child murder reduced to manslaughter. Certainly the details of a case are often obscure in news reports but how are we expected to feel when we read, for example, of a man found guilty of manslaughter for killing his 19-month-old son after the baby had given part of a meal to the family dog? The judge is reported as saying he was prepared to take a lenient course (probation for three years) because of 'wholly exceptional circumstances'. We are not told what they are but I challenge the most vivid and paranoid imagination to produce anything a 19-month-old child could have done that would seem to excuse its death at the hands of an adult.

It is true that what constitutes provocation in the eyes of the reasonable man changes from year to year. In the 1930s a man in a pub made some rude remarks about the King and a soldier standing beside him killed him. His plea of provocation was accepted by a jury and that, obviously, would be unimaginable today. So, in effect, provocation is anyway slowly being whittled away as reasonable men become ever more reasonable. Is it not time for that plea to be hacked finally off at the roots?

At the moment, horribly, the moral lesson for women at least would seem to be—if you want to commit murder, do it *now*, you *know* it makes sense. Pick up the rolling pin, hurl the glass ashtray, lunge with the carving knife the instant you are provoked and you have a good chance in law. Remember, girls, it's the heat of the moment that counts.

20 January 1975

115

Distorted Reflections

I HAVE ALWAYS LIKED reading biographies. It is the ideal literary genre for someone too prim, like me, to acknowledge a gossipy interest in the living—don't you *hate* gossips, aren't they *too* awful?—but avid for any nuggets from the private lives of the dead because that is perfectly respectable, an altogether worthy and informative way of spending one's free time.

And, of course, as a high-minded biographile I have always been deeply concerned that the author is getting as near the truth about his subject as possible. Well, I mean a nugget isn't a nugget unless it's a real nugget, is it? I don't want to raise my hands in horror and tut tut at something the subject may never have done at all. So early on, I eschewed all forms of biography where the author has Mary, Queen of Scots or Charlotte Corday or whoever *thinking* things. No use to me if I read 'Mary thought, "Ah me, would that I were a mere commoner and not the melancholy uncrowned head of an indifferent country" ' because we all know nobody could know now—never mind then—what Mary, Queen of Scots was actually thinking and I should immediately have to distrust all the other information offered. Pooh, pooh, I think at points like this, here we have a very *light* little work, suitable for lovers of romantic fiction I dare say but not of any value to the serious student like myself.

So I moved on to the next sort of biography, where the author says things like: 'One imagines Mary, Queen of Scots may well have thought, at that moment, "Ah me, would that I were..." ' and so on. It makes for a clumsy style, I grant you, but it gets so much more reliably near to the essence of the dear Queen, don't you think? And then, thank goodness, I discovered Stefan Zweig in my late teens. Mr Zweig meticulously winkled out any thoughts his subjects might have had and filled up the empty spaces with letters from, to and about his subject, each one carefully asterisked to an index that told you exactly where those letters were and even though you were never likely to go to the particular museum in Vienna or wherever, you did feel extremely confident that Mr Zweig's information was—above all—correct. *Echt*. Luckily for me, most biographers these days with any pretensions to academia do not put words unknown into the mouths of their subjects and from Mr Zweig on I have been nosing happily through the goings-on of famous corpses, secure in the knowledge that, give or take an insight or two, I was getting the real *This Is Your Life*.

But last week I had a rude shock. My girlish confidence was shattered. I realized suddenly that all my years of rubbing shoulders with Queen Victoria, Virginia Woolf, Gertrude Stein and Hitler may have been, if not entirely wasted, at least largely an illusion. An alarming sense came to me of a thousand bodies turning in a thousand graves, protesting with lipless mouths that no, they never did think like that, no they never were like that, no it was quite different, no, no, *no*.

The rude shock came from three different sources that all collided together at the same time. I was reading Mary Wollstonecraft's biography by Claire Tomalin. I was watching Germaine Greer on *Face Your Image*. And the same evening I came upon a whole pile of love letters I had written.

To take *Face Your Image* first, which is, as you know, a sort of on-the-spot verbal biography with the subject alive and well and peering at his or her biographers from a BBC studio. Various people—good friends, just good friends and mainline enemies—give their opinions, interpretations and memories of the Famous Person in the studio and the Famous Person says they're all talking a lot of codswallop or blushes prettily, depending on what's said. The Famous People may be humble and forbearing, like Lord Longford, and take a longish time to say codswallop or, like Germaine Greer last Friday week, say codswallop immediately.

Germaine was, at one point, confronted with a trim and tidy sort of girl who said, if I remember aright, words to the

117

effect that Ms Greer had toyed with the affections of some Italian gentleman at Sydney University and David Dimbleby, looking rather more nervous than is his wont, added that he thought the girl was saying Ms Greer manipulated men, or women could manipulate men like men were supposed to manipulate women or something. Ms Greer said codswallop, she was very much in love with the gentleman in question and he had thrown her over. I was forced to the conclusion that if, say, the Sydney University girl had chosen to write Ms Greer's biography over Ms Greer's dead body, a very different picture of Ms Greer would have emerged. In a living encounter you do, at least, hear both sides and the sides are obviously often vastly at odds.

My second source, Mary Wollstonecraft's biography, is an interesting and conscientiously researched book that relies quite heavily on letters. Mary Wollstonecraft wrote a lot of letters, as people did in those days, and Mrs Tomalin understandably uses these letters and others to explain to us M.W.'s character, her inner life, her attitudes to friends male and female. And perfectly logical it all seems. M.W.'s letters often took the form of outpourings on a theme of high-minded disappointment with the offerings of the beloved. Many of them incorporate a reproach of some sort.

'...I can only say that you appear to me to have acted injudiciously; and that full of your own feelings, little as I comprehend them, you forgot mine—or do not understand my character. It is my turn to have a fever today—I am not well—I am hurt...'

'I have formed romantic notions of friendship. I have been once disappointed and I think if I am a second time, I shall only want some infidelity in a love affair to qualify me for an old maid...I must have the first place or none...'

Or the even more querulous: 'My faults are inveterate—for I *did* expect you last night. But, *never mind it*. Your coming would not have been worth anything, if it must be requested.'

These excerpts were written when Mary Wollstonecraft was between fourteen and thirty-five and, as Mrs Tomalin points out, they have the same tone, the voice is unmistakeable. And she adds, using the letters as evidence, that Mary 'had set up an emotional patter she was never to break…she arrived at her own conclusions about the supreme power of the feelings…she blazoned her hopes and her disappointments. She could never wear a mask or keep a weapon in reserve.'

Biographers often have little enough to work with besides the printed word and obviously it is very tempting to take for fact what the subject writes. If you cannot believe what a person writes about their own feelings in a letter, especially in a love letter, what can you believe?

Nothing much, is the answer. Yesterday, looking through junk to find something else, I came across a bunch of my own love letters, there through the vagaries of time, the sharing of furniture, the forgetting of old suitcases once held in common. And though I read them who wrote them, I recognized myself not at all. For the first time I realized that letters, and most particularly love letters, are for the most part written out of a fantasy world that bears little or no relationship to the facts of the love affair. Falling in love is a most chaotic process and it so stirs up the sediment of emotion that the average love letter tends more to be an introspective battleground for old childhood fears and doubts than any clear depiction of present feelings, present love, present relationships.

My own letters amazed me. They were written to a man that I had absolutely no reason to think did not love me, as I loved him. But any stranger reading them, however intuitive, could not fail to have interpreted them as the last, wretched appeals of an unloved woman, desperate to prevent an inevitable desertion, furious at that coming treachery. Page after page bemoaned my forlorn state, accused my lover of heartlessness, described pitiful scenes where I apparently hung about waiting endlessly for a callous cad who kept not a single tryst. Spidery writing proclaimed my martyr'd understanding—'I *understand* that you love another, I *understand* I am nothing but a burden to you, I *understand* that if I were dead you would be relieved of a weight of guilt yada yada yada.'

And yet, to the very best of my recollection, I never once had any occasion to feel deserted, betrayed, unloved. Nor do

119

I ever remember waiting anywhere and being let down. I was blankly astonished at the whole distressing picture of suffering womanhood that emerged—who on earth was this pathetic and abject person? Me? Never. But coming upon these letters as a biographer, I would have no option but to depict this woman, myself, much as Claire Tomalin depicts M.W. Blazoning my hopes and disappointments. Never able to wear a mask or keep a weapon in reserve.

But now I know it ain't necessarily so. I wore a mask all right and I had plenty of weapons in reserve and, perhaps, Mary Wollstonecraft did too. But in the heightened tension of love, you write—not to your lover—but to yourself. You write of old unhappiness, childhood fears, rejections in the nursery, cold shoulders in the cradle. 'Daddy,' you moan to a staunch and devoted lover, 'why did you desert me, why did you withdraw your love, why did you never come when I needed you?' It is a form of exorcism. Perceptively, Claire Tomalin points out that Mary Wollstonecraft perhaps suffered from her parents' coolness towards her—'too preoccupied with their own interests and troubles to give Mary what she wanted of them, unable to fill the roles she wished to see them in and unappreciative of her efforts to impress them.' But she does not carry this perception through to the letters. Monologues from a lost infant.

In general, of course, love letters are a poor guide to real feelings. The writer says never, never has he ceased to think about the loved one for an instant since they parted. He may, in fact, have ceased to think about her for rather a long time and feels horribly guilty. Then there is the human wish to make love letters a work of art, elevating real enough feelings into something altogether more dramatic. And the curious paradox of falling in love: you resent the lover for arousing such feelings and so attack him. How dare you make me love you, you shall be punished. Or, on the other hand, how dare you love unloveable me, you shall be punished.

Worst of all, there is the power of a simple phrase to evoke something quite other than the occasion it describes. In one of my own letters I say 'we sat in an orchard and talked of love'. Note, not an adjective in sight. A plain, spare statement that surely must be true. And so it was, insofar as it went. I omitted to mention that the apple trees were puny and diseased and planted in an ordinary suburban garden, that I had a red nose from sunburn, that the mosquitoes were having a field day and that half-a dozen kids were crawling in the dust at our feet, irritating everyone and getting cuffed. Chekhovian in spirit, perhaps but hardly in the flesh.

All of which is not to impugn or decry the undoubted talents of Mrs Tomalin or any other good biographer. Only now I know that the truth about a person is even more evasive than I once believed and the truth about a woman evasive to the point of invisibility, so much more prone is she to fighting ancient battles and bewailing ancient wrongs while still having a good few trump cards up her black crepe sleeve.

17 March 1975

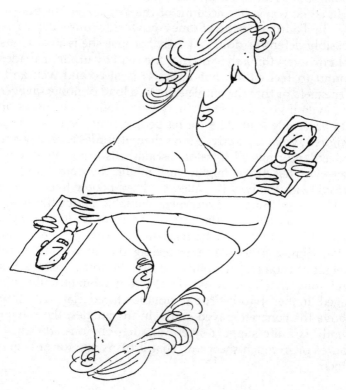

Extending the Family

I RECKON IT MUST GET pretty claustrophobic these days in the steaming jungles of South America, heaving as they evidently are with anthropologists, psychologists, archaeologists, zoologists, sociologists, ecologists, ornithologists, David Attenborough, the entire membership of ACTT and Uncle Tom Cobley and all. At least Miss Jean Liedloff, who lived there for two and a half years, is no sort of ologist. She is simply a laywoman and she has written about the lives of some South American Indian tribes.

In some ways, her account of the Yequanas, the Sanemas and the Tauripan in their Stone Age world arouses cynical and possibly defensive doubts, partly because she is so obviously sold on everything they do that the twitchy urbanite reader is bound to feel either that Paradise is alive and well and in Venezuela or that the whole thing is a load of noble savagery. But even if you suspect she may have omitted the occasional less agreeable trait, like eating people, say, or exposing girl children, what is positive about their attitudes is very positive indeed and rings all sorts of rusting bells inside anyone who has ever felt there might, just might, be something very wrong with the way so-called civilized people live.

The main thing I found most enviable about the lives of these Indian tribes is the fact of the tribe itself, the myriad close, till death do us part relationships that prevent, among other things, a woman ever feeling the unique and stifling weight of total responsibility for her children's welfare, body and soul, that is imposed on Western woman willy, nilly, caged in her two-bedroom double-glazed flat, 19 storeys above the concrete-paved earth. In the jungles, the extended family is a life support sytem of such obvious efficiency, a source of so much sheer joy, that it turns me, for one, grass-green.

Today, in our society, it is all too common to read of attacks on the family. It has been blamed for every ill that afflicts modern mankind, from loneliness to a fear of spiders to schizophrenia to the class struggle to the oppression of women and there is, I think, much more than a grain of truth in every single allegation. But certain facts are easily forgotten in the heat of the battle.

The family under attack bears little or no resemblance to families down through the ages, those rambling structures of aunties and grandpas and cousins of sisters that sometimes encompassed whole villages and provided, if only by their variety, almost every sort of help and experience needed by human beings young or old. The nuclear family, two adults and 2.04 children, is as artificial and unnatural and against the deepest instincts of mankind as its backlash—the attempt to do without a family at all.

A lot of people, particularly younger people, have revolted against the nuclear family and tried to put in its place an equally artificial extended family, the commune. Sometimes, given members of strong principle, great energy and (preferably) a small private income, communes work. Mostly they do not. The strains are immense, if only because the choice of commune members is made consciously and has none of the necessary glue in the form of blood-ties or legal relationships that are generally recognized as having social meaning and, therefore, a sort of social imperative. Human nature being what it is, it is all too easy to leave a commune in a huff whereas most people will try quite hard to resolve a quarrel with blood relatives partly, at least, because they know the ties will not disappear, even if they do.

So neither the nuclear family nor the commune are very successful in giving the ordinary human being what once the 'natural' large family supplied. Not is it possible, on a shrinking planet, to turn again and breed. Unless the human race is quartered by some holocaust, I cannot imagine a future solution in the do-it-yourself large family. Are we doomed, then, never to regain the lovely, large, companionable networks of the Yequanas, the Sanemas, the Tauripan?

It seems to me that there *is* a solution, however

unconventional and even far-fetched it may appear at first glance. Many of us already belong to an extended family, a strange, subliminal and shadowy family that we do not recognize because it is not yet acknowledged by our society and there are no words for the relationships therein. This family, oddly enough, is created by divorce.

Massive pressures from various sources force us to assume that the natural state of humanity is monogamy. It is made the easier to believe because there is some truth in it. But the whole truth, as any detached observer of social behaviour must admit, is that human beings are serial monogamists and would, given freedom from outside pressures, quite often replace one loving and sexual monogamous relationship with another and, possibly, another in an ever-lengthening life span. Polygamy, practised by half the world, is the male's acknowledgment of this truth and, surprisingly enough, though women had no say in the matter there is much evidence that they too, given the *fait accompli* of a new wife, were resigned or clever enough to see its advantages—an extra pair of hands to peel the potatoes, an extra pair of arms to cradle the infants and, later, a friend. The western world's form of serial monogamy is divorce, a poor thing at best, cause of untold misery, creator of as many problems as it solves and the splitter of even the nuclear family into its smallest and most lonely atoms. No answer at all.

Even so, even in all its bleakness, divorce creates an underground family that needs only to be stripped of its coverings, its shame, its inherent drama, to produce once more a natural extended family that has all the advantages of blood ties, legal relationships and very slight coercion so much a part of the old 'bred' family. Just suppose that this was the conventional pattern of society:

A young man and a young woman fall in love. That love creates the wish to spend their lives together, they go to some public place and they promise, in public, to stay together till death do them part. The only difference would be that they leave out those slightly bleak words 'forsaking all others'. Then they go home and get on with it and if they never wish for others they may live happily together, alone, for ever after. But—and it is the vital but—if one partner or the other does again fall in love and feel that life is intolerable without the presence of the second beloved, then divorce will no longer take place. Instead of the disruption of lives, the splitting of children from a parent, the pruning of in-laws, the abrupt curtailment of what may still be a perfectly viable relationship between the husband and wife, albeit a changing one; instead of a dwindling family we could see the beginnings of growth. There could be a coming-together. The new partner would join the original two and there would be a second marriage without a divorce. The first wife or husband would gain a friend and helpmate, the children a third parent. If the new partner was already married, the two married couples would move in together, with children, and a real extended family would begin to take root. No loneliness, no anguish of children bereft, no sudden change of circumstance for the old partner, no leaving of district or friends, no drop in income.

Instead, more wage-earners, more houseworkers, more people to care for the children and share the chores. The acceptance of change might be difficult but can it be *more* difficult than the isolation of divorce? We are told that children suffer from divorce and still we divorce. Could we not accept a stranger for their sakes?

Since most people who now divorce tend to marry once again, the new extended family might eventually consist of eight adults and accompanying children. Obviously, if everyone insisted on marrying early and then three or four more times, the original extended family might get a trifle too extended, accommodation might be strained.

And now emerges the shadowy family that already exists, become concrete and viable because named. Everyone who has ever been divorced, anyone who has ever had sisters, brothers, parents, children who have been divorced, knows in their bones that under-the-counter relationships exist. We have merely to dig them up and expose them to the light of day.

The woman my ex-husband marries is my relation. I have something profound in common with her. I will get to know her, even *in absentia*, quite intimately. I am, at the very least, curious about her, concerned in what happens to her. At present, she is perforce a distant, unknowable and apparently hostile figure whom I may invest, in my bitterness, with mythical virtues or sins, unlikely beauty or equally unlikely repulsiveness.

But suppose she became my official sister-in-law? Suppose I was faced with her daily in curlers at breakfast, in tears at the sink? Suppose she made delicious cakes or got on very well with my most difficult child? Suppose, in other words that she became no myth but familiar for better or for worse. I am forced to accommodate her, I chose her no more than I chose my own sister and the probability is that I will grow to like and, in the end, love her.

There are many other currently unacknowledged relationships that could be used to form a new family. I am not related to the child my husband's new wife bears. There is no name for the connection between us but who could deny that there is a connection? That child is a blood relation of my own children and so every instinct tells me there is something between us, too. Call the child my side-son, me his side-mother and reason sets in. I can talk about our relationship, communicate it, respond to it, make it fruitful. If the child lives with me and I help in his care, love will grow between us where none was before. Can that be bad?

A child has no blood or legal relationship with the child of his mother's first husband and that husband's second wife. But if that first marriage produced his half-brothers and sisters (are you still with me?) he will feel very strongly that he has. How, after all, can he believe that his own brother has a brother who has nothing to do with him? And his instinctive feeling is right, the true test of the unacknowledged ties that adults do their best to pretend do not exist. Why should we have to deny a child what he and we both know is true—mere divorce does not sever relationships, it simply drives them underground. Instead of being used as a basis of a bigger family, we prefer to put a tourniquet on them and allow them to atrophy.

Doubtless there are many who will see this suggestion as a charter for one long orgy. Others will say it is against human nature. It isn't and it isn't. In fact, it is merely a reconstruction of the ways in which human beings have lived

126

for countless generations with only one added ingredient, the woman has her rights, too. The way of exclusive relationships is life-denying instead of life-enhancing and in it fester unpleasant and sometimes violent emotions like jealousy, engendered by a society that continually insinuates that we are somehow less desirable, less ourselves, if the one we love also loves someone else.

We have accepted that human nature is not given over to monogamy; that acceptance goes under the name of divorce. But can any of the miseries of divorce be compared to growing pains in the attempt to get together? To me there is only the comparison: the pains of, say, a kidney stone with the pains of childbirth. One must be endured for nothing, the other for something grand, positive, a Continuous Concept.

Heal a broken home today. Invite your husband's mistress to move in. Build your own tribe—the blueprint is to hand.

8 September 1975

Mum's Rush

AT THE END OF A BBC-2's 'Controversy' programme (Dr Mia Kellmer Pringle talking on 'Young Children Need Full-time Mothers') I was left high and dry, beached on my bed, mouth opening and closing like a full-time goldfish.

I mean, there they all are on the teeny screen. Good, worthy, clever psychiatrists and anthropologists, sociologists and teachers, getting terribly emotional about the quality of caring and potting and loving and heaven knows what else a child absolutely has to have from birth to at least age three, if not age five, or *après eux le déluge*. But what is the reality? We, the English, lead the world in our indifference to and often positive dislike for children. Clichés are clichés because they are said so often because they are true. We love doggies and moggies and budgies and horsies but we never have much cared for kiddies. One man I know spends £8 a week feeding his Irish wolfhound, more than he spends per fortnight on his child and you will observe more men clutching pets in vets' waiting rooms than clutching children in doctors' waiting rooms.

Also, take a look at the astronomical lolly spent annually on pet food, a particularly schizophrenic industry because it consists of chopping up big animals who don't love us for the delectation of small animals who do. As for our actual treatment of children, we have the worst reputation in Europe for neglect and cruelty and physical punishment and, if we have the money, we send them as far away from us as possible.

And here we are, all of a sudden or (to be accurate) all of a non-sudden because the subject keeps coming back like baked beans whenever our nation gets depressed or uneasy or faces unemployment, going on and on about how working mothers create bitter, twisted kids who kick the guts out of football trains, can't read at age 15 and enter loony bins upon reaching their majority. On account of maternal deprivation. A note in *Time* magazine mentions a new book by Lionel Tiger in which he discovers that Israeli kibbutz women now want everything the old-fashioned woman wanted, from feminine roles and lipsticks to looking after their children because they are suffering from, guess what, maternal deprivation. This may or may not be so (anthropologists etcetera rake over Israeli kibbutzim so frequently they'll soon remove all the top soil) but what is fascinating is the number of men I know who, upon reading it, ran round in small circles shouting hurrah and goodie goodie, meaning they were jolly glad a new experiment in living seemed to have failed and never mind the frightening numbers of depressed non-kibbutzim mothers in their own society.

Dr Mia K.P. also talked a lot about raising the status of motherhood because she thinks if we did this, women would leave the factories and laboratories and sweat shops and go back home to be full-time mothers. Personally, since half the people in the world spend at least one day a week worshipping Mary the mother, I don't see how much higher you can raise the status of motherhood. Ever since the world began we have sung, preached and made up bad poems about mothers: the world's two greatest powers have practically gone berserk about them, the US with Momism and the USSR with Hero Mothers. What more has Dr K.P. to suggest to raise the stakes? What she has, in fact, to suggest is logical enough in a system that rates people's status by how much they earn—she wants mothers to be paid.

Now whether or not this is a good idea is entirely beside the point. Women are already poorly paid in the mainly servicing jobs they do outside the home. In France, apparently, they pay mothers two-thirds of a teacher's salary and, amazing though that is, you know what teachers' salaries are like. And recently a leading insurance company rated the worth of a wife with two young children at up to £71 weekly. But to imagine, first, that we are ever going to prise any money out of any government for the next 100 years for mothering and, secondly, that you will raise their status by paying them poorly for staying at home is to take up permanent residence in cloud cuckooland. Worse, it is completely to misunderstand why so many women leave their children and go out to badly-paid work in the first place. A recent survey in factory-land revealed that women did it for adult companionship, to get away from isolated sub-standard homes and, last of all, for extra money, however badly needed.

What those who share Dr Kellmer Pringle's opinions have to face is that the fact of women working is now irreversible and will increase in spite of bishops howling of juvenile delinquency and in spite of the combined budgets of advertising and consumer industries who portray all women at home with children because they can't think what to sell working women except deodorants. Working women now make up half our work force and, as Iceland has just proved, if they withdraw their labour even such a small and organizable island falls apart.

When women had no other option they stayed at home and looked after their children (with the help of nannies and other surrogate mothers). The moment they saw a possibility of getting away they did, in their thousands. Did anyone write learned papers on maternal deprivation when women worked down the coal mines, in the potteries, in the mills, in the fearsome 1840s? In the fearsome 1940s, it would have been unpatriotic to write about maternal deprivation because of evacuation. It was, after all, to save the kiddies from Jerry's bombs and only coincidentally to free women for war-work.

Even today, how much do governments care about the many one-woman families where the mother has to work, whether she will or no? Has anyone yet seen fit to pay her an allowance to stay home or even to work out cast-iron laws to get maintenance from vanished fathers? And has any academic been concerned with writing papers about early *paternal* deprivation? Well, good God, of course not. It wouldn't be at all convenient to find out anything about *that*.

So what is all the excitement about? I believe it is about change. We cannot bear change, it gives us heart attacks and ulcers, respiratory ailments and repulsive skin diseases. And we live in an era of enormous change, we see the shadows of new beginnings hovering over us and we scuttle like bunnies back into our dark and dirty burrows, back to the evil we know. Safe there, we sit twitching our noses and searching out a name to give the shadow, a scapegoat. What easier than half the world's population who are so obviously, so shamelessly, so ostentatiously changing: women. So the cry goes up. Disaster? Despair? A stock market crash? Stop the women, halt them, shoo them back where they came from, make them accept guilt. So much more practical than doing anything at all about bad housing, poverty, isolated and uncompanionable lives, inadequate day care and scruffy child minders. You tell them their children are suffering, doing badly, growing into horrid human beings, drunks and junkies, work-shy and mad and it's all their faults. And make the solution sound so simple, so wise. Just stay at home until your children are three (or possibly five). Is that so terrible? Three short years for the future of the next generation? Well, no. Except that most people have two children, two years apart, which makes six years and, if you want any more, it gets nearer ten.

But will they reward you for your unselfishness and sense of duty by welcoming you back into your laboratory, your executive chair, your archaeological dig? Will they hell. The ox-tongue factory for you, love, and lucky to get it.

So, once again, women are left to work things out for themselves and it is, even if you reject the guilt propaganda, a frightening dilemma. There is, in all honesty, mounting evidence that the way very small children are treated has a profound effect on the rest of their lives. No wonder those thinking women who would, perhaps, make the best mothers, are often made wretched by decisions they are driven, at times, to feel their own mothers were lucky not to have had. No good brooding about how it would be OK if you lived like an advertising lady in a large country house with a dozen home robots pouring sunshine into the bowls of eternally grinning kids because you actually live in a tower block that stinks of urine or you haven't anywhere to live because no one wants your children.

Serious thought—and, in the end, solely your own

thought—is necessary because you are the one who will be giving up an interesting job, chances of promotion or even an uninteresting job that at least provides independent money and a giggle or two along the way. The facts show clearly that society does not want your baby, does not need it (though, of course, it knows that someone will bear babies enough to keep things running, that being human nature). So do you really want a child or is it something you feel you ought to do to prove your femininity, please your mother, assuage your curiosity or pad your old age? If your husband wants the baby, it must be discussed between you at least as seriously as buying a new car. Who will pay and what? Who will service it, clean it, repair it, make decisions about it? Will the driving be shared and, if so, to what extent?

In my experience and in many others', children not only do not heal a tottering relationship, they often put unbearable strains on a hitherto happy one, turning the man into a complaining wage slave who shouts at the children and seals himself off at the pub and a woman into a frustrated nagging harridan with little else on her mind but nappies and boiled cabbage. I have seen young girls, bright as butterflies in their fine Sunday plumage and their platform heels, playing darts with the lads and laughing their way along pavements on the arms of boyfriends. And, like butterflies, die—in one year slovens with hair in curlers, alone, pushing prams, scowling at husbands and screaming at kids, their brief lives over.

In fact, this is the nastiest question raised in what is, at best, a messy and dubious debate. What are women *for*? It sometimes seems to me, brushing aside all the verbiage and the surveys and the fine words, that the Dr K.P.s of this world mean they are there for raising men. Little point, after all, in staying at home giving full-time mothering to two small daughters so that they may grow to the age of twenty or so without a single twitch, happy as clams, full of the kind of ranging intelligence they tell us large doses of the right kind of maternal love can foster and then, what? A plunge back into motherhood. Lovely, caring, intelligent, quality motherhood.

The paradox is that only if they have sons will there be any end product to all this quality mothering. Only sons can, without bishops howling and psychiatrists threatening, flower, make use of quality motherhood to create, to compose, to discover, to explore, to invent, to fulfil themselves. Because only boys, deprived of maternal love and care, will become hooligans who burn down buildings and kick in telephone booths and rob trains. Girls, maternal deprivation or no, will on the whole not. Caring for them will make them good and conscientious mothers. Not caring for them will simply make them poor mothers.

3 November 1975

Sex and the Single Gorilla

THE OTHER DAY—in light hypnotic trance due to the children discussing how long it would take, if you bit through the bottom of a car going at 50 miles an hour, to grind your molars to the gums on the road below—I had a revelation. I suddenly realized that sex, that modern obsession, that emotion apparently accountable for all our joys and sorrows, that coincidentally multi-million pound industry, was never meant to be enjoyed.

The knowledge, I now realize, had been simmering away in my subconscious for some time without surfacing, so conditioned was I. There I sat in front of the telly, watching films of gorillas humping other gorillas, stallions heaving over mares, bulls looming over cows, elephants leaning on female elephants, and lions banging lionesses. There I was, knowing about dogs and cats and mice and rats. Yet the obvious took years to dawn. The animals were not enjoying it.

The male gorilla went bumpety bump, with an expression of ineffable boredom on his human face, while the female chewed a banana leaf. The stallion, it is true, pawed the ground a bit first, but only in the way an athlete might, preparing for the high jump and, in the end, he couldn't manage it at all without human intervention. The mare gave a faint sigh and stared gloomily at the ground. The bull got it all over with in two seconds flat and the cow blinked once. The elephant looked exhausted and the female pulled another branch off a tree, and the lion was quite obviously fed up with the whole idea. As for cats, the whole business is for them a tortuous sort of duty, accompanied by much irritable biting and loud complaints that wake the neighbours. Yet watch an elephant scratching himself against a stump or a hippo taking a mud bath or a lion munching a springbok and you can see the pleasure on their faces.

Once the knowledge has been admitted, it explains so much. Only mankind has put sex on a pedestal, where it never belonged. Brainwashed into the erroneous belief that paradise lies beneath the belt, we rush about in small circles worrying. But what a terrible waste of effort and time and talent if sex was only ever meant to range, as I now suspect, from a mild sort of itch to a very pleasurable experience on a par, say, with admiring autumn leaves or eating a dozen jolly nice oysters. The female gorilla obviously preferred her banana leaf and good luck to her—she and her mate and others of the sub-human species having been doing their best to show us the truth since time began and we, in our arrogant way, have chosen to ignore their experience and assume that because we are an altogether higher form of life, we can get a great deal more out of sex.

Sex has become a right, and not just your average sex but fantastic, transmogrifying, transcendental sex at that. We demand it and, if we don't get it, we change partners, go to doctors, lie on psychiatric couches, take monkey gland and say our husbands do not understand us. It is as if everyone had decided that since they could all hold a paintbrush they all had a citizen's right to be Vermeer.

Once I met a little Chinese lady, small and neat, with bobbed hair and a Mao suit. She asked me in her delicate small voice please to tell her what was this Politics of the Orgasm in America. I gazed down upon her from my great western height and tried to explain, my cheeks mantled in blushes. 'Ah *so*,' she said eventually, nodding politely, but behind her inscrutable oriental cheekbones was incredulity. Was she to believe that these pink and large-nosed giants were truly concerned with such irrelevancies? Gently she began to talk of women's roles in China, of their work in the rice fields, of their joy in children, of their building of irrigation canals. Adults who had allowed children their childish things but knew the time to put them aside.

Pity the poor marriage counsellors. The sex advisers who continually grapple with people's sexual problems based on high expectation from a mundane activity. In come the couples who, after years of marriage, say the lust has gone out of their union. Do they say 'naturally', or 'of course it has, you twits'? Not at all. Brainwashed as the rest, they scratch their dedicated heads and recommend sex clinics, advise grotesque positions, hand out illustrated booklets in full colour, advocate peculiar undies. Why not, they say, have sex in the middle of a field for a change? Or buy some technological gadgets for an extra frisson? Or do it on the bonnet of your car or in a plastic dustbin? Or ask a friend to join you for a wee touch of the voyeurs?

But they never, absolutely never, tell the truth. They never say that sex is better than a smack in the belly with a wet fish but not a whole lot better. Apart from anything else, they have financial motives. Fred and Ethel Bloggs aren't going to thank them or pay them if they say yes, dears, you'll make quite nice Sunday painters but Vermeer? Forget it. So Fred and Ethel jump up and down in despair, shouting that there's something wrong, that they're missing out, that it's Fred's fault because he's always tired or Ethel's because of her bloody migraines. How should they know that it's not their faults because it isn't a fault at all. Just normal human and animal behaviour.

Next time you feel the glories of sex are passing you by, take a look at the faces of a couple of mating gorillas. It'll cheer you up no end.

10 November 1975

Freedom Frighteners

I SHALL LAUNCH into a description of my emotional state as we near this sombre Christmas of 1975 because it may mirror yours and serve as a dreadful warning to us and to Them. I have a psychological block about psychology but I know what I feel and I also know that what I am presently feeling makes a nice fertile breeding ground for the worst sort of violence, the mindless howling lynching hang 'em kill 'em kind that no longer cares what its target is as long as the dogs of war are slipped.

The ingredients are mainly composed of a continuous back-and-forth inner argument, an endless effort of the reason to suppress the emotion, fewer and fewer outlets for either in any way acceptable to both and, therefore, an ever-shrinking estimate of oneself as a 'nice', pleasant, tolerant human being. In the end I fear that the simple friction of these emotions scouring away at each other will create, like Boy Scouts' sticks, the fire next time. Or, to put it in a more domestic way, the steam will eventually blow the rubber off the pressure cooker and the stew will hit the fan.

Examples of this process, picked at random through the past weeks: I sit and brood upon the distorted values of our society, the mental and physical greed in the midst of a starving world, the selfishness and materialism, the I'm all right Jackism. And then upon the stage comes the Archbishop of Canterbury who voices some of these thoughts and immediately renders them unacceptable to me with conspiratorial nonsense about 'the enemy at the gates', an inexcusable ignorance of the distress of the unemployed, of historic oppression or, for that matter, of any of the vital issues of our time, including the fact that his own business, religion, has to take much of the blame for at least two bitter wars now being fought on our planet.

137

The Archbishop's underling, the Bishop of Southwark, showed so much more awareness of the real issues that he was immediately reviled by Establishment Christians everywhere. So the part of my emotions that agreed with the Archbishop met head-on with the part of my emotions that was appalled by his words and impotence set in. I cannot send my s.a.e. to Lambeth Palace, I cannot support his call to...what? Prayer? Chat-ins with others of goodwill? I suspect those others and I believe that what Dr Coggan calls goodwill, I would call complacency or ignorance. No action possible here.

I set myself to try to understand the obvious distress of older, middle class people. I tell myself how bewildered they must feel as the standards they have been given and have lived by are pulled out from under their feet. And then I read the Barclays Bank advertisement, across two pages somewhere, with the middle class man's tragedy encapsulated in his *possible* inability to pay next year's subscription to some country club and his middle class wife's horrible revelation that she *might* have to turn her flower garden over to veg. Cor lummie, what a turn-up for the books. The crocodile tears dry up on my steaming cheeks.

I read of vandalism and see vandalism, for that matter, as the playground below my window is systematically pillaged, burned and sledgehammered out of existence by prosperous-looking teenage thugs. Vandals throw fireworks into the laps of wheelchaired women, new centres for spastics are demolished, schools torn apart, whole villages terrorised. My Jekyll turns into Hyde. Punch crunch. Take *that*, you bully, you punk, you lout. In the film track of my mind teeth fly, jaws break, blood runs, I stir the stew so vigorously that it splashes red on the stove.

Next day, some pompous magistrate fresh from his country estate and his rich wife pronounces on the need to bring back the cat for young hooligans and defensive fury grips me. All right for some, isn't it? But what about the lads? Drunken father, door-mat mother, beatings and quarrels and an IQ either near ESN or, quite possibly, too high for anything that station in life is likely to require and a magistrate wants them cured by bloody weals on the back.

138

Marvellous. This time, my film script has my hands round the magistrate's neck.

I meet some freaks, some squatters, and they infuriate me with their high-flown talk of universal love, of the way they care so deeply for others, of the cosmic yin and yang and they don't even bother to pay the rates that ordinary working people pay to keep the pavements mended or give an old lady meals on wheels. I seethe. And then they are raided and harried and abused for smoking a little pot and hard-drinking judges condemn them to prison and I seethe again.

I hear of an IRA bombing that tears the limbs off an innocent passerby who quite probably wants just what the IRA wants, the English out of Ulster, and horror streaks through me, the black bile of vengeance burns my throat and my film actress self machine-guns the faceless assassins with manic joy. Rat-a-tat-tat in my kitchen and blood streams down the tiles. Then I go into my local pub and a grey-bunned lady sipping her glass of stout says if she were running the country she would have Them go into every Irish home and kill one member of the family in reprisal. Stunned, I stare at her everywoman's face and my machine-gunner self is wiped out in revulsion against her tweed-coated murderess. My emotions, like two cataracts meeting, foam up and collide. I go home and kick the cats.

Ross McWhirter is gunned down at his front door and I am appalled. But minutes later some inner computer runs through its programme and pops out a card saying better Ross McWhirter than him or him or him. I did not know Mr McWhirter personally and I always disliked his public activities. I have not forgotten the anger I felt when I sat down to watch the Andy Warhol film and was presented with a black screen because Mr McWhirter had decided he thought it obscene. I have not forgotten my disgust at his urging of the nation to Stand Up To The Unions. I was outraged by what I saw as his blindness, his intolerance, his apparently wilful ignorance of causes for the things he deplored.

But I am much more outraged that his assassins have forced me into inhumanity, into making some arbitrary choice of victim that I would never willingly have made. To some degree death always forces this choice on the living—if a young man dies, we think of the older, the sicker; if a child dies, we think of almost any other adult—but I heartily resent my own inability to resist the choice-by-murder.

Then I am infuriated by students at Southampton University who rejected an appeal from the university's Conservative Association to send a telegram of condolence to Mrs McWhirter. Good God, does the death of a woman's husband have to be seen in political terms? Is she to receive no comfort because A and B and C, all too young to know anything of grief and suffering, pompously decide it is against some inhuman principle of theirs? I go home and kick the kids.

Later, I watch Mr Norris McWhirter on television. He looks worn and sad and I am very sorry for him. Awed by his experience and impressed by his courage, I listen, willing to give him my sympathy, my goodwill, my ear. He says he has a right to live under the Queen's peace and I nod yes, yes, why not indeed? He continues:

'When parents of children cannot carry on their Christmas shopping...women cannot walk in urban streets for fear of attack...or when anybody exercising a small dog cannot do so for fear of being mugged, then surely the bell tolls for thee.'

A certain unease pimples my skin, which I try to suppress. All right, a trifle exaggerated, a mite scare-mongering. But then, as he goes on talking, my heart sinks. Yes, we have the right to freedom of speech, to worship as we wish, to assemble, to travel, to strike. But a right to ownership of property? A right to inherit wealth? A right to private medicine and a choice of education that most people could never exercise because they haven't the money? Come *on*. A chill runs through me when I hear the name of his new organization—the National Association for Freedom. I have learnt at some cost that those who understand nothing of causes or history or suffering always talk of freedom, patriotism, the flag, the Queen and democracy with extraordinary ease. They are also good at ringing phrases about active citizenry, defence of rights, the need to be prepared, to stand up and be counted. And when I hear that anyone or any organization is labelled 'non-political', that is finally when the bell tolls for me.

I do not exactly distrust Mr Norris McWhirter. I believe he may honestly think his National Association for Freedom is non-political. But I know what non-political means, I am familiar with the shorthand thereof. We live in a society that believes in the profit motive, believes that men will never work for any other reason, thinks that final virtue resides in large houses and expensive furniture and public-school educated sons, cares not a whit for the pillaging of our planet in the name of free enterprise and will sell guns to anyone as long as there's a buck in it. If you believe in this society, you are non-political, you don't have to be political because it already exists, it is taken for granted. But anything that seems to threaten this society is, of course, political.

So once again my honest sympathy for another human being in distress can find no outward expression. I cannot stand up and be counted because I do not like my company. I distrust the simplistic approach, the large worthy headlines and the nasty small print. These people, for all their human distress, are really street salesmen who stick their feet in your door and ask if you think every woman should have a vacuum cleaner. On that level, none of us would be too naïve to ask the obvious question 'how much would it cost?'

I am left, once more, beached, impotent, stranded, inactive, unable to register my ordinary human sympathy for fear of it being used against others for whom also I have ordinary human sympathy. I am barred from all organizations, whether run by the Archbishop of Canterbury or the *Guinness Book of Records*, whether they intend to keep death off the streets, stop murder in the night, enable old ladies to walk their pekes or any other obviously worthy cause because I no longer believe that is *all* they want from me. The Right will accuse people like me of being cowards, twiddlers of thumbs while London burns and I am sorry for that. The Left will say I am a bourgeois individualist because they always have some clause in small print that I can't agree with.

The fear continues. Emotions churn, stirred by high-flown phrases that sit easily on the mind and are almost instantly paralysed by ice-cold reason that tells me high-flown phrases are used to gain general agreement for eventual manipulation. I am political in the sense that I dislike the values of the society I live in. I am non-political in the sense that no other society offers me better values. I admire the achievements of the Chinese but their techniques do not apply to our needs. I admire the Soviet Constitution but only Sakharov and his friends try to implement it. Our own Labour Party is too busy darning an old sock to think of buying a new pair and Margaret Thatcher is fully occupied marching the Tories back to the nineteenth century. I do not espouse bloody revolution because the people alive in 1975 are just as important as those who will live in 2075—life is life, no matter when it is lived.

But if heat is applied long enough, if friction continues without visible solution, meaningless conflagration will certainly occur. And the flames will inevitably devour the wrong people for the wrong reasons.

15 December 1975

End of the Affair?

THERE WAS THIS LITTLE MAN sitting in the audience while learned persons discussed sexual matters. Came involvement time and the learned persons asked of the audience: hands up all those who have sex once a day? A lot of hands. Once every three days? A lot of hands. Once a week? A lot of hands. And so on until the final question, who has sex just once a year? Only the little man's hand shot up, a great beam across his face, his whole body radiating joy and delight. But why, my poor man, said a learned person, are you so much more cheerful than anyone else here when you only have sex once a year? Because, said the little man, quivering in ecstasy, *tonight's the night.*

Which story I know, deep in my woman's heart, has some Freudian connection with the way I feel about the Anti-Discrimination Act and the Equal Pay Act, both of which come into force today, and about International Women's Year, which ends in two days time. Is this, I ask myself, the end of the affair? Was it great fun but just one of those things? Some letters tied with blue, a photograph or two? Shall I be left to sing the blues in the night, like my mamma done tol' me. Oh come now, pull yourself together. January, 1976, is not the last day of IWY, it is the first day of International Women's Decade, so for goodness sake let's not all fall asleep as we did after we got the vote. You in the corner with your eyes shut, sit up and pay attention.

International Women's Year was a Good Thing. Admittedly, it had its longueurs but I, for one, shouldn't have learnt what I did learn if it hadn't happened. And, like all learning, you get as much from the things that aren't said and done as the things that are. Like it was interesting to find out that the UN-sponsored conference in Mexico was given only a third of the grant awarded to the environmental

143

conference in Stockholm and the food conference in Rome. A girl likes to know where she stands. You may argue that world food and world environment are more important than women, and I might agree, except that everyone keeps saying both are threatened by overpopulation and that, most definitely, has to do with women. Not too sensible, really, countries getting together about either subject and then going home to, say, Saudi Arabia or Egypt or Italy or the Lebanon and condemning or forbidding contraception, to the horror of their own hard-working women's organizations.

It was interesting, too, to see the often rather eccentric way people and countries used International Women's Year. The Yemen Arab Republic mitigated their Islamic punishment for a woman taken in adultery—stoning. Now, when the judge passes sentence, he rules that the stones shall be very small and thrown from such a great distance that the woman has a good chance of not being hit. I kid you not.

A lot of people here thought that IWY should be marked by making Princess Anne second in succession to the throne instead of fourth. No wonder HRH doesn't support Women's Lib. At our own reception to inaugurate IWY, the guest of honour was HRH Princess Alexandra, and the Mexico Conference was outstanding for the number of wives acting as mouthpieces for their husbands: Mrs Al-Sadat, Mrs Viola Burnham, Mrs Lea Rabin, Begum Nusrat Bhutto, Princess Ashraf Pahlavi, Queen Alia of the Kingdom of Jordan.

In Swaziland they declared a Woman's Day and made a flag from local materials to decorate the Queen Mother's car. In Cuba, Fidel Castro presented a record album of his speech on women to a woman's organization. Ms Gloria Steinem was asked, in Mexico, to use her influence to change the words 'women's revolution' because 'the phrase tended to antagonise many who were sympathetic to feminist aims'. Bahrain proposed that they might hold an exhibition featuring women's role in society. The Cyprus Broadcasting Corporation has planned a number of special programmes geared, guess what, to women. Crumbs, girls, aren't we going a little too far?

Altogether, the Mexico Conference adopted 34 resolutions on the status of women and 'other' issues. Each resolution invited, urged, called on, requested, suggested, re-recommended, stated, considered that, declared, recognized, hoped for and asked for priority to be given. Pretty please.

Here in England, the Women's National Commission, which was the United Kingdom Coordinating Committee for IWY, put out news bulletins of its successes. First Ever Achievements included HRH Princess Alice being made Dame Grand Cross of the Order of the Bath and Baroness Elliott of Harewood being winner of the Tweeddale Press 'Man of the Year' Award. Hip, hip. Other amazing breakthroughs: an IWY Commemorative Tankard for all those beer-swilling ladies; a one-day conference on 'Women and Smoking'; the WRVS children's fashion show in Worcester; the IWY Cambridge Steering Committee on housing, entitled 'Every Man Must Have His Shed'; a Service for IWY in Liverpool; a Cavalcade of Costume in Bristol; and an International quiz for IWY in Jersey.

Many other happenings managed to squeeze themselves under the all-embracing IWY umbrella. Women journalists received hundreds of press releases beginning 'This is International Women's year and Freda Bloggs is a woman, so will you please come and look at her paintings, bracelets, home-made chutney, sculptures made entirely of sanitary towels and old bras.' The women's peace groups informed us that Moira Brennan is the first girl to gain an O-level in piping, and even the Fawcett Society, in its usually excellent listings of women's achievements, got carried away and included Leonora Cohen, whose achievement was reaching her hundred and second birthday.

Never mind. I'm being less than fair to many organizations by picking out only the quirks. Though I still believe the whole idea was originally intended as a bit of diplomatic flattery to women so that we would be bemused and bedazzled and begone, even the worst intentions gang aft agley. At least now many of us know what we don't like and don't think was properly done, and that, in itself, is a painless step forward.

And a great deal of good has happened during the year, though most of it owed little or nothing to the label IWY itself. Our own Sex Discrimination Act, Equal Pay Act,

Social Security Pensions Act, and Employment Protection Act are comparatively powerful pieces of legislation that, given our own determination, will make a vast long-term difference to women's lives. The National Joint Committee of Working Women's Organizations has protested strongly at discrimination in education and stereotyped sex roles in school books, and the male jokes that greeted this are a measure of the need. The women of the Common Market have just gained a legal right to equal opportunities in employment, training and working conditions, and the enterprising Americans started a women's bank. There has also been a rash of first-ever appointments, from our own female Chairperson of the GLC to a new woman Prime Minister in the Central African Republic. And the best thing of all was the women of Iceland's contribution to IWY—an almost 100 per cent one-day strike that brought everything to a halt and made the women's point that they were essential in the running of their country.

But there is still plenty to do. Disgracefully, the Church remains a bastion of discrimination, though many good men and women inside are fighting for change and the Archbishop of Canterbury himself voted for women's ordination. There are many inequalities in the field of tax and welfare and the National Insurance system operates entirely on the assumption that every wife is a dependant. Women patrials do not have the same rights as men and abortion is still a bitter battleground. Nor is it easy for most women to earn their equal pay, since provisions for their children are derisory.

Yet IWY has taught a lot of us that we are very well off indeen compared with our sisters in the Third World. Though progress is being made, particularly in the professions, the plight of women in rural areas is actually getting worse. Planning, done by men to lighten other men's work, often results in increasing the women's burden. A new plough in a village enables a man to prepare more land more efficiently. But the traditional women's tasks, weeding and planting for instance, are thereby extended. In one African country, women do 55 per cent of the agricultural labour in an old-style village and 68 per cent in a modernized one.

When poultry schemes were introduced no one bothered about the extra water necessary (25 litres a day for 100 chickens) and fetching it was left to the women. Men are becoming better educated in order to cope with new technology—women are becoming more illiterate, more than ever isolated from the modern world, and sometimes isolated from men too as the men leave the land for the cities.

And it is women in the Third World who most often pay the penalties inherent in a changing world. Their men, eager to avail themselves of western goodies, salve their consciences and save their faces by putting women on an ethnic pedestal, making them practise rigid religious rites and keeping them encumbered in veils and masks, sure that this way, no matter how much they themselves rush about in fast cars and European suits, their true culture is safeguarded. So perhaps the most important of the resolutions taken at the Mexican Conference concerned women being integrated into the development process and participating in the decisions that form that development.

As IWY draws to a close, many women are asking the same question—where now? Certainly the Discrimination and Equal Pay Acts will only work if each of us makes sure they do by taking any complaints to the Discrimination Board (if we can squeeze past all the men already lined up moaning about pensions, unfair dismissals and so on). But I believe what women all over the world most need now is a organization on the same lines as Amnesty International. The English started Amnesty, could we not also start an international watchdog-type agency here for the benefit of women? Amnesty searches out cases of people imprisoned for their beliefs and, through groups all over the world, protest by letters, by lobbies and through embassies until the government of the country in question finally gives way to pressure and releases the prisoner.

Surely, as women, we could do the same thing on behalf of other women prisoners of sex? Pester various governments until they have implemented laws to back up UN, Mexican and Berlin resolutions. Take up individual cases of women in need or at risk, as was done, for instance, with Joan Little, the black American woman accused of killing her prison guard? Keep track of all important policy decisions and insist women are included in those decisions, whether about poultry schemes in Africa or polygamy in Arab countries? We could call it the National Association of Guardian Sisters. NAGS.

29 December 1975

Same on You

MANY THINGS WILL NEVER cease to amaze me and one of them is the belief apparently sincerely held by those who vote Tory (whether governors or citizenry) that the Reds under their beds spend their entire time thinking up ways to make the lives, liberties and pursuits of Englishmen and women conform exactly one unto the other.

'Damme, sir, if those Bolshies aren't out to crush every trace of individuality in us,' stammers a Blimp from Bucks. 'We must guard our liberties with our lives or the Left will achieve their aim and reduce us all to dreary little cogs in the great State machine,' says another in Herts. 'Those so-called champions of the working class whose secret wish is to regiment every one of us, stamp us into the same mould, invade our freedom of choice, and compress us into the identical grey breeze-blocks, of a Socialist society,' bellows a third from a platform in Berks. Margaret Thatcher announces to America that Harold Wilson is standing on people's heads to stop them growing taller or words to that effect and, most recently, they have all joined forces to bewail the ghastliness of Socialist engineering that seeks to stamp out, compress, and legislate away even the precious differences between the sexes. Just like China, they inevitably moan, where everyone wears a Mao jacket and you can't tell your father from your mother.

You get the picture, you've heard it all before. If you're a conservative with a big or little 'c', you believe it. If you're not, you may say it's an appalling misrepresentation, a pack of imperialist lies, fascist propaganda, the dying rattle of Capitalism or whatever else comes to mind, in a more or less apoplectic way depending on your temperament. But a closer examination of human behaviour reveals, in fact, a far odder state of affairs than either side seems to realize.

149

First of all, it must be obvious to the most short-sighted observers, if they pause for just a moment, that human beings are, by choice, positively lemming-like in their rush towards conformity. We all seem to want to look, talk, think, and live as much like other groups of human beings as is economically possible and though we may pride ourselves on our individuality, it sits upon us like the frill on a lamb chop—a very standard variation. It is rare to find a face that doesn't remind you of another face, a gesture of another's gestures, a character unlike another's character.

Only love makes one person wholly unique, and love is blind. About the only thing we possess that singles us out are our fingerprints, and I believe there is a growing doubt upon even this score. My mother, for instance, is as much of an individual as your mother, but put her in a queue for a cuppa at Dickins & Jones and several moments pass before I can pick her out from all the other ladies with neat grey hair and modest spectacles and boxy suits and polished shoes and nice green lizard brooches upon their left lapels. I dare say she would have the same trouble with me among my friends, with our unkempt hair and unmade-up faces and waving hands.

Go to any pop concert and match your own children against the other be-jeaned, be-booted, be-Indian-beaded crowd milling about, all doing their own thing in exactly the same way. And if we are not naturally conformist, Tchernikoff would not have his green Chinese girl hanging in a million living rooms, flying ducks would not be a joke, and Hermes scarves would never sell.

So all of us show far more fondness for uniformity than for individuality. But, curiouser and curiouser, even those people who have traditionally regarded themselves as the bulwarks of individuality against encroaching Socialist conformity, the rich and powerful and well-connected who have a nearly absolute choice about how they will lead their lives and could live as differently as humanly possible from anyone else, don't. Not only don't but actually fly in the face of their freedom and conform more carefully, more conscientiously, and at greater expense than any other section of our society.

150

They begin their devotion to conformist careers by attending preparatory and public schools where, in conditions of unrelieved gloom and discomfort that would horrify any self-respecting working class lad, they strive to become more alike than peas in a pod.

The uniform, almost unknown to State schools, is de rigueur and the 'better' the school, the richer the parents, the more conforming the details of that uniform become. There are public schools where intricate rulings hold sway about what buttons on what garments must be buttoned or may be left unbuttoned. Where the tilt of your boater or the position of your hands as you walk are matters almost of life and death. Where the paths or even the sides of roads upon which you walk are regulated. Where you may not even talk to whom you please without incurring penalties. At Eton, élite of the élite, it seems to be a career in itself to grasp the complexities of attire. And, interestingly, once a boy has actually made it into the Pop oligarchy of the school and is given, at last, options on clothing, he takes up every option as if it were an edict, from the fancy waistcoats and spongebag trousers to the flower in the buttonhole. As one old Etonian put it, 'Pop clothes are not compulsory but I never knew a boy who wasted a second before stuffing his buttonhole or buying his coloured waistcoat.'

Their rich and powerful parents have never, to my knowledge, dreamed of protesting at any of the rigid rules and regulations, even when the child of their bosom is being bullied and beaten to within an inch of his individual life (as long, of course, as the beating is administered only by sixth formers in stick-up collars and not nasty little fags living in identical wooden cubicles). Whereas, in the bleak drear State machine of the comprehensive, children wear what they will and parents often fight tooth and nail to preserve their infants' privileges, having been known to keep the kids away from school for terms on end for the right of those kids to wear rings on their green-varnished fingernails or bovver boots and hair to the clavicles.

Nor is language sacrosanct—no freedom of expression in the 'good' schools, no individualist nonsense there. Early on, the wretched children learn the particular words allowed at particular schools and use them slavishly. Jonathan Raban, one of the most recent of former public school boys to write about this (in the *New Statesman*), quotes from a letter he sent home in the first days of his first term at a new school, packed full of all the in words, from 'wet' and 'fellows' to 'ragging'.

And I can still remember my own brother, fresh from his first public school term, stalking about the house on holiday, talking of 'bloods' and 'yobbos' and saying 'is it the *done thing*?' to every suggestion of activity or behaviour from climbing a tree to having tea with aunties. Further than that in conformity, at age 13, you cannot get.

I understand, too, that girls—the subject of so many *vive la différence* sentiments in later *Times* letters—were and are treated much like their brothers, sent to boarding schools modelled on male boarding schools, infused with the same obsessional attention to clothing, forced to crash about sports fields, and, in general, given to understand that they should be as similar to boys as possible, though a certain resemblance to horses would not be frowned upon.

And after this? Once adulthood was attained, once school days were over, was there not a sudden flowering of the freedom, the individuality, the non-conformism so cherished in adult theory? No, there was not. Everyone simply continued in the way they had begun, exchanging school uniform for work uniform, a pin-stripe suit, a bowler hat, and a clean white hanky. I had a boyfriend once who was something to someone in the City and I embraced, regularly, at least four men every time I went to meet him, so similarly faced and barbered and clad were they all.

Others paid good money to get into those social groupings aptly named regiments, where they were promptly regimented to their hearts' desire. In regiments they spent their days playing all sorts of conformist little games like (in the Royal Welsh Fusiliers) eating leeks with one foot on the table and one on the chair and a drummer drumming on St. David's Day. Or, in the Worcestershire Regiment, always wearing swords when they sat down to eat or, in the Brigade of Guards always breakfasting, lunching, and dining in hats or, in the Minden Regiments, always sporting a rose in the hat on Minden Day, though no roses grew at the time of year when the battle of Minden was fought or, for that matter, anywhere near the place it was fought. Or, in the Highland Regiment, always passing the glass over a finger bowl before drinking, in honour of Bonnie Prince Charlie. Everything done was supposedly to mark some event or other but was really kept on to satisfy the insatiable upper class appetite for good-formity.

Even if you remained a private citizen and did no work at all, the rules pertaining to social life were quite enough to keep you busy, what with the ladies coming and going depending on who was drinking or smoking what, when. And remembering always to put the milk in after the tea and say the hounds were speaking when they were doing nothing of the sort.

After all, Nancy Mitford was able to weave a many-editioned best-seller out of these rules of behaviour and language; and so rigid were they in the time of, say, Jane Austen that nearly every movement had its meaning and everyone knew exactly where they were. As a *Guardian* writer has pointed out, people keep reading Jane Austen because of their nostalgia for those conformist days, which hardly supports the contention of the present and increasing Socialist mould.

Many of the rich and powerful made no attempt even to live in individualist houses. 'Ghastly little Socialist boxes, all exactly the same, that's what they want for all of us,' trumpets some red-faced old boy regarding a council estate and then off he trots, back to his Nash terrace where each house apes the next with a meticulousness unknown to council estates and none is even separated from the others. And were these famous terraces built in the humdrum workaday towns? Not at all. They line themselves up in the pleasure centres of England where people lived for fun, in Brighton and Cheltenham, in Buxton, Scarborough, and Lyme Regis. And was John Nash only patronised by the middle classes, the gentry, public bodies? Not at all. He was the favourite architect of the Prince Regent himself, who could have built any folly his heart desired and *chose* Nashian conformity. One of Mr Nash's best-known efforts on behalf of his royal

153

patron was Regent Street, exceptional for its featureless monotony and a butt, in its first days, of vulgar and philistine caricaturists. In fact, all the élite of England, secure in their illusion of individualism, thought this most conformist of architects the absolute bee's knees.

What's more, further back yet, in the days of the First Elizabethans so generally accepted as individualists to a man, Good Queen Bess imposed Sumptuary Laws that decreed exactly how each section of society dressed and carried prison sentences for nonconformist garb.

Strange paradoxes all. The very people who believe themselves to be manning the barricades in the battle for freedom of choice, for individuality, who would howl the place down if any Government suggested they do half the things they do by choice; who yell the loudest against the flattening, mashing mincer of socialist levelling, are actually the products of lives so conformist that, beside them, working class life is one riot of colourful iconoclasm and the hated Reds are eccentrics to a man, given to such awesomely individualist statements as Lenin's 'So long as the State exists, there is no freedom; when freedom exists there will be no State' and Marx's 'The administration of men will be replaced by the administration of things. . .the State is not abolished, it dies away.'

As I always say, it's a funny old world. Do you always say that? Oh good.

5 January 1976

Birth of the Blues

EVERY SILVER LINING has its cloud, which is to say (apart from any Monday morning blues) that every step forward contains an inherent step backwards, that every gain incorporates a loss, even though that loss may not be noticed by a particular individual at a particular time. To me the most general step backwards built into all the more recent steps forward is the increasing control we have over our lives that forces us into the increasing anxiety of making decisions.

For most of the time that mankind has been on this planet, resignation must have appeared a most valuable trait. Since a large percentage of the things that happened to you were quite out of your control, the ability to resign yourself or (the optimist's phrase) make the most of events, was essential to any sort of happiness. No wonder that the ability is enshrined in most religions in some form or another.

But today, resignation in the face of almost anything except death is called by a score of unpleasant names, from apathy to cowardice, and even the extreme, death, is not entirely exempt. Most of us have a very strong impression that death itself could be avoided if only we gave up smoking, took up swimming, ate fertile eggs, retired to a clean-air zone or thought beautiful thoughts. Nothing, we feel, is inevitable, if only we take the right decisions at the right time.

Quite suddenly, not more than about 10 years ago in a few countries of the world, one of the most inevitable human fates became controllable—the reproduction of ourselves. For the first time, many young men and women actually had to take a decision before bringing a child into the world and, awesomely, a decision entirely dependent on personal wishes because our planet does not need the children it already has.

155

Worse, in these days of nuclear families, most couples have no experience at all of babies or children, so they must decide, on the scantiest of knowledge, whether they will take the sort of gamble that will alter the whole course of their lives.

When I was a child, one of the things I least understood about adults was their perverse refusal to use their enviable freedom. There was I, a long-term prisoner in my parents' home, manacled to the arbitrary whims and commands of the occupying Brobdinagians. Go to school, wash your hands, eat your greens, wear a woolly, sleep at eight, get up at eight, do what you're told. And there *they* were, powerful infants with not a soul in the world to prevent them staying up all night, moving to the Casbah, eating 16lb of jelly babies straight off, watching telly till their eyes charred or doing any other single thing their hearts desired. And what did they do? Surrounded themselves with made-up rules, handcuffed themselves to the dreariest of routines, ordered themselves to trek daily to boring jobs or clean dreary houses and, in every way, made their lives a great deal more shackled and slave-like than mine. What fools these grown-ups be.

It never, of course, occurred to me that I, the child, was at least one strand of the whip that bent my parents' backs, that kept them going round and round like mice on a wheel instead of shooting off in all directions like glorious Catherine Wheels. I was born before the age of reproductive decisions and so were my children. I suppose the pill was circulating down in Puerto Rico and other foreign testing grounds but, in my early twenties, I caught not a glimpse of it. Now, I often ask myself if my own children would be here if I had been a post-pill woman. Obviously social and emotional pressures are still strong, grannies, neighbours and friends still eye with interest the flat belly of the newly-married girl and our consumer society still forces upon us the image of the happy family rather than the happy couple. I think quite a lot of the pregnancies that end in abortion have to do with the attempt to form a vague possibility into an obvious reality so that the woman *must* decide.

What exactly are the advantages and disadvantages of having children, shorn of all rationalising sentiment, viewed from a distance, before love for the children has entered the picture, before the womb has known a change? Those who have never dreamed of asking themselves the questions do not need the answers—I imagine that they are what are called natural mothers or fathers and there's an end on't. I was not and am not and I believe that, for better or for worse, I am in the majority, if the truth were told. This says nothing at all about the love parents have for their children when born—we love what we have to love (or, of course, batter it or kill it).

The disadvantages first. In my experience the most pervasive, the most overwhelming and the longest-lasting is that from the moment a child is delivered and lies beside you in a cot, you are never again completely free from worry. The umbilical cord may be cut but its thin elastic shadow remains. Sometimes the worry recedes so far that it is only the very faintest cloud on the horizon. Sometimes it looms so large it blocks out everything in sight but it never, ever, disappears. The new flesh is part of you and what happens to it through life happens to you, and often, more painfully. No woman, once pregnant, is completely unaware of that pregnancy for more than a few minutes of the time. No woman, once a mother, can escape that awareness for very much longer. At times, to be truthful, the weight is enough to sink you and that weight is certainly at the root of the incoherent fury women often feel towards the father who leaves. Though he abide by every gentlemanly rule, though he pays the bills, though he visit, he does not bear the weight and envy of his freedom can burn like hellfire.

The second disadvantage is more obvious and more practical—the loss of freedom for many years. That loss may vary greatly and a nice balance of money and psychopathy may leave some parents spectacularly exempt from this penalty. But for most of us, the coming of children is as much a curtailment of personal liberty as the curfew imposed on evenings out to the constant possibility of being aroused in the small hours by a knock on the door. Our lives are no longer our own, our choices are reduced to near invisibility. A schedule descends like a cage on even feckless mothers: mouths must be fed (if only with fish fingers), bodies must be kept clean (if only once a week), teeth must be filled, minds nourished, nails clipped, a way and place of living somehow established and kept. A woman is trapped in her house, a man made hostage to an employer, more cautious in claims for autonomy or even, paradoxically, for better pay. If the mother works, she must be grateful to the job round the corner with compatible hours and the hell with promotion, interest, more money or anything else that makes that job otherwise intolerable.

The third disadvantage is the slow transformation of love for your partner into the packhorse syndrome. Each becomes the symbol for the other of the worries and lack of freedom imposed by the children, eyes that once saw a desirable face now see only bills. Spontaneous love-making is the first casualty, assassinated in the children's infancy by any sudden cries, buried six feet under by ubiquity—the kids are always there as they grow older, needing something, wanting something, or simply creating merry and unignorable hell.

I know couples on their own after years who wander about the house and speak without looking at each other, strangers passing in the night. Who, say their eyes, is this person inhabiting my bedroom? Could it have been with him/her that all this started? The original impulse has long been forgotten, vanished beneath an avalanche of old skipping ropes and broken roller skates.

So, to me, the great advantage in having children grows out of the second disadvantage, the loss of freedom. Oddly, I find freedom at least as burdensome as its opposite. I do not like the idea that I cannot live where I wish but I like even less the idea that I could live anywhere. I do not care to think that I must do what I do but I am terrified to think what I would do if I could do anything.

Pressures force you into jobs, into places, into ways of life and out of these pressures emerge jobs, places, ways of life more to your liking. And there are no pressures quite like children. Through them I have been forced into experiences no one could choose; physical and mental pain, absolute joy, recognition of my ties with others and work of all kinds from washing dishes and selling ladies' corsets to writing for the *Guardian*. None of which I could initially have managed without the constant vision of the little beaks open in the nest, waiting for the worm. Some people can and all honour to them. I couldn't.

The second great advantage of having children is that they are your lifeline to the past and the future. It may not seem worth all the attendant troubles, merely to learn about bunking off or the names of the Bay City Rollers, and there are other, less exhausting ways to learn, but I doubt if I would have done it. I am, through my children, made to live more lives than my own and live my own life again. And I understand, year by year, more about my parents and their parents. Being a parent is, if you like, a form of compulsory Adult Education.

So, weighing again the advantages and disadvantages, in a cool and rational state of mind, given my life over again, would I have decided to have children? Would I, without any necessity, deliberately set out to hamper myself in nearly every way? Cause myself endless self-imposed anxiety? Pay a very high price for joys obtainable elsewhere at half the cost?

The answer is, I do not know. I love them more dearly than anyone else on earth, I think I would die for them and I greet each advancing year with delight, notching off my porridge to eventual glorious release. It's called maternal schizophrenia, my disease, and the pill is not a cure.

12 January 1976

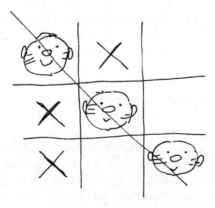

Lots of Sex, Please, We're British

YOU'VE HEARD OF SWINGERS. You know, those people who wife-swap and all that, down in leafy Neasden and places, the dormitory suburbs. Rather gruesome, really. A kinky side-effect of the pill. A bit desperate, I shouldn't wonder. Not for the likes of us, except for a juicy exposé in one of those Sunday newpapers we wouldn't have around the house.

Actually, I met some swingers the other day. It turned out they do rather more than wife-swapping a lot of the time. In fact, you could say wife-swapping was a mere hors d'oeuvres on a very à la carte menu. They invited me to a party where they meet and have sex together. This invitation made me much more nervous than when I was wandering about on the Lebanon-Israeli front. I told them all I wasn't going to join in, of course, just make notes in my little book. Then I made myself up very carefully in the bathroom mirror. Well, you might not want to join in but you don't want people not wanting you to join in, do you? And I put on a pair of my tattiest knickers so that, no matter what sudden temptation assailed me, I would resist. I am a member of the NUJ, after all.

It never came to that, not this time, because the man who was giving the party said his central heating had broken down and a cold orgy is not on. But I did learn some very interesting things about swingers that I will pass on to you as matters of public interest. The people I met were of various ages. They were nicely dressed and friendly and courteous. The women were comely, their hair sparkled, their teeth shone. The men were well set up, they smelt of after-shave, their teeth shone. They had come as presents for each other and they were most carefully packaged. They estimated that there were some four thousand of them in London alone and mentioned contacts all over Europe and the States, friends who dropped in now and again. Sometimes they had parties of twenty or so, sometimes nearer four hundred. They were busy making plans to go over to Germany for carnival time, five parties planned there already. 'I was raped at one on Old Ladies' Night,' said a man. 'I've been back ever since.'

I talked to many of them, including one true impresario of sex, in an effort to understand what made them tick. By the end I was beginning to wonder what made me tick, a much more mysterious thing. Because they have evidently done what D. H. Lawrence was always on about. They have transferred sex from the head to where it was originally located, the loins. They have not done away with love. They have simply separated it, without apparent guilt or even much thought, from lust. They antedate the Tree of Knowledge. The Eves do not know their nakedness, the Adams feel no shame, they have not eaten the apple nor glimpsed the serpent. Beside them the glint of Mrs Whitehouse's specs appears positively corrupt. Yet, oddly enough, many of them have the same aim as Mrs W., or the Archbishop of Canterbury. Give them their way and they'll stamp out paid sex. They believe in marriage and they attend parties to preserve those marriages. One circle also practises a form of therapeutic sex with remarkable kindness and democracy. Because sex is their pastime, their hobby, they offer to people with problems sexual solutions that would hardly occur to the best-trained social worker.

I have myself, for instance, commiserated now and again with the various problems of the disabled and the old. But in my conventional way I had barred thoughts of sex in connection with such people. Why? A kind of sexual fascism is the only answer. But these swingers think of sex in connection with everyone. Thus the impresario:

'There was a woman I met through my work, in a wheelchair, paralysed from the waist down. What, I said, does an attractive lady like you do about boy friends? She was only 40 or so. Oh dear, she said, it's been years but who'd fancy me? Lots of men, I said. I introduced her to a swinger, he went over, they had a chat, watched a bit of telly, and got down to it. She couldn't do a lot but what she did was fantastic, and he told her so. She's a changed woman now.'

The impresario comes into contact with a lot of such people. He has ladies with scars and fat ladies too, and lots of men like fat ladies. Impotence? Men often say to him, well, I'll come along but I can't do anything. They can at a party. They don't have to join in, no one does, but the impresario has never seen one who didn't. He thinks a lot of men are impotent with one woman because of the responsibility and when there's none, no pressure, they're fine.

The impresario has something like a thousand and one names in his head, known personally to him. Some of the women are, he says, what used to be called nymphomaniacs. Many of the men are fully paid-up swingers, stalwarts to be relied upon with anyone.

Lots have fantasies of particular kinds. Bondage—restriction without pain—is popular with the ladies. Some people like being beaten, others like beating. He recalls that once he got his own wires crossed. He lay in a bed regarding the Queen's back garden while a girl strapped his back for some ten minutes. Then he turned and said diffidently, are you...is that...are you OK now, on account of my back is a bit sore. Oh, she said, I thought it was *you* wanted it. My arm is killing me.

The computer in his mind sorts people out into matching fantasies so that everyone has a good time. But the fantasies are well controlled, in a party situation. A girl might say she'd like a gang bang with a whole football team and he'd arrange it but nothing can go wrong because others are there. He doesn't fool around with the fantasy, either. A girl wants a football team, she gets a football team, not 11 blokes in Chelsea T-shirts. Football teams are very co-operative that way, as are many surprising people. The impresario rings up film stars who come to London if any of his circle ask for them and, often, they're pleased to comply, with no complications, in a group. Swingers do not want people for their frame or their bank accounts, only their bodies and their fantasies and then only once or twice. Millionaires, says the impresario, are very enthusiastic. Often they have difficulty relating to the opposite sex or to their own. Think they're being sought after for their money. But in a party they can't think that and they relax. One of them said I don't think anyone knew who I was. Or cared, said the impresario.

A number of ladies, he tells me, have masochistic fantasies. But his ladies don't have to get themselves married to battering husbands to work them out. They come to parties, get their satisfaction—as much as they want and no more—and quite often it's out of their systems. One girl came to him and said she'd always wanted to strip in front of an audience. He had a strip-club owner among his members so he arranged that she should carry out her fantasy there. She did and she said to him after, that was fine but I never want to do it again. It's over.

One man I met assured me of the same thing. A man, if he's a swinger, all he really wants to do is give the woman pleasure in whatever way she wants and, at a party, she can say what she wants, be equal. The word gets around very quickly if you're the wrong type, impolite, not clean, you know. We don't mind people watching, voyeurism is very popular, but there was one man who came to two parties with six girls and told them what to do, without doing anything himself. We barred him then. We don't like that sort of manipulation, not privately, if you see what I mean. We've never had any unpleasantness, have we? Oh, well, there was that Irishman who got a bit riled when someone made a remark about Guinness, but that's it and that wasn't much.

The 'straight' swingers have no particular fantasies, just preferences. Many are married couples and conventional ones at that. I talked to two girls, one 33, the other 25, both married. The 33-year-old is a housewife with one child, married for six years. She had a fair amount of sexual experience before, but only with one boyfriend at a time.

'The thing that puzzled me, they were so jealous. If they even thought you might be seeing another man it was like an atom bomb hit the place. I never fully comprehended this; if a relationship is good, why worry? But they did. Then I married and my husband had less experience than me. So we started going to parties. We're more in love now than we were. If I heard he was going out with another woman *alone*,

163

I'd be very jealous, I'd try and stop it. I'd fear love, you see. A party situation is very different, it has nothing to do with love. I don't ever wish to go out with other men, I don't fancy other men—only at parties and I have them and it's over.'

The 25-year-old said that before she and her husband went to parties they each secretly had friends on the side. She found the involvement depressing, she was continually torn between another man and her husband. Then they sat down together and said this is ridiculous. We both want other people sexually, occasionally, but doing it this way is going to break our marriage. Let's have sex with other people together. So they did. She goes once a fortnight ('I think of myself as averagely sexed'), her husband once or twice a week, alone. She is happy with this because she knows he is not emotionally involved. You can't be, at parties, she never heard of anyone who was. And it is so nice to come home and be alone together. She doesn't have orgasms at parties.

What happens at these parties? You meet at someone's house and, usually, there are one or two couples you know and the rest are strangers to each other. That's the way it's supposed to be. You have a drink (not too much and no drugs allowed), something to eat, a little chat. A man comes over and says what a pretty necklace you're wearing. Then you go upstairs and begin. There are two or three beds in each room, you can look at other people, change round or not, just as you prefer. Some houses are well known, designed for parties. One has a gallery where you may look down at others. One has spectacular pictures, large rooms, a fantastic sound system and fantastic sounds. Swingers often have cards with their names and telephone numbers and sticky backs, so they adhere to the naked flesh of someone they fancy and haven't got round to this time. Some men I met said, in a modest sort of way, that they went to four and five parties a week and sometimes even shaved and went straight on to the office.

As I listened to them, their nice healthy hair shining, their nice attractive faces glowing, their friendly hands stroking, I was reminded more than anything of a newish kind of religious group. They have a message, they believe you will benefit, they know the change it has made to their lives, they

164

want to convert you too. They proselytize, they draw you in. Their eyes are as earnest as a Sally Army lady's under her bonnet.

I shall try to nerve myself and attend a party later. But I do not think it will turn me on. I am, you see, hooked on sex in the head. The kink for me is the excitement of one person, the way he smiles, the way he walks, most of all the things he says. Sex with everything seems a mite bland to me, a bit Butlins, Skegness, instead of the outer reaches of Afghanistan. But I see no wrong in those who manage a division, and it is quite likely that more people would attain more sexual happiness with sex located firmly in the loins. I am not innocent as they. For me, sex is dangerous, a continuous background threat, a shadow in the dark. I like it that way, I know no other way. The swingers have domesticated sex, tamed it, controlled it, made it into a hobby like bridge or stamp-collecting, though a hobby very helpful to others. To each his own. But, in the Garden of Eden, I would be the pervert.

16 February 1976

Heads Who Win

FOR THE PAST FEW WEEKS, in common with thousands of other parents, I have been preoccupied with what the headmaster of my son's primary school calls 'a momentous decision'. At what school should the fruit of my loins spend the next five or six years of his life, given that we are not evicted from our flat and can, as a nation, continue to afford schools at all?

On one level it is a momentous decision. I happen to have been reading various autobiographies lately wherein such decisions were tragedy or turning point to the writer on the lines of 'If I had not had Fred Fribbs as my form master / science teacher / chaplain I would never have become Archbishop / won the Nobel Prize / remained sane /gone mad'. My God, what a responsibility I have to my child, to make sure that the school I choose will enable him to meet / not meet Fred Fribbs's equivalent and have his life transformed. On another level, it is a decision compared to which choosing a new lipstick is momentous. I went to 14 different schools merely because I happened to be around when they were and met not a single Fred Fribbs, one way or the other. I remember absolutely nothing of all those thousands of hours of teaching, emerged virtually unemployable and learnt all I know in the University of Life, not to say a typing school.

However, some decision has to be made. The first step is the arrival of one's child with a pink pamphlet listing all the schools in the district the child could attend—in some parts of the counry all two, in London a fairly bewildering variety. I ponder the list. Whether grammar, comprehensive, voluntary or church, each write-up is more glowing than the last. Sudden new possibilities impinge—what about a ballet

166

school, a drama school, a school on a ship? Could I produce a Nureyev, an Olivier, a Nelson at the stroke of a Biro? My son says no, he'd rather not be a dancer, an actor, or an admiral, thank you. There is a short and slightly acerbic exchange between us about lack of vision and the spirit of adventure and we get down to more practical things.

One very practical thing became immediately evident. If I did pick schools A, B, C or D, would my son be able to get there and back daily without a helicopter? The ILEA do not send you underground or bus maps but these are essential weaponry in the early decision-making process. If, as I imagine hopefully though unrealistically, my child is going to become involved in a host of extra-mural activities from stamp collecting to optional Lithuanian lessons, he can't be expected to make his way home in winter, in darkness, on three buses and an underground train without risk of meeting an early and sticky end.

So trial by transport begins. I track down school after school on maps and scratch them off because there is no simple way to get to them and first years are not even allowed to bicycle to school. The next lot are eliminated on what I might call vaguely ideological grounds. Or what they might call vaguely ideological grounds. I do not think the Jewish Board of Education would accept my son as a Jew, which is annoying because they might have the best schools. Roman Catholics ditto. Being English, my son has, I presume, the loosest of rights to go to a Church of England school but church membership is usually taken into account and I can't produce that at the drop of a hat. Besides, I have a feeling that both me and my child would be worms in the bud, flies in the ointment. All church schools have at their heart what I would call superstition. And faith in a god, plus ritual worship of same, is not my idea of the best compost for free thinking.

Heavens, how the list has shrunk. Transport and God have done for fifteen out of the original twenty-three without even venturing out of the house. My own dislike of the direct grant system, allied , admittedly, to my own inner knowledge that my son would never be accepted, does for another two, girls-only schools for three more and, lo, there are only three schools left, three green bottles hanging on my wall.

Armed with these three possibles, I attend the primary school parents' meeting to assess five visiting secondary heads. The primary school head gives us a short speech on momentous decisions and we all look suitably solemn and canny. The head then explains to us for the fourth time about how little we need worry about the marks on our children's tests, due back shortly from the ILEA. My son is not aware he has done them—not, I fear, a hopeful sign. The head, a kind man, is evidently quite horrified at the idea that any of us might take any notice at all of these tests. He says most children will be in the 50 per cent middle bracket and then squirms, reddens and nearly collapses under his desk at the ordeal of having to pronounce, in public, such obscene phrases as 'low' and 'top' 25 per cent. The 'so called lower' he says, blushing. The 25 per cent, dare I say it, 'top' he says. He appears to be on the verge of a thrombosis. The parents stare at him, beady-eyed. A father clears his throat and says but surely the marks do make some difference to his choice of schools. The head convulses again. Only, he moans softly, the tinciest winciest difference. Practically invisible to anyone without the strongest bifocals. The parents' eyes bead a little more. They know the facts, that only a top 25 per cent bracket will give them a grammar. The atmosphere is loud with unspoken thoughts, uneasy fidgets.

Embarrassed for us all, I lower my eyes and read the prospectus of the local grammar, presently in the throes of a threatened amalgamation with a local boys secondary. The grammar says it has the *utmost* admiration for the secondary. It goes into impassioned detail about the amazing *facilities* offered by that secondary. It congratulates its colleagues at that secondary for their *outstanding* achievements. *But*, it says, it is overwhelmed with *fear* for that secondary and its pupils, if the Government insists on merging their incredibly *humble* grammar school selves with such *genius*. Might not a *lowering* of secondary standards take place? Pause for shudder. *All right thinking* parents are implored to prevent this appalling fate from falling upon the boys of the *secondary* if they have any heart at all. *No merging*.

Raising my wet eyes from this cockle-tearing appeal, I see

that we parents are now invited to ask questions in informal groups of the five visiting heads. My mind becomes a perfect blank. What on earth am I supposed to ask? Not, obviously, what I really want to know, viz: which one of you is going to be the most tremendously interested, kind, and encouraging to *my son*, deeply appreciate and love and help *my son*, above all other children and sacrifice all your time and talents to the service of *my son*.

I wander from group to group. The *Sunday Times* magazine has recently suggested certain questions parents may profitably ask of secondary school heads. Several parents have obviously read them. One after another they say, forcefully, 'What is the staff turnover at your school?' And then, relieved beyond measure at having asked anything at all, they fall back stunned. The teachers' answers are polite and evasive but no one is listening, collapsed as they are in a self-congratulatory daze. This meeting is to prove to parents that they know the questions, and the answers are quite immaterial, if not impossible. Will we be rated the 'top', 'middle', or 'lower' band of mothers and fathers? Will we pass the tests?

In another group a father and a teacher confront each other on matters of the highest mathematical principles. 'Geoff,' says the father, 'does his multiplication like this—he puts the noughts at the back. Do you put your noughts at the back?' Deeply obliging, the head takes out a piece of paper and, together, they quickly cover it with noughts back, front, and sideways. I drift away.

My son's form master, seeing my disarray, ushers me over to another head. Panicked into honesty, I say the first thing that comes into my head. My son is rather a gentle boy. Umm. Do you, is that, will he...umm? The head fixes me with a spiritual eye. 'At our school,' he says slowly and musically 'we aim to turn out very gentle children, yet with an inner core of tempered steel.' Ah, I say.

The next turn in the gavotte is a parents' meeting at a particular secondary school. Interested parents sit around a large table thinking with envy of all those deplorably uninterested parents now having a pint round the pub. We eye each other surreptitiously. What sort of parents are these, who may mix their children with ours at this school? 'That woman with the big eyes, I recognize her' whispers my husband. 'Big eyes?' I hiss back. 'Those are ordinary sized eyes in an extremely small face.' I am not having my child's future biased by the possibility of interesting encounters at PTAs.

The wonders of the school are spread before us. Language laboratories, drama centres, sequestered playgrounds for the newcomers, dedicated teachers, incredible sports facilities, metal work rooms that could produce a Concorde, science laboratories that could split atoms. I want to cheer at the end, I am overwhelmed. All this and not a penny to pay. Other parents are unmoved, they look stern, suspicious and unforgiving as if they were stumping up the fees of Eton for these facilities.

At the next school, things are less organized. Small family groups wander about in the gloaming or edge their way along the walls of lighted classrooms, staring at scrawly essays entitled 'My Dad.' My Dad has a bad temper and shouts. My Dad says, when I eat a banana, don't leave any for me will you. My Dad gets furious if we play when he is asleep in his chair. My Dad is the best Dad in the world. I roam about, unsure what to look for. Broken windows? Graffiti? A budding Michelangelo? You've seen one child's painting, you've seen them all. I am disgusted at my own lack of enterprise and collar a large boy trekking across the playground: He says the school is OK, he supposes, for a school. He says yes, there's quite a bit of fighting. The head had just informed me that to hit another child is 'our most serious crime'. The lad goes off, cuffing another lad.

Finally, we are collected by a teacher who carts us upstairs and down lab talking all the while. I and another mother are gripped, strangled by politeness. We ooh and aah at each new room as if the Queen were showing us round Buck House.

During the next week, I march round one more school. The teachers comment often on how boys are being taught to sew on buttons and girls to repair cars. Everyone seems delighted at these revelations. Quite *right*, they keep saying. Why *not*, they repeat. I think, sourly, that only last year they were probably writing letters to the *Times*, saying that mixing classes was the end of civilization as they knew it. After each visit my son announces his absolute intention of attending this particular school. All his friends announce the same intention. One head says he thinks too much time is spent on 'difficult' children and at his school they concentrate on the helpful children, awarding them merit badges for helping old ladies to cross the street. 'What a *good* idea,' chorus the parents. Another goes into lengthy detail about what he does to help 'difficult' children. What a *good* idea, chorus the parents.

Rumours fly. Parents talk to parents, children to children. My friend had a daughter there, had to teach her to fight. Other girls. My friend says they just caught five boys doing the parking meters, made all their meter-breaking tools in the woodwork classes. I think that is rather enterprising. No I don't. My son arrives home with fearful tales of the toughness of A, B and C. Robert's going to C, he says, because his older brother is there. For protection. Would Robert's oldest brother protect you too, I ask, humbly.

I ring up a last school to make an appointment for the following week's Open Day. A kindly female voice says so sorry but it's all booked up. I ask for the next Open Day. So sorry, there are no more. I ask for an appointment with the head. So sorry, he's had all his appointments. You mean, I say, that my child couldn't come to your school anyway, that it's booked up? Oh *no*, says the kindly voice, shocked. He has *every* chance. But if I've never seen the school, talked to the headmaster? I know, she says sympathetically. It *is* difficult, isn't it?

Finally, the climax. The marking assessment. I have a wild moment's dream that the head will say your son, *my son*, is brilliant. At everything. We have never had, in all our years, such an incredibly intelligent, talented and, yes, so charming a child. The head says fair, not at all bad, poor, could do better, quite good at.

I have, it turns out, a mixed ability child. And I am a mixed ability parent in a mixed ability world. I wander away from the primary school and slowly my head empties of all the last few weeks' phrases. Streaming, banding, setting, remedial, pastoral, project. Come September, some school will take my son. Come some July, and he will leave that school. As we all have done, are doing and will do, for ever and ever, amen.

1 March 1976

Femina Sapiens

THE NATIONAL CONFERENCE of the Women's Liberation Movement in Newcastle comes hard on the heels of the Brussels Tribunal of Crimes against Women. The women who were most effective at the Tribunal in terms of helping a lot of other women were those who had gathered together cold hard facts about a particular crime rather than those who simply told of their own ordeals. A harrowing story of rape in Norway or France remains just that, a harrowing story. Women, listening, 'know' it to be true but there is a fearful gap between such intuitive knowledge and the factual ammunition needed to take action against it. One woman alone, in a paper entitled *Femicide,* supplied exact figures on women murdered in her country, the United States, and the proportion (one in ten) whose deaths were a direct result of sexual attack.

'Give me facts,' said an elderly Belgian woman barrister, 'and I will take off my clothes and walk naked in the streets to draw attention to them.' She knows what every woman knows, even if she tries to hide it from herself, that injustice, fear and even violent death stalk the second sex. But she also knows that emotion is not enough. Essential, always present but, by itself, not enough.

Sadly, there is a deep revulsion in some parts of the Women's Movement against facts and against those women who deal in them. Indeed, so powerful is that revulsion that many such women have already been alienated from the movement; women with analytical minds, women who are emotional only up to a point and then argue the need for proof, for statistics to use for further action. Various charges are levelled against them—that they are not truly committed or involved, that they are doubting Thomasinas, that they have been co-opted by the male system, worst of all that they reject emotion and subjectivity, the women's virtues, and try to be rational and objective. And therefore are men with men's minds, rams in ewes' clothing, traitors to the women's cause.

The underlying assumption here is a curious one—that the masculine mind and the masculine approach is rational and logical and objective. Therefore women must all the more cherish their own innate natures—emotional, illogical, subjective. But the slightest move towards closer examination immediately shows this assumption to be almost absolutely untrue. Men have run the world, whether in governments or only in the family, since recorded history and that world has, as far back as I can see, been anything but outstanding for its logic and rationality. Take any one of the most powerful influences of our time, or any time, and you will see that they stem almost solely from an emotional source, from prejudice, illogic and irrationality.

The plight of many women, the reason they were at the Tribunal, is the result of blind irrationlity. The kind of fear and hatred of women obviously felt by some men and manifested in rape, in beatings, in torture and even in pornographic rape films is not rational. The price men pay for their oppression of women—anything from the burden of the mortgage to continual fears about their virility—is even less rational.

Religion, the worship of gods or a god unknown and unknowable, is another obvious example of male irrationality that has held sway, in one form or another, throughout man's short life on earth. Each civilization laughs at the previous gods and immediately sets to creating gods of their own who are, of course, the *true* gods, though they are so suspiciously like the old that a Martian might not be able to tell the difference. A little readjustment here, a slightly new angle there and *voilà*, down on your knees.

Were the witchhunts that swept Europe and spread to the New World a rational exercise? Was the Inquisition logical? Does it make good sense that some doctors today are devoting their energies to measuring changes in the electrical charges of the body so that a woman forbidden by her religion to have intercourse without reproduction in mind may have intercourse without reproduction in mind, by studying her volts instead of using the pill? And remember, for religion read 'men'. Women only decorate the altars.

And what of the other great irrational institutions so many accept as gospel? That the colour of a man's skin says something absolute about his nature. That such colour differences are worth waging wars about, making slaves about, creating completely separate societies about. But, for that matter, men are quite irrational enough to make deep divisions between peoples of the same colour. We are perfect human specimens and you are frogs, wops, wogs, bohunks, taffies, yanks, huns, japs, gooks, niggers and kikes. Does all that strike you as the product of logical minds?

There are a hundred other examples. George Orwell was taught that the lower classes smelt and never quite got over that emotive barrier, in spite of knowing better than most that you do tend to smell if you work hard and have no place to wash. Hitler raved, ranted, and used film to depict the Jews as dirty, depraved and hideous, thus paving the way to the gas chambers. Quite ordinary politicians lean heavily on emotion in their speeches and a lot less heavily on facts. Even the most apparently detached news report usually packs in an emotive word or two—the baddie is obese, the goodie chubby.

All of which proves just one thing, that men are the antithesis of women's picture of them—they are emotive, irrational, illogical beings who have shaped the world to their image and they have consistently spurned, ill-treated, exiled and even killed those few among them who have sought explanations for what the rest infinitely prefer to believe is magic of a kind. 'Earthly minds, like mud walls, resist the strongest batteries,' said John Locke, 'and though sometimes the force of a clear argument may make some impression, yet they nevertheless stand firm, keep out the enemy, truth, that would captivate or disturb them.'

And yet men dare say, praising a woman who attempts a rational stance, 'she has a man's mind'. Worse, women believe this definition or why would they say, in disparagement of such a woman, 'she has a man's mind?'

174

There is no evidence that women's brains differ in structure from men's brains. There is no evidence that women who try to be rational are less 'feminine'—how can they be, when men are so obviously irrational?

Of course, dealing in thought as opposed to feeling is much harder work for very little reward. How do you prove your allegiance to other women? By total acceptance, blind faith, in anything another sister says. How do you prove yourself a traitor to those sisters? By applying logic, by refusing to be swayed *just* by emotion, by daring not to believe in all of the women all of the time. By, in fact, applying those brakes to emotion that men hardly ever apply, that few Germans applied to Hitler, few Italians to Mussolini, few Russians to Stalin. I should not be required to sob and scream to convince you that I recognize the extent of women's oppression. I should not be required to talk only of hatred and never mention a victory, celebrate a gain, on pain of instant ostracism by some sisters.

Nor should women be made afraid of success because it might put them beyond the female pale. This is an ancient symptom of oppression and the blacks, in their time, went through it and recovered. I remember the time when to mention a well known black man or woman to another black would automatically call forth a sneer, an insinuation that the 'star' must have sold out to the honkies. There are women in the movement who are doing the same thing to other women today. Successful (hard-working, talented, useful) women are suspect. When Kate Millett visited London last, after the publication of her autobiography, *Flying*, she talked to a group of women of her problems, anxieties, and difficulties in thus exposing herself.

But what did her first questioner say? Predictably, a confusion of accusations—that she had sold out to the media, that she had lost touch with the grass roots, that she was in some way tainted, contaminated, no longer 'pure.' So do women apply male irrationality to other women. You are a success. Women are not successes. Therefore you are not a woman. And thus does the Women's Movement deprive itself, not necessarily of its best brains but certainly of a variety of brains. *Cogito, ergo non sum.* We are in danger of

175

losing, by ostracism and derision, one half of our potential, the rational half.

The Women's Movement today is still—perhaps because of this emphasis on emotion—overly protective of itself. Confidence, it seems, has not grown, in spite of legal gains. Movement women too often suspect any part of the media over which they do not have absolute control. '*Spare Rib*,' I have heard it said, 'is OK because they will take what we hand out, without question.' This, presumably, applies to the rest of the feminist press. The national press is damned because it will not. There were, of course, very good reasons indeed for this attitude. When the Women's Movement began, male reporters (and many female) could only be relied on for two things: total ignorance of the aims of women and a laugh a minute at the means. On no other subject would so many editors have allowed so many manifestly uninformed reporters their say. But the years have passed and confidence should have been gained. There is no need for the ghetto mentality any more—not because men have suddenly become so much more sympathetic (though many have) but because women themselves know more.

And then there is the curious horror of ego-tripping felt by the Women's Movement. The horror is understandable enough if it were generally applied but it is not. Ego-trippers abound but are forgiven as long as they appear to be swept away by overwhelming forces apparently beyond their control. Any other form is not. Bertrand Russell, in his essay, *Can Men Be Rational?* says that stupid egotism is much more anti-social in its effects than intelligent egotism. 'If all men,' he writes, 'acted from enlightened self-interest the world would be a paradise in comparison with what it is.'

But he does not pretend that the ego can be entirely discarded. Nor did Freud. Nor does any honest human being. Stupid egotism is that which gives immediate satisfaction without any long-term aim. Intelligent egotism is that which realizes ego satisfaction but channels it to other people's good. The latter is too often condemned in the movement, the former not enough.

And, with egotism in mind, I pass on to money. The necessary evil behind every venture, every conference, every

176

good. Women, outside the power structure as they generally are, have little or no money. They struggle continually to raise desperately small sums for desperately large needs—refuges for battered wives, rape centres, newsletters, films, books, fares to meetings, rents for buildings. But part of the reason for this endless struggle is the refusal—understandable, even praiseworthy, but ultimately self-defeating—to cater to the egotism of the rich.

Those who have money, even those who have only a little, like to be seen to be giving, if only for income tax purposes. Men know this well enough. If you give to a male cause you are offered your name on letterheads, on broadcasts and in newspapers, on park benches and hospital wards and the bricks of theatres. You are often given another name to put before your first—Sir, Lord, Dame, Lady. Do women do this? Not at all. Their way is quite opposite. If a woman gives money to a woman's cause and then expects anything at all in return, she is all too often reviled, rejected, put down as a capitalist, an authoritarian, an anti-movement woman. Whether all this is true or not is beside the point. Money is money. And a refuge, a crisis centre, a book, a film, a magazine, a woman helped is justification enough. Unless, of course, the purity of your soul, your feminist credentials, are more important.

22 March 1976

More a Parent than Real

NO SELF-RESPECTING CHILD-CARE manual would be seen read without at least one chapter entirely devoted to the relationship between parents and offspring: how to understand, how to cope, when to come forward, when to step back. Adolescence is generally accepted as the crunch in the relationship and if that is dealt with in the right way, hey presto, parents and children live happily ever after.

But is that the experience of many people? And if it isn't, where are the manuals that guide us through the thickets from then on, when we, the children, are middlescent and our parents aged? A host of vexatious parental problems may dog our footsteps all the way and yet, because everyone seems to have entered into a pact of silence about the subject, there is no help conveniently to hand and we are shamed into an outwardly conforming silence ourselves, at a cost that can sometimes make strong men weep.

Freud, of course, wrote a great deal about the effect our parents have on us in adulthood but in his case histories, full of women whimpering about Big Daddy and men sobbing of Oedipus complexes, it is as if Father and Mother were merely the names of youthful diseases that have left the skin ravaged rather than two individuals who may have been very much alive, epidemics still raging through their children's psyches.

The only aspect of the subject that has been frequently aired is the practical side—who's going to look after granny, the scandal of our old folks, Mrs X dead for three weeks and her daughter living just round the corner. The practical side is important, God knows, but I get this uneasy feeling at times that the plight of a few of the old, at any rate, must have something to do with what they have made their children feel about them. The old lady standing at her gate complaining that her children never visit her reveals only one side of a story. The destitute old man, father of five, must have left some paternal clue behind him worth looking at before we sweep it under the carpet. I know that there are plain selfish children, too busy making money to repay unselfish parents. I know small flats have little room for babies, never mind grannies. But it seems to me that something else, something deeper, must be wrong, too.

The conspiracy of silence starts with our own children. The *pas devant les enfants* syndrome. We do not discuss our feelings about our own parents with our own children because...well...wouldn't it be letting the side down somehow? Undermining our own authority and our expectations of automatic love? And if we revealed to our teenagers that though Grandpa is jolly nice to them he wasn't always jolly nice to us, mightn't they let slip something to the old folks, even round upon them in accusation and *then* what would happen? What old wounds would not open and ooze poison upon us all?

And the more careful we are, the more we smile and kiss and hide, the more unimaginably huge becomes the imagined penalty for honesty. As the years pass, we water the few stunted roses on the poor soil but never, never dare to dig down deep and pull up throttling weeds so that a mass of sturdy roses can bloom in their place. Oddly, I think that if an adult does have parental difficulties, it is the adult who suffers most. To begin with, many elderly parents have more than one child, more than one egg in their basket. If one child disappoints them, another may not. The child of those parents has only them, one mother, one father. They, parents, tend not to remember the details of their behaviour with their children. As age creeps up, so do illusions. They may truly believe they have always been as mellow, as mild, as they are now. They count off the picnics, the new clothes, the money scrounged for a 'good' education and congratulate themselves.

Only the child recalls parental sins, the sarcasms, the betrayals, the mean punishments, the frights and fears because only the child was truly vulnerable, impressionable, and quite defenceless in the family cage. Benevolent or not, parents in a nuclear family are despots, dispensers of ex-cathedra dogma that may go contrary to everything the child senses himself to be, life to be, but cannot prove or even balance for years to come. This process often leaves indelible scars on the child and no trace at all on the parents.

Nevertheless, instead of talk, the conspiracy of silence descends. We are now, at least on the surface, all adults together and we will pretend, in front of strangers, brothers, sisters, in-laws, and our own children that Granny and Grandpa were, are and always shall be, lovely people. Apart from anything else, there are physical barriers now because you know what they do, the old devils? They disguise themselves, they dissemble, they pretend they are no longer the people we once called Mum and Dad.

They grow white hair, shield their once-fierce eyes with spectacles, put on an old man's stoop, an old woman's hunch, temper the familiar bellow, the familiar fist with a touching tremble, a stutter softens the cutting tongue. And just when we reach the age of revenge, the age when we could be coherent about what we resented and still resent, when we could clear out the past debris in a great blast of honesty and, perhaps, start again; there they are, old. Vulnerable, defenceless, pathetic. Caged by age as we were caged by them. Vengeance may be the Lord's but it cannot be ours. The air, at every meeting, is filled with unspoken words that must remain unspoken, now, for ever.

But must they? Convention says that once the hair whitens on the head the human being beneath must be protected from harsh words and home truths. That common humanity demands that they be tucked away from the hurly burly of reality. That the elderly are in a special category, an age when they cannot be considered entirely human, when they are obviously too old to be capable of growth or change. But isn't this the ultimate condescension? Am I right to assume that my father, your father is 'beyond hope', beyond even the hope of throwing out the rubbish and starting again, two adults in an adult world?

Many adults seem to think so. They appear to believe that the only decent thing, once parents are older, is to lead a life of lies, that this potentially most intimate of relationships is not 'real' at all since they assume it would wither at the first hint of straight talking. Over and over again we hear it. 'I would tell my mother but...you know...she's getting on.' 'I'd like my father to know but...well...he'd probably have a heart attack.' 'For goodness sake, *don't* tell my parents.' Said, sadly, about almost everything that really affects the adults. Marital problems, separations, worries over children, ways of spending money, deeply held ethical or political views, jobs, religion, fears, anticipation, anything at all that distinguishes man from animal. All smoothed over, left out, censored, denied.

'Hullo, mother. How are you? I'm fine, he's fine, the children are fine.' (I'm having an affair, he's got a girl, our child's been arrested, I'm having an abortion, I'm pregnant.) 'Oh, we're decorating the bathroom. Yes, green, I thought.' (I'm having a nervous breakdown, I hate you, you hate me.) 'Lovely, dear. How nice, how lovely, oh, good.' (Help me, I'm dying, I'm madly in love, I can't pay the mortgage, I've got debts up to here.) Every single major event in our lives must, apparently, by definition be hidden from our parents. In case they get upset. In case they upset us again.

One girl I know cannot bring herself to tell her mother that the girl she shares her flat with ('Yes, Mother, Susan's very well too') is also her lover. The core of her existence, the centre of her every thought but Mother mustn't know. So a once healthy relationship is doomed by lies to superficiality and so, in the end, to no relationship at all. Impossible to hide three-quarters of your life and still believe another loves you. Loves who? A baby in a pram, a toddler staggering in a garden, a lanky schoolgirl in a tunic? Both connive at this slow gangrene—the girl through assumptions (how can she *know* Mother would not understand, shouldn't she give her the benefit of the doubt, anyway?) and the mother through refusing to listen to the words behind the words. Each censoring out the other's needs, heading for indifference and the eventual sourness of deception.

And parents, in spite of the convention that says if they are ageing they must be harmless, can show in amazingly subtle ways the most blatant hostility to their adult children. No one, I submit, can be quite so unforgiveably rude to other

181

people than an elderly parent to an adult child.

'I'd feel so much happier if you had a nanny looking after dear little Mark.'

'Funny Mark should cry so much with you, he's an absolute angel with me.'

'Darling, I'm sure Aunt Beth would love to stay with you but you do live in rather a pig-sty, don't you?'

'Dear John,' (the husband who has just left you). 'We always got on so well together.'

'Poor little Mark, come to Granny then. Who's got a hole in his sock, mmm? Whose shirt needs a good iron? Granny'll do it, don't you worry.'

A friend, aged 35 and twice married, who has strong left-wing views, actually got up the courage to voice them, briefly, to her staunch Conservative father. 'I don't know where you get your opinions from,' he said. 'Pillow talk, I suppose.' Telling me afterwards, she said if it had been any other man she would have hit him. But this one was her father and 65. He was allowed to get away with it unchallenged. At the cost of another dive in the relationship, another inward promise never to reveal true interest, true feelings.

The question is, do parents really want to know their children in adulthood? Or would they rather meander on, falsely smiling, pretending that the familiar face is really familiar? Sometimes I fear it is only the adult children who want to be known, who cannot bear the hypocrisy of putting on a front for Mother and Father, concealing their real characters and hating that concealment, hating—eventually—the people who make them conceal. And so, slowly, they drift away. Visits become more and more infrequent, the lies grow, thick as thorns, between them. Intolerable to sit drinking tea, smile round the Christmas cake, nod round the television together, pretending to be present and, in fact, light years absent.

Inner distance creates outer distance, falsehoods sap energy, it becomes physically impossible even to get into a car and drive to the parental home. You are my mother and a stranger. You are my father and a man who passes in the street. I sit next to someone in a pub and he knows more about me in ten minutes and I about him than both our sets of parents. If I had robbed a bank you might be justified—though the parents of bank robbers seem to accept and often still love. But I haven't. I have committed no crime except that of being myself rather than your conception of a 'good' son or daughter. It hurts me to lie. It hurts me more that you do not want to know that I am lying, that you cannot tell, that you do not care.

I wish there were some social formula for settling old grievances and beginning again, some special birthday when convention demanded a struggle, a meeting, a confrontation and then forgiveness, between parents and children. Then, perhaps, the children would not carry unnecessary loads through to the fifties and parents would not deserve the final vengeance—isolation, loneliness. Is the 'happy family' act worthwhile, just for the neighbours' applause? Are people, as they age, beyond change? Should we give them the dignity, bleak though it may be, of honesty or do we meekly join the act, please the neighbours and sacrifice all hope?

If you are a parent with long-grown children, do you think you know them? Or would you rather not know them, rather make them up, fend off their reality with the threat of weeping eyes and little-old-lady sobs? Have you retreated into old age and shut the door and will you then complain that the children never visit, that they treat you badly, that they ought to come for Christmas, for Easter, for holidays and it's all their fault they don't? Isn't that the price you pay for inventing your children? A mask where a face once was. A powdery dust where life once was. A polite ritual where love once was.

29 March 1976

183

Life's Rich Travesty

FIRST THE GOOD NEWS, said my lodger. Someone's thrown a brick through the window and I've got syphilis. Wearily, I put down my shopping bags. Women do get weary. There you are, you see, I said. There you bloody are. How d'you mean, said my lodger. Syphilis is what I mean, I said. That's what you get, isn't it, for being so bloody promiscuous. My lodger looked hurt. I'm not promiscuous, he said. Anyway, what's wrong with being promiscuous? Oh shut up, I said.

Where are the vicarage lawns of yesteryear, the chink of teacups and smell of lemon curd, the soft conversations, the how nice to see yous and you are looking wells and do have another éclair? In moments of stress my little finger crooks in memory of gentler times. Strawberries and cream, panama hats, sunshine on the snapdragons and the light laughter of children in Fair Isle and frills. Life I only see today in ads for Ribena.

In the untidy bedroom, glass stalactites lay over the floor, winking evilly. At the window beside my typewriter, a jagged hole gaped. If I had been writing at the time, the knife-edged slate that did the job would have scalped me. Could I have claimed for industrial injury? Would my editor have paid me compensation, wounded at work? Down below, in the adventure playground, the little psychopaths roam, their eyes bright and empty. One in a Jaws T-shirt is throttling one with a patch on his bum saying If You Don't See What You Want, Come Inside. Two are hacking away with knives at the walls of the playhouse. Three are setting the treehouse alight. Those kids will go far. Rampton, Broadmoor, Dartmoor.

My life was never meant to be like this. I was destined for finer things. I should have married Roger and lived in

Shropshire in a statelyish home. OK, so Roger was a chinless wonder who spent his days galloping about the countryside slaughtering all creatures great and small but I needn't have joined him. I could have sat in my boudoir embroidering things, far from slates and syphilis. I can hear my lodger moving about in the room next door. To hell with him. I am a respectable married woman and I have a headache. At my age, I have a constitutional right not to have to put myself in the other person's place or see their point of view. A citizen's prerogative not to be understanding. Other people write letters to the newspapers condemning everything—why shouldn't I?

Look, I said crossly to my lodger, I'm sorry. That's all right, he said gloomily, crunching Kellogg's Cornflakes. Think of it this way, I said. You only ever eat six cornflakes so you'll die of scurvy long before syphilis gets you. Crunch, he said. And don't use our towels, I said. You can catch it from towels. You can't. You can. Course you can't. You can too. Why didn't they tell me that at the clinic, then? Aha, I said. They don't tell you that at clinics because if they did you could say you caught it off a towel and that isn't going to help them stem the flood. Is it? Why are you being like this, he said. Because, I said...

So we had a long talk. No it is not shameful to get syphilis. We dare say an amazing number of very nice and worthy people get syphilis. Only nasty people think it's nasty to get syphilis because it's connected with sex and they think sex is nasty. We admit that the only reason I haven't got syphilis is I'm happy having sex with only my husband and that's my good fortune, isn't it, not my virtue. Right. If I was single I might have syphilis, mightn't I? Right, I might. And is there anything wrong with having sex with lots of people if the urge takes you and them and no one gets hurt? I suppose not, I say grumpily. All right, no. Except getting syphilis, I add meanly. Humph, said my lodger.

Couldn't I have one day in each week when I don't have to examine my attitudes? Can't I have a Tuesday, say, from nine to five, when blind prejudice rules, OK? But it is true that my lodger is not promiscuous. Syphilis only needs one. He's already done all he can, rushed down to the clinic the minute

185

he was told. I bet it looks like a bloody underground map there. Jean from Wimbledon slept with Charlie from Baker Street slept with Madge from Piccadilly slept with John from St. John's Wood slept with Ted from Edgware. All change at Clapham. It wasn't like that in my day.

Re-examine that attitude, if you please. It wasn't like that in my day because we had to frustrate our natural sexual desires because we didn't have the pill and the pill is a great boon and blessing to mankind, far outweighing the bother of an occasional dose. Besides, it was like that quite often. I remember my Uncle Hubert, a very correct gent, got it from a lady in the Regent's Park Hotel and gave it to my Auntie Maud. There was a lot of coming and going in our sitting-room and I can't say I understood much then, ear pressed to the wall, but she divorced him for it. Is that better or worse? Auntie Maud didn't bother to understand, not her. Ladies had some rights in those days. Out, she said, and Uncle Hubert went, looking ever so crumpled and forlorn. I thought it was in sickness or in health, I said cheekily to my Auntie a few years later, on our way to church. God didn't mean *that* kind of sickness, she said, and don't be cheeky. I envy my Aunt Maud.

I mean, you don't know where you are today, what's wrong or right. Take the tax men. They've been rifling through my drawers for over a year now, politely insinuating. I had to go down and tell them no, I don't have a Swiss bank account or a horde of stocks or shares or yachts anchored off St. Tropez. I keep saying to them why don't you tell me what you think I've done and I'll tell you if I have or not, but they won't. They just go all inscrutable, thus costing me and the ratepayer small fortunes in accountancy bills and me an honest working woman with nothing but bills up my sleeve.

Why don't they leave me alone and track down the real tax dodgers? By God, I could put them on to a few good things if I wished, instead of the two and sixpence I might not have declared, through sheer inefficiency, 10 years ago. I know people doing the markets, earning their weekly five hundred quid for the five winter months and taking off to Spain all summer in their Bentleys and schooners and not paying a penny's tax and getting thirteen fifty a week in social security mailed to their door, yes sir.

I went down to see just such a couple the other day and they were sitting on the velvet Regency sofa rattling antique sabres and peering through the velvet curtains now and again, between bottles of Scotch. Someone had threatened to get them that night, one of the heavies. Chuck a bomb through their letter-box or something. Listen, said Rosie, reeling over and fiddling with my handbag. Keep this for us, there's a love. If they do us over I want you to have it, to look after sonny boy. And she wept whisky all over my blouse.

Next morning, searching for the car keys, I dig in my handbag and there's five thousand pounds, in twenties, in plastic bags. If I'd put it on Rag Trade the next day I'd be sitting pretty now. If I said I'd lost it, what could they do—as it is, the cat tried to tear the notes up, making a nest for her kittens. I should report them, shouldn't I? A citizen's duty and all that. Patriotism, in a slump. But that would be grassing, that offends against another code. Besides, I like them. They put a bit of colour in my upright life.

The thing about being upright (at least as far as bureaucracy is concerned) is it weighs you down like an albatross; it gives you no joy. Having a vicarage upbringing only works with vicars because only they know the rules. You go out in this wide world and you find those rules aren't only inoperative, they're considered downright daft. Please sir, it was my fault sir, I cannot tell a lie. Aw for God's sake, gel, put your hand down: what are you, some kind of nut? Pay a parking ticket—you must be joking. Use electricity from the mains—I've got a mate can bypass all that. The tax man—tell him you're just here minding the shop for a day. VAT? Say Miss Tweedie's gone abroad indefinitely and you're minding the flat. You're not paying good money for licensing your car, are you? Any trouble, scarper. You didn't buy that radio, did you? I've got 12 here fell off a lorry.

Myself, I think some of the trouble comes from living in a mixed economy. Makes for mixed-up people. How can you have doles and hand-outs and free teeth and council houses and family allowances *and* private property and expense accounts and multi-national companies bribing away and no

187

wage ceiling and inheritance *and* expect people not to try their luck with the lot? Not to say the muddle of a small island containing paupers and millionaires, priests and punters, landed gentry and squatters, porn merchants and Poor Clares, soldiers and mercenaries and a hundred gradations of class and colour.

All part of the rich tapestry of life for the tourist, I dare say, but an uneasy mix for the residents. And in the mix of socialism and capitalism, how can you ask people to make sacrifices and tighten their belts when they know perfectly well there are hundreds of sizes of belts and bellies? Even children know today that virtue resides in wall-to-wall carpets, big cars and Caribbean holidays. You got money, you can't be all bad.

Don't be greedy, you say to your children, try and put others before yourself, money isn't everything, how would you like to be hungry! handicapped! beaten up! orphaned? Yeah, they say, gazing glassily at a television commercial offering them the good life round the swimming pool. Cor, you aren't half lucky, they say, when the boy next door gets a portable colour telly, bought out of undeclared profits. *Things* won't make you happy, bleats Mum. Yeah, they say. Do you try to make clear to them that you can't afford such luxuries because you are paying tax and rates and National insurance stamps and 8 per cent self-employed and the neighbours aren't? Do you explain, when they say Brian has time to play with us, how come *you* don't, that Brian happens to enjoy being on the dole (being careful to add that lots of people don't) and you happen to work. Why don't you go on the dole then, they say. Because, you say, if I did, you wouldn't have a television to watch. Thought you said *things* didn't make you happy, sussed you up good there, ha ha.

I dip into Marcus Aurelius now and again when the going gets rough but he does seem a little remote these days. Look, Marcus, when it comes right down to it, you were an Emperor. And you must admit it is a little easier to hold yourself aside from the hurly burly when there's someone to keep your palace clean and wash your toga and get your food, however frugal you choose it to be. Retire into thyself, says

Marcus Aurelius. The rational principle which rules has this nature, that it is content with itself when it does what is just and so secures tranquillity.

Well, apart from a long argument about what just is, I have noticed one perturbing thing. When I do what I think is just, I do not secure tranquillity. The Emperor didn't hold with clipping his children or anyone else's ears if they did him an injustice but, if he had, he might have found what I have on several occasions. Tranquillity. How do you reckon that, M.A?

But then, he says, when a man has done thee any wrong, immediately consider with what opinion about good and evil he has done wrong. For when thou hast seen this, thou wilt pity him and wilt neither wonder nor be angry. For either thou thyself thinkest the same thing to be good that he does or another thing of the same kind. It is thy duty then to pardon him. But if thou dost not think such things to be good or evil, thou wilt more readily be well disposed to him who is in error.

Gotcher. Because I take it Marcus Aurelius is pointing out what Freud discovered a lot later on: you only get really angry about people doing the things you want to do and aren't. Which means I wish to be promiscuous, throw slates through people's windows, cheat the electricity, the tax, the VAT, be given stolen goods free and go on the dole while making a fortune on the side. Consolation prize: it also means militant anti-abortionists aren't (unconsciously) that crazy about babies, anti-pornographers have dirty thoughts, racialists envy the blacks, and Jehovah's Witnesses are something else again. The sound and fury of the belief is the test of the paradox.

But the conscience that stands in the way of doing what you deeply want cannot be harnessed, rewarded, strengthened in a mixed economy. Perhaps it sounds ludicrous to bring politics into unconscious feelings but it seems to me that is what politics is largely about. In China, a very unmixed economy, the reward for a conscience is, at the highest level, public praise and respect and, at the lowest, the knowledge not only that no one else is managing to indulge his selfish desires but that if they are, you have a duty to stop them.

189

No wonder, in moments of stress, our leaders tend to use war-time slogans like Dunkirk or the Battle of Britain. War, like the Chinese regime, was a great equalizer. Rations made sure no one got more food than you, bombs fell on anyone (in principle, at least) and you could even report someone in good conscience if you thought them subversive in some way. Those who would rather be dead than red are protesting against the same thing. Though, come to think of it, the dead are rather more equal than the red.

My lodger just came in and said the clinic said you can catch syphilis from towels very occasionally and, anyway, he hasn't got it, after all. You see? There is no justice in this world.

26 April 1976

God the Mother Rules—OK?

RECENTLY I READ A snippet about women in the United States who were altering prayers and hymns by substituting Her for Him, Mother for Father and Goddess for God. Oh ho ho, did you ever, sniggered the writer. Put them in straitjackets and take them off to the funny farm.

One of the continuing small surprises for the enquiring atheist is the widespread ignorance of believers about their belief. A viewpoint peculiarly limited—parochial is, I suppose, the *mot juste*. Is it wildly unfair to say that if you picked the first avowed Christian off any pew and set him the religious equivalent of the 11-plus, he would fail?

The one I picked was quite hot on the Church version of Jesus's life: who he was born to, where he was born, how he died and where he died, though in between was a bit of a blank, apart from a vague image of white robes, long hair, sheep and children. He knew about Judas and he listed three miracles, including the resurrection but he didn't know the number of apostles and only remembered five of their names. As to any historical realities of the time, nothing. The Sadducees, the Philistines, the Pharisees and the Samaritans were simply emotive words, the Old Testament an almost complete blank other than the bit about Moses in the cradle and parting the Red Sea. Nor had he any idea at all about the beliefs of the Jews (except that they killed Jesus, of course), the Buddhists, Islam, Taoism, Shintoism, Hinduism or any other ism. Religions that preceded Christianity? The Greeks had a lot of different gods and the Indians (Red) had the totem pole.

Indeed, without wishing to be unduly critical, my experience even of those who have taken up religion full-time, priests and vicars, monks and nuns, is that though they

191

may have a detailed knowledge of the mystical side of things, the mysteries, the ritual, the dogma, they are almost as ignorant as my random sample of historical realities. Which is, of course, not entirely accidental. Historical realities and, worse, historical perspectives, have a frightening way of shedding light and reason on corners that, to the believer, are best left dark.

That reporter from the States automatically assumed that his readers would join him in his titters at the absurdity of women who, not content with equal rights, are now pretending God could be female. He has, like most of us, the comforting idea that history started yesterday and will stay that way for ever. Because God and God's son are male today, so they always were and always will be, amen.

Brother, you couldn't be wronger. Slowly but surely a vast and ancient international jig-saw is being pieced together: antic temples here, swollen statues there, papyri drawings, carvings and writings from all over. And already the puzzle, half-finished though it is, is as exciting and significant as would be the revelation of a mother to a child who supposed itself an orphan from birth. Because it appears increasingly certain that a male God is an *arriviste,* a mere *nouveau riche* upon the contemporary scene. Before Him, for literally thousands of years, disappearing back into the trackless wastes of pre-history, the people of the world shared one central figure of worship. A She, a Her, A Mother. The Goddess.

Merlin Stone, sculptor and art historian, has spent over 10 years on the trail of the Goddess and the results of her detective work in museums and ancient sites in the Near and Middle East have been published in *The Paradise Papers.* It makes a beautiful whole of many scattered clues until now undiscovered, ignored, misinterpreted, or—shamefully often—unacknowledged; an anthology of archaeological material that fairly bellows Ms Stone's central thesis. The impulse to worship came from the mystery of birth and the performer of that mystery, apparently entirely on her own, was woman.

So the explanation of a Goddess, the original Mother of humanity, came about as naturally and, when you think

192

about it, as obviously as all the other apparent miracles of life and the Goddess was made manifest in the millions of statues, large and small, of big-bellied women. Statues we all know about and we have all been encouraged to dismiss as unimportant, mere fertility symbols, evidence only of cults, of strange rites practised in corners by heretics instead of what they surely are—endless variations of the same central belief held by many peoples over anything up to 25,000 years.

The face behind the clouds is a woman's face, women are her chosen priestesses and handmaidens and unto women shall go all kinship lines and rights of inheritance. Call her Ishtar in Babylon, Ashtoreth in Israel, Astarte in Phoenicia, Athar in Syria or Ate in Cicilia, call her what you will in the Mediterranean, the Near or the Middle East, even in old Ireland—by any other name she is the Goddess, the Queen of Heaven.

Ms Stone opines that the core of all theological thought is the quest for the ultimate source of life and ancestry worship occurs (and occurred) among tribal people the world over. Add that fact to the observations of anthropologists like Margaret Mead and James Frazer—that in the most ancient human societies coitus was not linked with reproduction—and you have woman the life-giver, the sex that gives birth.

What, then, more logical than to posit a First Ancestress in the Sky? Robertson Smith, writing of the precedence of the female deity among the Arab and Hebrew peoples, says: 'It was the mother's, not the father's, blood which formed the original bond of kinship among the Semites as among other early people and in this stage of society, if the tribal deity was thought of as the parent of the stock, a goddess, not a god, would necessarily have been the object of worship.'

How did women fare when the Goddess reigned in their lands? Merlin Stone brings together the researches of many archaeologists and anthropologists to find out and the answer is as predictable as it is revealing of the purpose of religion. If you have a God in heaven, men rule on earth. If you have a Goddess, women take charge. Diodorus of Sicily, observant traveller BC, reported that the ladies of Ethiopia carried arms, practised communal marriage and raised their children communally. Of the warrior women in Libya he says: 'All authority was vested in the woman, who discharged every kind of public duty. The men looked after domestic affairs and did as they were told by their wives.

'They were not allowed to undertake war service or to exercise any functions of government or to fill any public office, such as might have given them more spirit to set themselves up against the women. The children were handed over immediately after birth to the men.' Are you listening, Colonel Gaddafi?

Professor Cyrus Gordon, writing of life in ancient Egypt, says: 'In family life women had a peculiarly important position for inheritance passed through the mother...this system may well hark back to prehistoric times when only the obvious relationship between mother and child was recognized.' The message is as clear and as apposite today as ever. Though you gain power through error (the misunderstanding about the father's part in reproduction), once the system is working for you (matrilineal descent) you can hang on for a very long time in the face of the most damning facts. Patriarchal gods know all about this, too.

Mind you, in spite of probable male suppression under a goddess, there is a plethora of evidence that the goddess made it well worth their while and that under her sexually permissive reign there were more tempting compensations for being a mere man than ever there were for a mere woman in a god's world. Subjugation, says the God, is your punishment. Subjugation, said the Goddess, can be fun. Because one thing is certain. It took eons of bloody struggle to put the Goddess down. They came out of the northern countries, those eventual victors, migrating in waves over perhaps a thousand, even three thousand years, to the lands of the Goddess, armed with their God and the realization that power for men could only come when a man knew his own son. And how could a man know his own son? By caging women, by making her male property, by scaring her into believing that all hell would break loose if *she* did, that only by cleaving to one man from virginity to death could she hope to save her soul by a male God's intervention.

So battle commenced, fought as much against the desires of many men as against the sexual freedom of women. All over the territories of the Goddess are the myths that mark the traces of that battle. For years I have wondered at the stories of men fighting dragons—what did a dragon represent, what was its factual origin? Merlin Stone drops in another piece of the puzzle. The snake (serpent, dragon) was the widespread Goddess symbol and the living companion of her priestesses. So what was St George doing, fighting his dragon? He was the new religion fighting the old, the male squaring off with the female, an historical reality told in snake/man struggles in hundreds of nations and tribes from India to Turkey, from Babylon to Assyria, from Ireland to Israel and Jehovah's battle with the serpent Leviathan.

'But it was upon the last assaults by the Hebrews and eventually by the Christians of the first centuries after Christ that the religion was finally suppressed and nearly forgotten,' says Merlin Stone. The struggle rages still in the pages of the Bible, pages that as a girl amazed and fascinated me, with their constant emphasis on whores: whores of Babylon, whores of Sodom and Gomorrah, whores like Lilith and Jezebel, painted whores to be spurned by the sons and daughters of Israel. I had thought it then a sort of kink, a kind of mental aberration common to Jews and Christians. Not at all. The truth is far more tangible. The whore was the Goddess, the old religion. The sin—adherence to the old religion. The real sin—ignorance of paternity, female promiscuity.

And that whole battle, so bitterly fought over so many years, produced as its apogee the fable of the Garden of Eden. There is the serpent, creature of the Goddess, of the old religion. There is Eve, the woman, handmaiden to the Goddess and traitress at the heart of the new religion, potentially promiscuous and, therefore, potentially the underminer of male power, of patrilineal descent. She must be warned, threatened, terrified in order to save Adam from the temptations of the Goddess. If she will not accept a male God and reject the Goddess, if she will not accept one man and one man only, all her life, she will be thrown out of Paradise and bear her children in agony.

It is all there in *The Paradise Papers* and, for me at least, Merlin Stone crystallizes what has all along been obvious, however submerged. Even today, in the dour Protestant religions, the last lingering trace of the Goddess (Mary, carefully a virgin) is hardly allowed to surface. The Catholics, always more opportunist, gave Mary her place in the sun but exacted from the ordinary woman a terrible price for this concession.

Yesterday, I thought the leaders of all contemporary religions a blind and prejudiced lot for their refusal to allow women any more power within their churches than the arrangement of flowers upon the altars. Now I know they are simply afraid, afraid that the Goddess may return from her long exile and take over again, and that is curiously comforting, an explanation from weakness rather than strength.

This, then, was the original battle of the sexes. A Goddess reigned for thousands of years, a God for two thousand. Shall we soon, perhaps, learn to do without either?

7 June 1976

Laze Away

LAST SUNDAY I LAY BY THE Thames near Maidenhead, nailed to a small wooden jetty by the hammerhead of the sun. Slow worms of sweat slithered across my body. The river was flat and Limpopo green. Along its smoothness boats went up and down, ferrying cargoes of flayed bodies as if from some distant battlefield. It was dead on noon and dead silent. No leaf moved, no grass blade stirred. A butterfly flattened on a burning stone, a bee hung buzzless in a rose, an ant dropped its greenfly and nodded off. An invisible volcanic ash had stopped us all in our tracks, a perfectly preserved English Pompeii, a still life for tourists a thousand years hence.

Would Monday morning dawn on lengths of empty city streets, acres of vacant office desks and factory benches? Would the Red up in the sky forge an instant revolution undreamed of by Reds under the bed? Without a march or demonstration, a soap-box orator or a polemic pamphlet, a single coded message passed between one man and another? Would the workers of England, each off his own bat, lay down tools for ever, refuse ever again to do what a man must do, refuse on this Monday to start again, earning a living?

Because, under a broiling sun, what living is needed? The itch to possess, the drive to make money, the duty to labour, fades and dies, lingering only as a faint memory of some illness once suffered and now gone, leaving the body drained and whole again. As the sweat trickles and the eyelids swell, as the skin mottles and turns brown, getting and spending seems an odd, outmoded activity, a fever that once upon a time consumed and then was burned out. Almost impossible to think what it was all for, the bustling, the shoving, the rushing around. Televisions and carpets, toasters and washers, fur-trimmed coats and four walls? Who needs them, when even wood is hot and metal a danger to human flesh? The sun burns away all the dross of the consumer society: it turns things into ashes. What madman driven by what insane greed would endure wage slavery in order to accumulate more than the bare necessities?

The sun is an agent of subversion more powerful than any plot devised by man. Pulsing in a shining sky, it beats ambition, competition, acquisition to a powdery pulp. Its flaming rays pump out one overriding message—why bother? Why ever bother? What did, what does, what ever could matter enough to move one glistening limb? Let economic disaster hit, let the pound fall to the level of one aduki bean, let industry fold its tents and steal away, let the banks close and the petrol pumps dry and the machines run down and the bills mount, and still there is no motive even for turning over from belly to back. Fame and fortune, invention and progress are children's toys left out too long and now cracked, rusted, useless, disdained by owners and scavengers alike, artefacts of a civilization past, treasure trove for future archaeologists.

I lie half asleep, listing my needs. One torn and sun-bleached dress, one pair of sandals, a rug to smooth my sleep, a well for cool water, a river for fish and for washing, a patch of ground for beans and peas, tomatoes, and lettuce. Somewhere back there, in the city, four walls are packed with possessions now obsolete, unwanted. Outside, a car. A boiling, searing, four-door cage with seats to tear the skin off rumps and a wheel to char the hands, belching filth, groaning for fuel, capable only of restless movement because we are never where we want to be. Detested spin-off of an industrial revolution that has spewed non-biodegradable rubbish across our pleasant land. Down the river bank there is a spear of blue, a kingfisher. No stunted, whey-faced children crawled in mines; no woman stitched their fingers raw; no men coughed their lungs out to make a kingfisher.

The sun pummels out of human beings the questions hidden deep below the surface, under the compliant front. Why were people wrenched from the fields and packed into satanic mills, why were men and women prised apart, and set against each other, one to earn, the other to be dependent

198

and produce dependants, cut off from the tribe in ticky-tacky boxes? Why are great whales slaughtered to extinction so that cats may eat and comfort us in our isolation? Why are forests ravaged to produce a million billion bad books? Is there progress or only change? Do some live who would have died? Yes, but many die so that the few may live too well, taking another route to death.

Heart attacks and cancer take over from rickets, one country spews gadgets from another's starvation, technology gives us more crops filched from another's birthright. Before we knew of vitamins, our food was full of them. Now we have discovered them, they are fast vanishing, pulped out of the cardboard convenience foods that cook quickly so that we may rush back to the factory and make more. Under the sun, the questions breed and multiply. From the prison of childhood we are released into the prison of adult life, where the rules are unwritten and relentless. Thou shalt get up in the morning, thou shalt go to work, thou shalt earn and spend and earn and spend and sleep and start again. Ask not for whom the cash register tolls, it tolls for thee.

How were wars ever fought, under a hot sun? The first day of the battle of the Somme is made more hideous, if that is possible, by the fearful knowledge that it was a lovely summer day, that the sun shone, that the larks sang, that the poppies shone like blood across the wheat, that roses bloomed in Picardy. What ghastly impetus made it impossible for a flash of sanity to halt all action on that beautiful morning and save a generation? Was there no one in command capable of reading the message written everywhere that day? Last year, I stood in France among neat white crosses that rayed out across the green grass as far as I could see, each one sprouted from a young man's body. Last summer, it was hot, too. The butterflies fluttered in and out of the lines, the bees sucked pollen from the graveside flowers. I wanted to conjure those men alive, have them stand where their crosses were standing and give them another chance, another choice. As the sun began to burn on their dead-white flesh, could they possibly say they would do the same again?

In 1974, in Samarkand, Eden of the East, the conqueror

Tamerlane's imperial capital, the sun is sucked of its fury in the water-blue tiles of mosques and madrasahs, graveyard cool at high noon. Deep below the scorched earth is the green rock jade of Tamerlane's tomb, lame father of a dynasty of despots. In his time, men trembled before him and touched their foreheads to the ground, but I sat on his jade coffin and thought no more but that it was cool against my legs. In Samarkand, heat pounds and cracks on the dusty streets, reddening the eyes and blistering the skin, turning the sky into enemy territory so that human beings run from shade to shade like hunted men through hails of bullets. Heat like that demands submission in every facet of life—submission in building, in clothing, in mode of living. It is more omnipotent than Tamerlane ever was. It lays down the hours of work, it forces the planners to plan around it with cool courtyards and ancient tiles, canals that criss-cross every street, trees that shade every square. It makes for resignation because it rules.

By the fountains, girls in the rainbow silks of Uzbek costume wander here and there and raise their faces to the cooling spray. What do they think, these small, dark, ancient people, behind their half-Indian, half-Chinese masks? What do they think of the big blond blue-eyed Russians who swelter in their midst, paid danger money by Moscow for working under that sun? No stranger can know and yet it is clear that those sun-baked republics seem quietly to have conquered their conquerors. Out of Moscow they have drawn the bonus of literacy and sexual equality and an end to endemic starvation and disease, and to this bonus they have added the luxuries of the sun that icy Moscow goes without, stalls overflowing with saffron and pomegranates, melons, and grapes and oranges and lemons, fragrant tea, and fluffy cotton, glistening silks and mole soft leathers.

The sun, it seems, knows its own and, in the long run, drives out the Northern invader. The drums of Africa, echoing the sun, made the white men move uneasily, move and slowly leave. In the Caribbean islands, in India and Ceylon, in Singapore and Indonesia, Egypt and Guyana, now in Rhodesia, perhaps in South Africa, white skins—unsuited to the sun—draw back and yield up to the children of the sun, people whose skins are armoured, whose hair protects the scalp like the topee the white man must buy.

So we came back to our cool climes and now find a hotting up. Grey stone villages turn, in the new glow, into Mediterranean haunts. Geraniums cascade over every window sill, wind-blown squares fill with naked children and gossiping grown-up people walk bare-footed on cobbled streets, doors and windows breach the Englishman's castle and the roads are filled with music and voices and smells. Where shall we go for our holidays when our own beaches burn? No longer, surely, to the lidos of Italy, the seas of Spain, or the south of France? We shall bask in Wales and Ramsgate and set off to vacation in the cool Norwegian fjords or the winter twilight of Lapland. Come to Coldest Canada, the posters will invite. Cavort in the Cool of Siberia, Go North, Young Man. Packages to both Poles. Self-catering Igloos by an Icy Arctic Sea. Holiday crowds swarming back through Heathrow will carry the new souvenirs; no straw hats but sealskin gloves and snow-shoes will hang on tropical English sitting-rooms for the rest of the tropical summer.

And we, the English, so long conditioned to flatten ourselves in the smallest ray of sun, will move indoors, jettisoning our sun-tan lotions and panama hats, preserving jealously the whiteness of our skins, like old Greek ladies do. We will dress in black, grow pale outer circles around irises, mark of eyes burnt out by sun. Our houses will shrink inside, swell outside to balconies and porches. The long evenings we will sit rocking on our stoops, leaving our televisions to glare on empty rooms. We will sit on our vine-heavy verandahs and watch the Greeks and Italians, the Spaniards and the Arabs flocking to our beaches and wonder at their ways. Only mad dogs and foreigners, we croon to each other as we retreat indoors for our siestas, go out in the midday sun.

5 July 1976

201

Colour Blind

TO TRY, HONESTLY, to analyse the emotions aroused by black immigration to this country is becoming more and more difficult. Revealing emotion may, in itself, add fuel to the Powell fires because most of us are, at one level or another, racialist, if only through ignorance or misinformation or a lack of sensitivity to someone else's feelings. All too easily we find ourselves forced into one of two extreme camps, the 'goodies', motivated by a vague idealism, who blather on about understanding and the brotherhood of man, usually from a distance well removed from reality, or the 'baddies' who write anti-black graffiti on all available walls and make life a misery for Asians arriving at Heathrow. Nor is it made easy for any citizens, black or white, to find ways to come together in order to discuss these emotions openly and, by doing so, defuse them.

As things are, we understand almost nothing of the pressures affecting black immigrants, seeing them all as one homogeneous mass instead of separate peoples with separate cultures. And they, in their turn, understand very little of our anxieties or our divisions, particulrly the historical experiene of each class that has produced quite different attitudes to race. There is a dangerously deep rift between us and no obvious way to heal it before it grows too wide.

Both our governments have been, in their different ways, quite useless in helping us, the ordinary people of Britain, to cope with our ignorance and our fears or, for that matter, in informing immigrants for the same purpose. We did not know, for instance, of the large advertising campaigns directed at West Indians, encouraging them to come here for jobs we were becoming unwilling to do for the given wage. As far as we were concerned, the immigrants arrived out of the blue, putting immediate strains on our already scandalous housing problem. As far as the immigrants were concerned, we, in the name of the British Government, had asked them to come so why, mysteriously, were we so surprised and generally unwelcoming?

Great play was made at the time—still is—of our reputation for hospitality, our grand tradition of offering refuge to the oppressed, our common sense, our British maturity and, most of all, our responsibility to those whom we had once, under the umbrella of the Empire, occupied and exploited and robbed and grown fat upon. This is one of the meanest of manipulative tricks, since the facts—for a majority of the English—are very different. Members of the aristocracy and of the middle classes may feel this responsibility, this harrowing emotional necessity to make up for past sins. That, to put it crudely, is their bag. The bitter fact, for the rest of us, is that in the hey-day of the British Empire, when Queen Victoria reigned over half the planet, the gold poured from the colonies exclusively into the coffers of the rich. The majority of the English were living lives as deprived and as wretched as any enslaved peoples in foreign parts.

Melvyn Bragg, in his book, *Speak for England*, about his home town of Wigton in Cumberland, says: 'It's an interesting aspect of our history that the same men, literally, could at one stage in their careers be responsible for the administration of a large chunk of the colonial globe and, at another, for the employment of their own countrymen in conditions not very dissimilar to those they found in the backward countries overseas,' and he cites his grandmother's life story as proof. The few reformers of the day recognized this clearly. Such men as General William Booth and George Sims used the language of the Empire to describe what was happening to the English who lived around and about the comfortable houses of the Victorian rich.

'The woes of an Egyptian or a Zulu,' wrote General Booth, 'send a thrill of indignation through honest John Bull's veins; and yet at his very door there is a race so oppressed, so hampered and so utterly neglected that his condition has become a national scandal.' Jack London described the East

End of London in Empire imagery as a place 'where the sun, on rare occasions, may be seen to rise.' And General Booth continued: 'Hard it is, no doubt, to read in Stanley's pages of the slave-traders coldly arranging for the surprise of a village, the capture of the inhabitants, the massacre of those who resist, and the violation of all the women, but the stony streets of London, if they could but speak, would tell of tragedies as awful, of ruin as complete, of ravishments as horrible, as if we were in Central Africa; only the ghastly devastation is covered, corpse-like, with the artificialities and hypocrisies of modern civilization.'

Nor can the reformers be suspected of exaggerating their cause. Andrew Mearns, in his pamphlet of 1883, wrote, 'Eight foot square, that is about the average size of very many of these rooms. Walls and ceilings are accretions of filth. It is exuding through cracks in the boards overhead; it is running down the walls. What goes by the name of a window is half of it stuffed with rags or covered by boards to keep out wind and rain. As to furniture, you may perchance discover a broken chair, the tottering relics of an old bedstead or the mere fragment of a table but more commonly you will find rude substitutes for these things or more frequently nothing but rubbish and rags.'

And Mr Mearns continues with a list of the earnings of these free men and women: 'Women, for the work of trousers finishing, receive 2½d a pair and have to find their own thread. We ask a woman how much she can earn in a day and are told one shilling. But what does a day mean to this poor soul? Seventeen hours! From five in the morning to ten at night, no pause for meals, making in very truth, her shroud. Here is a woman who has a sick husband and a little girl to look after and by the utmost effort can only earn 6d a day, out of which she has to find her own thread.' Overcrowding was endemic. 'There are eight destitute children, their father died a short time ago, and on going into the house today the mother was lying in her coffin.'

These were the appalling conditions of the urban working class of England, our great-grandfathers, exploited by the same people who were exploiting the great-grandfathers of today's immigrants. The total disruption of families, the ruthless destruction even of the normal sexual relationships between men and women, that happened on the slave plantations of the Caribbean was even worse, but a dead child is a dead child, and you do not console the mother by pointing out to her that another child has had a slightly harder death.

And is it not, then, a bland and infernal cheek when the descendants of these exploiters turn on the descendants of the exploited in England and say we *must* understand, we *must* welcome, we must act as if we had received the riches from the black man's labour and therefore share our homes and our jobs, now? They, of course, need not share because, interestingly enough, black immigrants are not remotely threatening their jobs and their homes.

And out of this imposition of one group's responsibilities and history upon another with quite a different history, comes the inarticulate fear and anger that can turn, in the present vacuum, into vicious racialism. It is as if the Lord of the Manor, fresh from an awfully jolly stay and tiger-hunt and all that with the Maharajah of Poona, invites him and his entourage to visit and gets very tetchy with the under-parlourmaid when she complains at the extra work, largely because she is bewildered by the strange, dark faces. The ordinary Englishman or woman does not see that they owe anything to the immigrant for the simple reason that they do not. It would be nice, of course, if we were all able to rise to the occasion, to put off xenophobia and insularity overnight and become rational, kind and informed human beings. It would be nice, too, if the one legacy of the exploiters to the English poor—a profound belief in the natural superiority of the white skin—had been rejected, but when you are poor you do not make a habit of rejecting anything. Many black immigrants say the English working class today are deeply racialist. If they are, is it surprising? If they are, isn't it convenient? Much better for them to focus their indignation and rage at bad housing, rising prices, slum schools upon an industrious Pakistani shop keeper than upon an English government.

On a more abstract level, immigration poses knotty enough problems. It is one thing to visit other countries, noting various points of their culture, traditions and religion as you tour. It is another thing entirely to have those cultures transferred to your own doorstep. What is the ethical view then? Obviously, parts of those cultures will be merely different, therefore interesting, and therefore enriching. But other parts may go directly against your most deeply-held beliefs. The ordinary Asian woman, for instance, is a very unequal human being. There are women in Asia fighting for her emancipation. If these inequalities are my general concern, why should I not set about rectifying them? And yet I am advised that this would be tactless, wrong, an invasion, an insult. Why is a foreign culture here so sacrosanct, the bad with the good? Or is it simply an inverted racialism—their skins are dark, they wouldn't be able to cope?

If I am fighting to get rid of compulsory religious education in schools, must I suddenly be expected to switch tack and, in the name of some woolly liberalism, fight for immigrant children to have their religion made compulsory, too? Am I allowed to attack Christianity but expected to respect Islam and Hinduism?

Most crucially of all, if I believe—as I do, against many cogent opposing arguments—that the seed of racialism lies in and is exposed by the old, old question, would you let your sister marry one, is it not perfectly natural for me to express this belief as strongly to a black as to a white? Of course economic and political factors were the main reason for the expulsion of, say, the Kenyan Asians, but the Kenyan leaders were only able to implement their policies because those Asians had made no kinship ties with the Africans. Man has known since time began that the way to consolidate a position, ensure security in an alien place, is by marriage, and I believe that to show unwillingness at this basic level is always seen as a mortal rejection and insult. It is no accident that Enoch Powell's suggestion that the Irish should cease to be given free entry to this country was met with total silence—who, of the English, does not possess an Irish granny, Irish in-laws, an Irish second cousin twice removed?

We have many decisions to make with immigrants, about their place in our society and, so far, we are facing none of them. Do we want, eventually, a multiracial island in the American sense, where black and white children both are inculcated with the British way of life? Not, I would imagine, a popular policy with, for instance, the West Indians, who have had, if anything, altogether too much of this inculcation back home and are more concerned, now, to uncover their own identity. America had no history and so everyone was welcome to join in and make one. We have altogether too much history, and not much of it to the liking of the immigrant. And yet, somehow, we have to fill the gap in the many children, born here rejecting the parental culture and left now, high and dry.

Could we adopt the Canadian mosaic principle, where immigrants gather in groups and continue, undisturbed, to live by their own traditons? The Amish, for instance, live in a world of their own, using their own language, wearing their own unique clothes, rejecting even the modern facilities of electricity and machinery. But Canada, of course, is a very large country, able to lose in its thousands of square miles whole small nations.

There is no doubt in my mind that this country could become a richer and far more interesting place if our immigrants are happily accommodated. But the accommodation cannot be happy without honesty, without discussion, without some purposeful attempt to bridge the ever-growing gap. Effort is needed and a sometimes rather frightening exposure to possible rejection. It takes a certain amount of courage, for instance, to walk across a school playground and make a deliberate start at conversation with an immigrant mother. It takes effort to go to the public library and borrow books to enlighten yourself on immigrant backgrounds or persuade your local club, group, or society to invite one immigrant guest.

But it is not a very high price to pay if we wish, seriously, to avoid Enoch Powell's predictions of rivers of blood. I do not even think it ludicrously naïve to believe that a nationwide exchange of recipes for Lancashire Hot Pot and Chicken Vindaloo would be at least the beginning of a beginning.

12 July 1976

Bad Relations

INTO MY HANDS has come the journal of the Community Relations Commission, an issue entirely devoted to women, here and world-wide. Now the CRC does fine work in the field of race relations and has contacts with some 2,000 ethnic minority groups throughout England and the journal makes fascinating reading, not least for the sense it gives of the unevenness of women's emancipation, not only world-wide, which is to be expected, but less predictably in this country.

In fact, it occurred to me that there may be no other country in the world that presently contains such a variety of women leading such different lives. It is a near-cliché to point out the anomalies of, say, India, which has a woman prime minister and women a good deal less respected than sacred cows. India is, after all, a huge country and a developing country, anomalies are normal. But Britain is highly-developed, very small, has one of the most advanced legislative programmes *vis-à-vis* women and yet, within its narrow confines we find almost exactly the same anomalies as India—a woman leader of a political party and women in purdah, sharing, at least on the surface, only one thing, British citizenship.

No wonder, then, that the articles in the CRC journal seem, at times, not so much about women as about the inhabitants of different planets. Around half of these articles are concerned with aspects of the working of the Sex Discrimination and Equal Pay Acts which cover in theory the lives and aspirations of all British women. And their common denominator, whether they are specifically concerned with housing, education, law or child care provision is, quite rightly, the writers' anxieties that the domestic conditions of women's lives will prevent them from benefiting fully from the equalities and opportunities made legal for them on paper.

Eva Lomnicka, writing on education, says 'Discrimination occurs or is potential from the cradle—when many children are treated on the assumption that the social and economic roles of the two sexes are radically different—through education to employment. The Sex Discrimination Act does not presume to deal with private relationships. Thus nothing is, or could have been, done directly to affect the treatment of a girl in the home. But in her treatment in society, in the fields of education, employment, housing, and the provision of services covered by the Act, attempts are made to put her on an equal footing with her male equivalent.'

And Luise and Dipak Nandy say that 'we cannot afford as a society to neglect the importance of the role of child-bearing which women have traditionally peformed...but *if women are not to remain shackled to this role* (my italics) we will have to rethink the whole social mechanism by which children are to be reared.' All of which makes perfect sense except for one odd omission, considering the rest of the articles in the journal that examine the lives of immigrant women. The audience addressed quite obviously excludes a large majority of Asian women and their English-born daughters. As Eva Lomnicka ·points out, the Act cannot affect the treatment of girls or women in the home and (as she does not point out) Asian women are unlikely to benefit from what the Act can provide outside the home since they will hardly manage to *get* outside the home.

And Mr Nandy, himself an Indian by birth and a man who, on his own admission, believes that if a woman is confined only to child-rearing she is shackled, seems quite to have forgotten the Asian woman who not only has no chance, because of her culture, to poke her nose out of the door, but who is actually segregated almost entirely from the other sex, whose child-bearing and rearing role is her only role because she is given no choice whatsoever and, worse, who will be instrumental in training her daughters to this role. Mr Nandy quotes three reasons for inequality, one of which is 'in consequence of direct exclusion or disbarment because of membership of the group', in other words, because a woman is a woman. But he illustrates this by saying 'as when blacks are excluded from pubs or clubs because they are black' and he draws a little diagram of a box labelled 'Source of inequality—direct exclusion or disbarment', an arrow pointing to the result, 'Inequality', and an arrow pointing to the remedy, labelled 'Anti-discrimination legislation'. Which is, I find, a rather odd interpretation, since the source of Asian women's discrimination (and he is writing about women) is their own menfolk who, in the name of culture and religion, most effectively exclude and disbar them long before any white racialist has a chance to keep them out of clubs or pubs.

The other half of the journal concerns itself with a most interesting and informative collection of accounts of the lives of immigrant women, but they are, in tone, very different from the first half. The articles on the Sex Discrimination Act have an academic approach which does not conceal the writers' indignation at the injustice and inequalities of women's position. But the outlines of the lives of immigrant women reveal no such indignation. Here the writers, even though they be from the same background as the immigrants described, have put on their anthropological hats and show only the disciplined pleasure in noting other cultures common to academics. There is no sign of any passion, any criticism of the enormous inequalities that prevent Asian women from coming within sniffing distance of the legislation designed for them as citizens of England. Indeed, a kind of affection for the rituals of immigrant life is manifested that seems to me more suitable to describing the life style of the grey-leg goose.

It does not surprise me, then, that under these careful articles I kept hearing odd echoes of past times. Hooting upper class voices pointing out that the working classes are different from you and me. That they have their ways. That if you gave them baths they'd keep coal in them. That they like living in squalor. That a beating administered by a husband to an immigrant wife does not fall on flesh like yours and mine because to her, you see, it is a proof of affection. Or something. Unfortunately for this detachment, it is too short a time ago that things began changing for white Englishwomen.

For instance, I think I may have written the first article in this country questioning the God-given right of an Englishman to batter his wife without the unwarrantable intrusion of neighbours or friends into his sacred family life. At the time, it was considered extreme interference. Marriage was sacred and what happened between a man and his wife, even if that happening resulted in her terror, injury, or torture, was sacred too—no business of nosy outsiders and least of all the nosy State. Since then, as we know, refuges for battered wives have sprung up all over the country, police are willing to prosecute, neighbours to interfere and the law to condemn. But the attitude of non-interference has not disappeared—it has simply moved on to immigrant cultures, now labelled sacred in exactly the same way.

And, I think, for exactly the same reasons. *They* do not perceive things as we do. *They* have their ways. The white liberals say what awfully good things immigrant culture contains, after all, and the bigots say *They* are black, foreign, peculiar and simply do not feel as you and I feel.

But if the women's movement has taught me anything, it is that women almost always have more in common with each other than they have with their various male-dominated cultures, be they American, Brazilian or Aborigine. It is called sisterhood and it is real. Now by that I do not, simplistically, mean that I think an Asian woman newly arrived from a small village is going to feel, if I suddenly materialize in her kitchen, more affinity to me than to her husband. But I do maintain that if the barriers of sheer strangeness could be overcome we would find we had more in common than each one of us with many men. And because of that, I cannot for a minute feel that her subjugation to men, however many compensatory features it contains, is in any real way more natural to her than it would be to me. If I did, then, truly, I would be a racialist because I would be assuming that she and I were in very essence different, not sisters under the skin but alien beings, she in some way made for subjugation, me made for independence.

One of the articles in the CRC journal is about purdah as practised in Pakistan and in Bradford. It is written by Verity Saifullah Khan, who lived for six months herself in Bradford, in a modified form of purdah. On purdah in Pakistan, she writes:

'Interaction between men and women is limited outside a certain well-defined category of people. Secondly, the sexes are segregated before or at the time of puberty. Boys and girls no longer play together and must maintain the required social distance, or avoidance. Thirdly, there is a division of labour...evident from the age of puberty. Fourthly, women must at all times be modest in dress, movement, attitude and expression to avoid attracting the opposite sex. They must be virgins at marriage and must remain chaste thereafter.' And she goes on: 'The socio-economic variable is of crucial importance. The ideal purdah system necessitates a certain standard of living, the purdah household requiring more than one room and servants or children to maintain contact between the worlds (in the form of food, messages, etc.). Complete seclusion of women similarly requires servants or the men to collect water, fodder, and shopping. It is therefore only a small percentage of the population that can maintain the ideal...from the high socio-economic strata.'

But does this confined life change when women in purdah come to Britain and live under the Sex Discrimination Act? No. Indeed, according to Verity Khan, it gets more rigid. She cites the Mirpuri people who have emigrated to Bradford. There, in one front room and one back, the sexes divide. The women either do not leave their houses at all or only occasionally, veiled and chaperoned. Purdah is more strictly observed because the city of Bradford is an alien world and the Mirpuri woman 'must observe purdah in relation to all these unrelated men and most particularly towards other Pakistani men.' And the Mirpuri man himself is tightening the bonds of purdah for the women living in England. As Verity Khan says, 'the stricter observance of purdah in Britain...is also related to its importance as a status symbol. Strengthening the pride of the Mirpuri, it indicates to others in Bradford and in Pakistan his acquisition of a new and valued status...'

In other words, the new opportunities that come the way of the immigrant man in England, his higher earnings and better housing, are immediately and directly used further to

212

imprison his women, though Verity Khan is either too tactful or too anthropological to emphasize this in any way. Would she show the same forbearance if she were writing of some English custom that oppressed women? And what of the daughers born here and raised here, heading for purdah and arranged marriages themselves? In Pakistan, a woman in purdah at least shared a companionable and supportive women's world. In two rooms in Bradford she is often quite dreadfully isolated, a sad and useless appendage there to look after the children and vouch, silently, for her husband's prestige. Perhaps half the daughters of such marriages still accept their parents' wishes for them, but the other half need a great deal of support in their rebellion. If the support is not going to come from detached academics such as Verity Khan, from where will it come? Rumour has it that, so far, only some Northern registrars (male) occasionally refuse to solemnize marriages where they feel the bride has been coerced.

It will be said that because I am not of that culture myself, I have no right to comment. That I do not understand whereof I write, that there is nothing so marvellous about western culture and many better things in foreign cultures. All true. But once you get your eye in, once you shed a certain delicately inverse racialism, strange and therefore exotic customs and the trappings of more colourful religions should not blind you to the startlingly familiar skeleton beneath. There it is, in the cupboard, shorn of *sari* and *burqa* and *dupatta* and, just like our skeleton, it is female.

A lot is said about how race, in this country, is creating second-class citizens. Let us not add to our sins by condoning the growth of third-class citizens, English-born girls of Asian parentage, because we are too polite, too overcome by the wonders of 'culture', too diffident to speak out. Oppression remains oppression, however ethnically camouflaged.

19 July 1976

213

Africa's Dark Secrets

OF ALL THE ABUSES WOMEN HAVE endured since (as the weathermen say) records began, there can be none so starkly brutal and so cynically male-serving as the ritual mutilaton of the female genitalia. The mutilation is literally and metaphorically hidden from the public eye. Those who do it, those to whom it is done, those in whose countries it is done and those outside who know it is done all too often collude in a conspiracy of silence engendered by an odd but very potent combination of ignorance, custom, shame, poverty and academic aloofness. Men demand it; women comply; officialdom at worst denies it and at best transfers its practice to hospitals; international agencies are reluctant to become involved; and anthropologists discuss it with the detached interest they might accord to little green persons on Mars.

The subject is fraught. It so easily arouses a morbid sexual sensationalism that, like the sexual tortures it closely resembles, women to whom it has happened are reluctant to talk. But a few brave African women and their supporters in the West are beginning to speak out, to protest, to demand legislation and an end to the suffering and health hazards involved. Such mutilations concern all women, not only because the practice is a blatant assault on human rights but because it is, in its way, a caricatured version of attitudes that have their echo in our experiences. And it happens, most pathetically, to little girls.

The male's insistence on the virginity of his wife is hardly an attitude buried in the dust of history in Britain. I dare say a really keen researcher could root out remnants of the virginity rite in various remote corners of this isle. Like Hackney, say, or the trackless wastes of Berkshire. Its male-serving basis is obvious and we have a good idea of its emotional mainspring—the old masculine fear of the insatiable woman who, once introduced to the wonders of sex, will instantly become a nymphomaniac rampant upon any old bed.

So the physical manifestation of these worldwide male attitudes should come as no thunderclap from the blue. Our own gentil parfit knights buckled their ladies into iron chasity belts before they took off to enlighten the heathen. Some Africans do the equivalent today, only in their case women's flesh is used, which is more effective than iron.

There are two general types of mutilation. One is the excision of the labia and clitoris (clitorectomy or circumcision) and the other is the sewing up of the labia (infibulation). In some tribes only one is practised, in others both. Experts trace these 'operations' as far back as the Pharoahs of ancient Egypt and infibulation is still often called 'Pharoanic circumcision'.

Jenny left her home in Somalia and came to this country when she was 16. She is a beautiful girl, tall and lean and full of humour. Her parents were both Somalian, but her father was Christian and disapproved of the general Somalian habit of infibulation. So her mother had it done while he was away. 'I was seven years old when my mother told me I would have "habalays" in two days. I was so scared, my heart began to go bang, bang, bang. I couldn't eat anything, thought I would run away from home, but they came too early. They came at six o'clock in the morning and I was still in bed.

'The women think they are lost if they don't, that they will have no proof of virginity and then no man will marry them. Young men today feel just the same: I know one who sent his daughter back to Somalia for the operation and she was born in England. Mothers don't think about it, they just do it. You must marry and, if possible, the husband will have money so that he can look after the family later on. He expects a wife who is closed.'

Naturally enough, first intercourse is, again, a time of pain and fear. Jenny's mother belonged to a generation of women whose husbands expected, quite literally, to rip them open on the wedding night. Today this is done with a knife but intercourse must take place the same day and continue

215

frequently thereafter, to make sure the labia stay apart. Wedding bed as battlefield, the blood-stained sheets as proof of victory.

The old woman was summoned. Jenny knew she was doomed to endure the operation and she rushed out of the house to try to get help.

'I saw this man passing and I thought, because my father disapproved, so would he. I got hold of him and I clung and screamed don't let them. But he pushed me back. After the second time of cutting I was very ill, the wounds were infected and I lost a lot of blood. I was frightened even to drink water because it hurt me so to urinate. My father was very angry when he came home and he nearly left my mother over it but, in spite of that, my younger sister had it done too. Only she was four years old and I envy her for that. She was too young to remember it as I do.'

The idea behind this torture is, of course, to ensure virginity by almost complete closure—the smallest aperture becomes a cause of sad pride among the girls. Jenny says that all her friends had it done, that neighbours talk if the mother leaves it too long, that she knows girls who asked for it if it did not happen before they were ten, and that a friend of hers has just had it done on her own four-year-old daughter.

'The women who arrived were neighbours with no knowledge either of nursing or of hygiene. One was old and four were young and strong. They took me from my bed and held me and one sat on my legs. First they peeled the skin off the clitoris and then the old woman made two cuts right along the lips. The knife was so sharp I could hear it cutting the flesh. The pain was terrible, I can't explain to you how terrible. Then they pushed three long thorns that they get from a bush through the lips to hold the two cuts together. After that they tied my legs together and put me back in bed. The old woman came and took the thorns out after three days, until the cuts healed together and closed. But I couldn't bear it. I got up on the fourth day and fell down and the wounds broke apart.'

Even more horrifying is clitorectomy, the complete cutting out of the clitoris, an ordeal Jenny was spared. There is an account of this in a book entitled *La Cité Manquée et Magie*

216

en Afrique Noire published in 1972 but it makes such appalling reading I shall spare you. Suffice it to say that extreme and lengthy suffering is inflicted on small girls who, apart from anything else, cannot afford to lose much blood without risk to their lives.

One reader of a Senegalese magazine, *Famille et Développement*, relates how the practice was carried out on her elder sister, a girl much loved in her village. She bled from early one morning and died *'après une nuit d'angoisse'* early the next morning, leaving her parents, relatives and friends prostrate with grief. The reader says that though circumcision continued after this, the festival associated with it was abandoned, so distressed was everyone by the fate of her sister.

'The circumcision no longer has the magic aura of the past. It continues but we know it will come to an end and on that day I shall be the first to rejoice. I would not want others to lose their much-loved daughters and sisters like that, stupidly, a flower one crushes carelessly.'

But in the same issue, clitorectomy is defended by another reader. I quote excerpts, roughly translated:

'The suppression of circumcision doesn't seem to me a necessity for these reasons. A non-circumcised woman has more appetite for sex than a circumcised woman. Polygamy being the custom of our society, it would be difficult for a husband regularly to satisfy all his wives. The consequence is infidelity, source of family instability. And if the husband really wishes to accomplish this work, there goes his health. A man is not a machine.' And the gentleman ends by saying, 'One has also remarked that in countries where circumcision is not practised, debauchery is the rule.' His logic is irrefutable. No clitoris, no pleasure; no pleasure, no straying wife.

For the past two years, the American newsletter WIN (Women's International Network) has been campaigning against female circumcision with great dedication. The editor, Fran Hosken, has found it very difficult to collect facts because all concerned have their own reasons for concealment and the reaction from those in high places is one women have come to recognize in many other contexts. That

217

oh, come now, that doesn't happen much any more. Confronted with more evidence, a shrug. Well, it doesn't happen much any more. Confronted with more evidence, OK, all right, so it happens. It's not my business.

But Ms Hosken, in the admirable way of American women, has soldiered doggedly on. She turned up at Vancouver's recent Habitat conference and protested to the Somali delegate, among others. Yes, his wife and daughter were infibulated. No, no one wants to change these customs, there are other priorities. She explodes on paper: 'The Socialist/Communist revolution that continues in Somalia is run by men alone. They proclaimed equal rights on the outside while mutilating their own female children in an organized way at public expense in the public hospitals. How can women respect such 'revolutions' and their leaders?'

In another issue of WIN, there is a formidable bibliography on the subject and an account of a systematic letter-writing campaign mounted in maternity hospitals and health clinics in Africa maintained by religious bodies and welfare organizations. So far, the letters have been ignored, though a Mr Tanmundjaja, senior adviser to the Family Welfare Programme of UNICEF, says he shares WIN's deep concern and is making an effort to discourage the practice. The World Health Organization appears to have been strangled by its own red tape.

The most telling research is by a Belgian doctor, who says infibulation is practised on the southern coast of Arabia, throughout Somaliland, in Kenya (Kenyatta wrote approvingly of it in his autobiography), in Ethiopia, the Sudan and southern Egypt. Excision and clitorectomy take place in a broad band reaching from Kenya and Ethiopia to the west coast parallel to the equator. The doctor's chilling account of the 15 or so daily operations in Somalia's capital city hospital makes clear that there is no religious rite involved, and this was confirmed to me by an Englishman who had recently visited the country. 'There's no doubt about it,' he said. 'It is a straightforward business deal, nothing to do with rites of passage and all that mumbo-jumbo. A girl must marry as well as possible, men will not marry her without the operation, and so she is forced to have it.'

218

An article in *Tropical Doctor,* written by an Irish consultant obstetrician and gynaecologist, gives a list of short and long term results of circumcision. There are fatalities due to shock and haemorrhage. There is infection, damage to adjacent tissues, urinary disturbances, chronic pelvic sepsis. Infertility sometimes results. Obstetrical complications are frequent because a woman cannot give birth normally. First, the scar tissue must be cut and then resewn, and this is usually done by village women without anaesthesia or sterile instruments. The newborn sometimes sustain brain damage.

The article also documents more countries wholly or partially concerned—Ghana, Nigeria, Zaire, Congo, Katanga, Sierra Leone, Mozambique, many Bantu tribes in Central and South Africa, Brazil, Mexico, Peru, Moslem areas of Asia, Mali, Upper Volta, Niger, Mauritania, Senegal, Uganda, Dahomey, Togo. Nor is the list complete. African women asked the World Health Organization in 1966 to compile records of the areas where circumcision is practised, but they were refused.

Ms Hosken attempts to estimate how many women are affected. The population of Africa is more than 360 millions, of whom half are women. Thirty million women are town-dwellers and probably exempt which leaves 150 million rural women. Experts believe at least one-third of Africa is involved in the ritual. So Ms Hosken comes to a figure of about 10 million African women who are circumcised in one way or another.

'There are,' says WIN, 'few epidemics that take such a terrible, continuous toll. Yet no African health department nor international health institution, including WHO and UNICEF consider the death, torture and permanent maiming of female children their concern.'

I give Jenny the last word.

'Just because it is our custom does not mean we like it or that we do not mind the pain. Young women would be very pleased if it was stopped by the law. Otherwise, the change is very slow.'

23 August 1976

To Hell with Innocence

IF SOMEONE ASKED ME what country feels to me most like home, in the literal sense of resembling England, I should not name an English-centred nation like Canada or Australia, I should say Holland. I was there two weeks ago and I had no sense of strangeness. About the people and their lives there is a solidity, an ordinariness, even a boredom I recognize. The man and woman in the street are not overly fat and somehow aggressive like their German equivalents, not faintly manic like the Mediterraneans, not casual and loud like North Americans, not sleek and sportif like the Scandinavians. There is a sort of comfort in them, they are unexaggerated, they are friendly but not too friendly. In short, they are like us.

Which is why the huge divide between public permissiveness in Amsterdam and in London comes as such a surprise. There, just off the main street, just behind the largest department store, slotted in among shops selling Delft pottery and Edam cheese, briefcases and sheepskin boots, soap and coffee, are *les girls*, *les filles de joie*. The girls do not put coded cards in shops to marshal clients and they do not hang about street corners. They sit at square picture windows in their undies, framed in flocked wallpaper and cosy pink lights, for all the world like sweeties in a box. Behind them domesticity reigns, a kettle steams on a ring, potted plants line a shelf, a poodle scratches itself. I particularly remember one overstuffed blonde lady of middle years with specs, a cheerful auntie-figure, knitting in her window under the shadow of an old church, the large circles of her nipples clear beneath a snow-white cami-nick. Ladies like herself passed by, on their way to prayers.

And then there are the Amsterdam sex shops, again no

apartheid here, no special district, no back rooms for customers with uncommon kinks. The wares are out for all to see, the bases of display windows sprout with pink plastic stalagmites of wondrous variations and lengths, the ceilings drip with stalactites of black leather, there are startled masks of women's faces with accommodating mouths, and headless, limbless torsos and torsoless rumps, all 'met motor'. What fearful injury, one worries, could a short circuit inflict here? Now and again, someone pauses—usually a tourist—to get a closer look, to snigger or stare in bewilderment. The comfortable matrons in their high-rise hats push past without a glance, children clutching satchels skip past without a glance, it is just another part of life.

In a large neighbourhood cinema, four tram-stops beyond any night-life centre, I saw *Realm of the Senses*, the Japanese sex-marathon. The place echoed with emptiness. Beside me there were two young girls, on the other side two young men and a girl, in front of me a middle-aged woman in a felt hat and her middle-aged husband with his umbrella. The short film shown first was on someone's collection of erotica. Little wooden men with large wooden accessories were wound and little wooden couples jigged, magic lantern slides showed silhouettes of naughty masters and servants, outlines that left nothing, not even the relevant bodily fluids, to the imagination. There was a chuckle or two from the audience, a crunching of toffee papers.

The main film is, basically, one long coupling and there are no concealments of any kind, not a flouncy skirt, not a potted plant, not a wayward hiding hand. The middle-aged couple exchanged little remarks, passed each other chocolates and watched. At the end, the woman said to her husband, with a slight smile and an eyebrow raised, *'Mooie film, hoor?'* Nice film, eh?

Then I come to these white cliffs of Dover and it is another world, a teacup full of storms. Bill Grundy has been suspended for two weeks for allowing we-all-know-what to be said on television. Pauline Quirke's teenage programme has been whisked off the screen for its sexual innuendos, the kind all our children make. Women packers at EMI have refused to handle the Sex Pistols' latest record. Thames's *Sex*

In Our Time has been withdrawn. Mrs Whitehouse is prosecuting a professor for writing a rude poem and two Tory Members have attacked Lady Plowden for daring to label the Bill Grundy episode merely 'tiresome.'

I do not, myself, have strong feelings about the merits or demerits of women in windows, sexy films, four-letter words on television or badly behaved punk rockers, though I reckon Mrs W. *et al* are doing their best to put England into that once great money-making slot called 'Banned in Boston'. And for once I do not intend to argue whether or not action should be taken to suppress, censor or otherwise do away with these threats to our way of life. If that's your bag, carry it. What I do feel strongly about is the vista of middle-aged adults with their little paws in the air; the whole shock, horror, sensation bit.

My own upbringing took place before the dawn of the Age of Aquarius and I was, by a certain definition of the word, innocent. When, at the age of twenty, gossip had it that A and B were living together, that C and D were sleeping together, I felt shock, horror, sensation. I rubbernecked at A and B, I gawped at C and D, I scrutinized their faces for a glimpse thereon of Dorian Gray depravities. I had no idea of sex beyond the most straightforward and not a lot of that. When rumours first reached me of possible variations, shock horror sensation. I only knew one four-letter word and had never heard anyone say it and I thought Mary Webb wrote sexy books.

There are those who would, today, consider this an admirable state for a woman of 20 to be in, even if she is married, which I was. I do not. I think, in fact, that it was a form of mental retardation that happened to be sanctioned and encouraged by society under the name 'innocence'. For heaven's sake why, you may ask. What is so wrong with that sort of innocence? I'll tell you. Innocence is not a technical term: if it were, the word 'ignorance' would do as well. Innocence, to my mind, is not a state in which you are born, rather a state of rebirth: you must know a good deal of the world's practices and the evils thereof before you can begin to aspire to innocence. Unless ye *become* as a little child, goes the saying; not unless ye *stay*.

In my technical innocence I was more prurient than I am now. I saw too many people in terms of their sexual behaviour and judged them by my own ignorance. I did not see unmarried non-virgins as women who had, among other things, a sex life—sex was inextricably mixed up with sin. And, confirmed by society in my saintly innocence, I had *carte blanche* to be as much of a bitch as I wished. I was cold-hearted, narrow-minded, critical and superior, and I gave no man pleasure. My then husband, encouraged by the same society, admired my innocence and thus made his own bed to lie on, with me. It was no fun for either of us. Paradoxically, I also became a prime candidate for sexual victimization and turned, in my innocence, several perfectly nice men into monsters. Ignorance is not bliss, it is moral dereliction.

It seems to me that the watchdogs of our society today are mentally retarded as I was. They presume shock to be a virtuous emotion when it has no value at all. Shock is what you feel when you didn't know something could be and, as a full-grown adult, you ought to know, it is your business to know. Once you do, shock is no longer a part of your emotional repertoire, real or feigned. You are now in a position to do something about the causes of evil rather than shrieking hysterically and trying to suppress the symptoms.

In my opinion, people like Mrs Whitehouse are fringe people, carping and fiddling at the hem of life, unable to recognize real evil and therefore illiterate about real good. They patter about on the surface of life, convinced that sweeping crumbs under carpets and swatting flies with an injunction or two will earn them the Good Housekeeping Seal of Approval for a really good spring clean. They empty ashtrays and think this will stop smoking.

They have, it appears, no conception, in the careful net-curtained structures of their souls, of the weird and blinding chaos in which this planet swings, its stench of sulphur and its sudden stabs of miraculous light. They do not recognize an evil miasma if it emanates from a law-abiding pinstriped family man. Even less would they recognize innocence if it wears the wrong clothes.

No wonder that today's children find them such prime targets *pour épater les bourgeois*. They have grown up with a communications system that forces them to know about the evils of this world. They have seen a country denuded of foliage, its people massacred, by the Goodies. They hear, over and over again, of the international webs of corruption that bring down governments, in the bitter end. They have learnt that behind the most powerful and untouchably respectable men of our time lies, often, unimaginable greed. They are aware that a quarter of the world's people live, quite literally, by killing the other three-quarters. They are also aware that there is very little indeed that they can do about it. Except expose respectable values. Shall we show you, they say, in a world that has famine and unthinkable tortures, hidden genocide and corruption, what they *really* mind? Fuck. See? That's what they *really* mind. And they are, for the most part, right.

To go back to my original comparison, I conclude from, among other things, our recurring sexual brouhahas, that the English are still mentally retarded, still innocent, meaning ignorant, compared with the Dutch, for instance. As a nation we have one of the least savoury of histories *vis-à-vis* large portions of the earth and its peoples. We have, in our time, caused appalling suffering, we have deformed the development of whole races, we have demolished cultures and we have denuded natural resources. The Dutch did the same in their time—their colonization history is as shameful to honest Dutchmen to this day.

But perhaps the difference between us came during the war. The Dutch were occupied and we were not. They were offered seven guilders for a Jew, we were not. They had the chance to take up that offer, they had the temptation and the fears that drove some of them to fearful brutalities. At this moment, in Holland, they are deliberating on a verdict for a Dutchman who buried Jews up to their necks in the ground and then kicked their heads to pulp. Or got other Jews to do it, on threat of the same. We are still innocent in the technical sense. The Dutch are not.

It may be that the difference between us, their tolerance and our small hysterias about something so peripheral as sexual behaviour, stems from a true assessment of guilt. The Dutch know evil. They have seen it upon their streets, they

224

have felt its touch, some of them have committed it.

So they know that it does not reside in four-letter words, in shows advertising 'real focky-focky', in films of sexual obsessions or in fat ladies wearing white undies. When will we grow up?

3 January 1977

Suffering Sex

I cannot tell you all my sufferings during the time of motherhood. I thought, like hundreds of women do today, that it was only natural and that you had to bear it. My husband being some years my senior, I found he had not a bit of control over his passions and expected me to do what he had been in the habit of paying women to do.

I had three children and one miscarriage within three years. This left me very weak and suffering from bad legs. I had to work very hard all the time I was pregnant. My next child lived only a few hours. After the confinement I was very ill. With each child I seemed to get worse. I do wish there could be some limit to the time when a woman is expected to have a child. I often think women are really worse off than the beasts. During the time of pregnancy, the male beast keeps entirely from the female: not so with the woman: she is at the prey of a man just the same as though she was not pregnant: practically within a few days of the birth and as soon as the birth is over, she is tortured again...

THIS LETTER IS NOT from a reader of 1978, for which contraception, better wages, medical advances, and all our lucky stars be thanked. It is, in fact, one of 160 written in 1914 by working-class members of the Women's Co-operative Guild and now published by Virago under the paperback title *Maternity—Letters from Working Women*. I read them all last weekend, and I am still reeling.

To learn what marriage, pregnancy, motherhood and just plain life was like for these women only 65 years ago (and what are they but the tip of an iceberg whose base spreads back into endless generations?) is to feel such immense pity for them and such immense gratitude for being spared oneself as to think it impossible ever to complain about anything again.

For them, the marriage bells tolled the knell of everything that made their days worthwhile and rang in pain, life-long ill health, mental anguish, extreme poverty and constant heavy manual labour, inside and outside the home. Laundresses, seamstresses, domestics, farmworkers, paid a pittance themselves and often supporting out-of-work husbands, they had also to bear and bring up many frequently ailing children when they themselves were exhausted, ill nourished and diseased. Some mention drunk and brutish husbands but the majority speak well of their partners, even though the sexual act itself was almost always a prelude to wretched physical suffering and childbirth sometimes literally crippling—at least three women talk of being unable, after multiple births, even to walk and had to 'slip about on my hips'. Those of us who campaign today about the side-effects of the pill and the things still wrong with childbirth can only take on the ills of our own times but the letters in *Maternity* should also make us fervently aware of our blessings.

Over and above the pity and the horror, these letters raise a question touched on by the writer of the one I quote who compares women and female animals. It is a question I find insoluble—perhaps someone has either theories or specialized knowledge that might clarify it?

At the heart of all life is the necessity for the survival of the species and to that end, any trait, physical adaptation or experience that seems to work for survival is selected to enrich following generations. This master plan is quite ruthless, it cares not a whit for individual suffering as long as healthy reproduction is ensured. Yet it is shockingly clear that *homo sapiens* (especially the female of the species) has taken on some fearful and unnecessary burdens and aberrations in fulfilling this task, at least if compared to other species.

Take our nearest animal relatives upon this planet—the Great Apes. To read of their matings, reproduction, maternity and infant welfare is to conjure up a blissful picture compared to our own miserable history. It seems that a

227

female ape has three vital advantages denied to her so-called higher sisters, us. First, she can and does refuse the male when her body or mind so dictates and the male accepts her refusal. Secondly, the evidence is that birth does not damage her and, thirdly, her infants apparently survive at a much better rate than the human infants of the past. And from what I can gather of the observations of primate watchers, when natural conditions militate against her (age, ill-health, famine) the female simply does not come on heat and therefore cannot become pregnant. Her sexual cycle is obviously selected for the maximum health and survival of mother and baby.

A very different picture from that of females of the human race, who are 'available' to the male at any time from birth to death, in sickness or in health. Male zoologists such as Desmond Morris have thought up the most extraordinary explanations for this fact. Generally, they run thus: because of the long gestation and childhood of the human infant, the female had somehow to ensure the nurturance and protection of the father for a very long time. Monogamy or pair-bonding became necessary and to make sure this happened, the female had to offer the marauding male the carrot of sex-on-demand. Desmond Morris adds various frills to this theory—he believes that the female also refurbished her entire body in order to keep her man, switching buttocks to breasts and backs to fronts in an orgy of redecoration so that this poor near-impotent fellow would keep coming back (or rather front) for more.

Personally, I consider this theory not a million miles from ridiculous, an explanation so blindly male-centred as to ignore all other facts. The most cursory examination of social history (not to mention your next door neighbour) will show that men (and quite probably women) are anything but monogamous and only ever pair-bonded in an official sense because the male wished to ensure that any children his wife produced were incontrovertibly his. This applied as much to polygamy as monogamy, if not more so, which in itself undercuts the pair-bonding theory.

So it is obvious to me that the replacing of the animal 'oestrus' with the female 'open-door' policy is still a mystery.

More than that, it has actually enfeebled the race for hundreds of years and now has overpopulated the planet. Because of her constant sexual receptivity, a woman was subject to too many pregnancies, often could not feed her infants and was therefore at best an inefficient mother, and at worst a dead one. Of the children she produced, many died in infancy or grew up sick and ailing. The Co-operative women are sadly aware of this and frequently testify to it.

'A few details of my neighbour's life... she thought it was her lot to have so many children and so many sickly ones, but now she feels she has been to blame for many things—for the dullness and lack of energy in two of them; for the feeble-mindedness in a third; deafness and sore eyes in a fourth...'

'Then I lost a sweet little girl and I had a dreadful miscarriage...and after that I never had any more children to live. I either miscarried or they were stillborn.'

'A cousin (a beautiful girl) had seven children in about seven years; the first five died in birth, the sixth lived and the seventh died and the mother also. What a wasted life! There are cases all around us much worse.'

Are we not forced to the conclusion either that the female half of the human race was entirely dispensable, both in her role of childbearer and mother, or that somewhere back in the mists of time, when the first lady ape stood upright, something went hideously wrong with her sex life, not to mention her reproductive organs? Since the advent of reliable contraception, and only since then, has the constant availability of women to men made any sense at all and even now, if it were not so, we should not have to take the pill all the time and suffer those smaller consequences. It is hard not to think that all the woes of womankind, and children, too, began when the oestrus ended.

It is true that we do not have much information about primate sex life. Anthropologists have lately dogged their footsteps in hordes, and we know much more than we ever did of their habits. But does a female primate ever come on heat when she is sick? How long at pregnancy and after birth is the next oestrus? Why do some animals and birds remain monogamous for life without the lure of constant sexual availability?

And why is it only in the animal kingdom that a female may refuse a male, often apparently on a whim, and be sure that refusal is accepted? Since it would certainly have been better for the health and equally good for the survival of the human species to continue the sexual cycle of the ape, why didn't natural selection pick the human female who stayed sexually ape-like? That way she could have produced only enough children to care for properly, and survived herself—surely Nature's first rule?

Is everything really for the best in the best of all possible worlds?

2 February 1978

Whose Human Rights?

WHATEVER ELSE HE may or may not have done, President Carter has certainly put the issue of human rights on the world map, where it has caused an astonishing amount of ill-feeling. Or perhaps, when you come to think about it, not astonishing. The phrase itself sounds so innocuous, so self-evidently humane and civilized that, like peace, it has to be something we are all for. Instead, the issue is practically guaranteed to stir up controversy whenever it is more than superficially discussed. Contradictions and conflicts abound. One man's human rights are another man's bourgeois individualism and, worse, my human rights are often gained at the expense of yours.

Life, liberty and the pursuit of happiness by white Anglo-Saxon Protestant Americans not only deprive others of life, liberty and happiness but actually depend on so depriving them. The machinations of Nixon and the CIA effectively imprisoned, put to torture and to death a mass of people in Greece and in Chile and I do not imagine those who survive too much relish Uncle Sam's other hand wagging an admonishing finger the while and citing UN charters.

What, for a start, are the rights of human beings? Is it some sort of invisible layette handed to each infant upon birth by the Great Ombudsman in the Sky? Even those who believe in a God would be hard put to it to find the small print guaranteeing us anything more concrete than post-mortem harps and flowers. Moses came down from the mountain, Jesus came out of the desert and Buddha held forth from under his banyan tree but they all talked of human duties. Rights were barely mentioned and were anyway clearly understood to be dependent upon divine whim. 'Give us this day our daily bread' is only part of a prayer that Thy will be done and

231

if Thy will is a shortage of daily bread, so be it.

Obviously, then, human rights are a secular and man-made concept, a cerebral compensation for the imbalance and excesses caused as we drifted away from the instinctual bases of animal behaviour and built the neo-cortex over the mammal brain. No gorilla would need to ratify a list of gorilla rights because all of them are coded into him, synonymous with his own survival. But we are long cut off from such natural roots and so we must invent reasons and regulations for what animals do without thought. Our most sweeping invention, the Universal Declaration of the Rights of Man and Citizen, ratified by all the United Nations member States and the basis for President Carter's campaign, is pretty high-falutin' in its aims. Human rights, it announces, are such things as freedom from torture, freedom to form opinions, organize assemblies and have recourse to law against the abuse of power, all of which are very well if you already have the human right to food in your belly and a tincey bit irrelevant if not.

Most of us would agree that access to food is a basic human right if only because, without it, we are rather beyond caring about any other single human right. And yet what is the positon on food? One in three of us is not getting enough. A number larger than the entire population of the United States and the EEC are not getting enough to remain alive, never mind free. That human right is not mentioned in the UN Declaration and, moreover, nobody much seems to care. From such omissions comes the hollow ring to the rest of the list.

And a long list it is, at least in the developed world. Over the past year I have heard people claiming as human rights an extraordinarily wide range of things, apparently with no priorities. A few examples: free education, a home of one's own, travel, interesting jobs, unpolluted air, pets, cosmetic surgery, euthanasia, change of name, heat, a garden of one's own, books, rubbish collection, health, as many children as one wishes. The list, in fact, incorporates almost any desirable state you can think of, up to and including the right to pass exams, the right to go to Butlin's if you are handicapped and the right to a pleasant view.

232

No harm in asking, you may say, but actually there is harm in asking too frequently. Almost all these human rights, demanded by the rich nations, use up resources that deny other people in other parts of the globe much more basic rights directly connected with survival. My human right to a beef steak is your bowl of grain, my cobalt bomb is your malaria, my job is your dole, my healthy child is your dead one.

Even within the rich communities, paradoxes and deprivations abound. The right to walk the streets in safety may pre-empt the right to privacy with ubiquitous closed-circuit TV cameras everywhere. The right to demonstrate has already pre-empted other people's rights simply to exist without harassment.

Human rights are also frequently dependent on opting for particular political systems. Half our troubles today are caused by our wish for human rights that conflict with our democratic right to vote for the party of our choice. Those who believe free enterprise, competition, and the making of fortunes to be human rights often believe just as firmly (at least when misfortune hits them) in the human right to welfare hand-outs, free medicine, and government subsidies. Those who vote for socialism are often, once fortune hits them, the first to head for the nearest tax-haven, apparently believing that to be taxed in a welfare state is a violation of human rights.

My own universal declaration of human rights would go in steps, concentrating on one until that was universal and then adding the next. The first would be food, without which the whole concept is a travesty. The second, absolutely dependent on implementation of the first, would be the human right not to have life endangered by any form of governmental edict (individual criminal attacks would have to come much later on). Only then could I begin to contemplate such refinements as freedom, equality, and the vote. To my mind, looking at the state of human beings as a whole, these are very nearly metaphysical ideas.

20 April 1978

Cherchez l'Homme

I'd like to ask your opinion on something that has puzzled me for a long time. In my view many problems, especially those connected with sex, such as prostitution (both child and adult), child pornography, etc., would simply disappear if men would only control themselves. We women have been conned for generations into believing that this is much more difficult for men than for women, but I don't believe it. However, even if it is, they have no natural right to exploit women and children simply in order to avoid suffering frustration—a state that the other half of the population has to learn to live with.

Why is no reference ever made to the fact that if there were no male customers for casual sex and pornography, there would be few problems and no need to find ways of dealing with ponces and prostitutes? It is scandalous that about 100 women are currently in Holloway convicted of prostitution offences when, if anyone should be in prison, it is their customers.

Why isn't the basic responsibility of the male sex for the social problems I have referred to brought out strongly in every article and discussion on the subject, so that it would gradually get through to society who the real culprits are?

THIS LETTER PUTS ITS finger neatly on something that most of us are very carefully conditioned to overlook. It specifically mentions sexual problems but it raises, in fact, a hornet's nest of horrors in which the male—and the male alone—is implicated. Many women have become, over the past decade, properly outraged about their inferior status as women. But we have, it seems, hardly noticed a much more massive hood-winking of our sex in which we are instantly promoted from inferiority to equality and that is in all manner of what are inaccurately termed human problems, deemed to emanate from human nature.

I will give you an interesting example of this phenomenon in action. Arthur Koestler, a man I much admire except in his wilder metaphysical moments, has recently been preoccupied with worries about human aggression. As I understand it, he theorizes that there is some basic malfunction or failure of communication between the middle brain which engenders emotion and the neo-cortex which is the seat of logic and reason. And he points out that since aggression as an emotion is not able properly to be dealt with by access to reason, in a physiological way, the human species may be doomed.

All very convincing and, for a while, I was convinced. But then I realized, as so often before, that Mr Koestler was not in fact discussing a human evolutionary problem but a male view of an evolutionary problem. Women constitute half the human race and if there is some sort of physical block between the centres of emotion and reason that makes aggression difficult to control, then women must have it too. Yet women, though they may feel aggressive, have historically managed not to give vent to it. Therefore Mr Koestler is talking androcentric codswallop. There is no evolutionary cerebral malformation, only a lot of men who allow themselves to be aggressive and pretend this aggression is an intrinsic programming of the human species.

And we women have believed them. Sitting under our human being hats, we have wailed and moaned of human sin and the more liberal among us have beaten breasts in an orgy of *mea culpas* whenever crime statistics soar, muggings hit the headlines and murders horrify us. But we are brainwashed and we are wrong. Most violence, most crime and most vice is not committed by human beings in general. It is committed by men.

This letter-writer accuses men of sexual abuses and she is right. The creation, production, distribution and consumption of pornography is almost exclusively male. The motivation behind prostitution is male and the law that punishes prostitution is male-conceived and administered. Women do

235

not take indecent photographs of nude children, women do not molest children. But this male culpability goes far beyond sexual matters. We talk of muggings and robbery with violence, of assault and battery and grievous bodily harm as if such problems were endemic to the human race, but they are only endemic to one half of the race—the male half. The vast majority of muggers are boys and men.

We talk, euphemistically, of domestic violence, but which sex is domestically violent? Men. We talk of violence in the streets but who is violent in the streets? Men. We talk of corruption in public life, of widespread tax evasion, of embezzlement, bribery and a hundred other crimes, large and small, and we are talking about men. Hit-and-run drivers are mostly men, incest is almost exclusively instigated by men, wars are started and fought by men, our hideous modern weaponry—up to and including the neutron bomb—was invented, made and may eventually be used by men.

A month ago, I monitored a fortnight's newspapers for reports of violence and vandalism. In every case, the felon was a man. Worse, in a disproportionate amount of times, the victim was a woman. Yet so easily is this central fact fudged that you often hear adults discuss juvenile delinquency when they mean boyhood delinquency and even mothers chatting anxiously of children's unruliness when, ten to one, they mean their sons.

I do not argue that the female sex is inherently better than the male. A combination of oppression and powerlessness may well be rather more responsible for our comparative virtue than any genetic sainthood. But if we really wish to attack the rotten roots of our society, it will do us no good to obscure the issue. Human nature is not the cause, male nature is. The identikit of the suspected villain has a *man's* face, the police—our society—want to contact a *man* for questioning.

As always, even the male thriller-writers put up a convenient smokescreen. The truth is—*cherchez l'homme*.

27 April 1978

236

True Confessions

I was married 20 years ago to a man who was vital, witty, sometimes charming, but often vicious and violent. Half-way through the marriage I fell in love for the first time—with a man who treated me with gentleness and respect rather than criticism and abuse. I therefore felt that my affair, which lasted four years, robbed my husband of nothing he had ever had.

The break-up of this relationship caused me to have a mental breakdown, at the end of which I confessed my long-standing 'misdemeanour', hoping to establish a more honest and mutually rewarding marriage. The news shattered my husband. I achieved nothing except bitter, venemous outbursts, informing me that I had no idea what I had done to him by my confession, that he had had many chances to be unfaithful but had thought it wouldn't be 'playing the game'.

Finally I have decided to sue for divorce and now I have been informed on good authority that my husband had had at least three affairs before he ever found out about my infidelity.

Tonight I asked him if he would have preferred never to have known, for my liaison to have been conducted discreetly, without any rocking of boats. His answer was an unequivocal yes. He further avers that I am the odd one out in wanting to know the truth always, however much it hurts. He says I am asking to go through life exposing myself to pain. Perhaps so, but especially in marriage shouldn't relationships be built on trust and honesty?

IN THESE DAYS OF open-ended marriages, this problem—to tell the truth or forever hold your peace—is probably on the increase. Many younger couples do not consider marital infidelity a major hazard and some count its future occurrence as part of a charter of individual freedom. That is, in theory. But to tell or not to tell about specific infidelities is something else again. Personally, I have come to think that sexual infidelity itself causes less real pain than its accompanying circumstances. The demand for honesty is not so much a desire for confession as the wish to avoid what must otherwise amount to a web of lies—he wasn't at that meeting, he was with *her*; she didn't visit her mother, she visited *him*.

It is a nasty enough shock to admit that your own dear partner can be as devious as the next person but it is worse to have to acknowledge that your life for the past month/year/years has been lived not so much in lies as in unreality. What you believed was happening was not happening. What you believed was not happening was happening. The mind collapses into disarray.

Then there is often an overwhelming sense of foolishness. An ignoble and petty reaction, perhaps, but it burns like acid. There you were, all the time, a daftie, a loon, a sucker, without perception and doubtless, a figure of fun to them and to the world. Self-confidence chars to ashes. Perhaps—oh perish the thought—They talked about you, discussed your shortcomings, gave away your deepest secrets, tittered over your gullibility. The chances that they actually did are remote but each of us is condemned to sit alone at the centre of our own tiny universe, shivering and betrayed.

Another ignoble reaction (are they all ignoble?)—when They were doing what They did, what were you doing? Scrubbing the floor? Changing the nappies? Sweating blood to pay the mortgage? Buying loving birthday cards? Hateful. Uncontemplatable. *Unfair.* If hell hath no fury like a woman, is it because she was scorned or because she was stuck indoors minding the kiddies while he was having himself a ball?

Curiously, even a partner's choice for infidelity matters. Many people love to hate their 'rival', building up an image so monstrous as to be positively insulting to themselves—why, one longs to ask, should the spouse who chose you also choose a tarty, bird-brained trollop or an anaemic mouse of a man? Is a monster easier to hate than your spouse? For myself, I had rather my husband took up with a woman I could admire or like, whose attitudes I shared, whose motives I trusted. That way, at least, I wouldn't feel so totally rejected.

I am convinced that the anguish of discovering, rather than being told about, infidelity (and being told is quite painful enough) is a combination of all these things and all of them combine to wipe you out as an individual. Infidelity causes as much of an identity crisis in the 'wronged' partner as adolescence—more so if you yourself do not recognize it and so fail to give it due consideration. The emotional backlash is too easily labelled jealousy or righteous indignation or dismissed as a vaudeville cliché rather than being pinned down as something a trifle more complicated. Like 'Who am I?'

My own hopes for the marital conduct of an affair would be total honesty. I do not wish to be banished from my husband's inner life because such intimacy is a part of friendship as well as love. So if he gets seized with lust or even love for another woman, I want to know. The furniture of his mind is changing, however slightly, and I am interested in the new décor. Therefore some intimation from him, of the kind likely to be given a friend (no voyeuristic details, ta) would be welcome.

Given it, I am enabled to preserve some dignity in my own eyes and feel that I am at least being treated courteously, with due regard to the chores of marriage (children, bills, the work of the household) which must go on, moon and June apart. The whole business might well cause me acute distress but living in lies would be much more distressing. It is possible, of course, to gamble on not being found out but even if the gamble paid off, the insult implicit in that attitude would out.

There is one final point: a question, if you like, of sexual etiquette. If you are sleeping with someone else, I consider it a duty to inform your partner. What more humiliating than to realize that you have been physically sharing your mate with someone else, without being given the right to a decision about the disposal of your body in one way or the other?

Better honesty and pain than ignorant bliss and the threat of a discovery that could cause infinitely more bitterness and ruin, besides whole chunks of memory from the past.

25 May 1978

The Unacknowledged Network

THERE IS A YOUNGISH man who lives on my street and he is always around. I see him in the mornings ambling down the High Road, I see him in the afternoons pottering in his front garden, I see him any time of day playing with his three small children, stuffing local postboxes with local bumff, chatting with neighbours on his doorstep or theirs. Last week I mentioned him to a friend. I said, 'There's this man down our road, he doesn't seem to *do* anything.'

A second later, skies darkening, thunder rumbling, lightning sizzling, alarm bells screaming in my head, I grovelled on the kitchen floor, tearing my hair, wringing my hands, begging forgiveness from the Great Goddess. Years of feminism cracked across like the mirror of the Lady of Shalott. What was I, after all, but a Pavlov dog or better, a Pavlov pig, conditioned beyond redemption into making the piggiest remark of them all. That man was doing what women do, he did not vanish from my ken at 9 a.m., and return at six. *Ergo*, he was doing nothing.

My sisters of the hearth and home, forgive me. My only excuse is that I, too, have fallen victim to the brainwashing of a male world. Far below the level of consciousness I have absorbed by osmosis the male belief. Men are paid for what they do and therefore what they do in the home is nothing. Shocked by this involuntary treachery, this male face beneath the feminist front, I did penance. Meticulously I listed what women do, that frequently evoked half-joking list often quoted when the question of women's monetary value comes up, and some assessment is attempted of what they might be paid, were their services offered on the open market. Nanny, charwoman, chauffeuse, cook, hostess, sex object, gardener, handywoman, decorator and so on and on.

For which the payments usually mount up to a weekly three figures that we can all have a good giggle about and promptly forget.

But this time I dredged up from the bottom of my mind a whole lot of other things women do and I had to dredge them up because most are undertaken so automatically, and are so much a part of simply being a woman, that they are invisible, taken for granted even by women themselves. And these things worried me because already almost all single women and well over half of all married women are working in paid jobs outside the home, as they have every right to do, and yet if women disappear from the home, who then will do these endless invisible tasks?

For example, a quick survey of the past two weeks taken from the experience of my women friends and myself. A son had to be taken to hospital and, once there, sat with for four hours so that he would feel easy in uneasy circumstances. A mother had to be visited in hospital so that she did not feel lonely and unloved. A father had to have meals cooked and house cleaned while the mother was in hospital—can't cook scrambled eggs for himself, poor old boy, and too late to learn now. One aunt and one stepdaughter needed birthday presents and cards to be bought and sent off. A daughter needed a birthday party to mark a coming-of-age.

A mother-in-law had to be written to with news of family doings and inquiries as to aching feet and general well-being. Two letters had to be written to distant friends for how should they stay friends without occasional letters? A child's school had to be visited for talks with teachers, another school had to be provided with jumble to raise money for the children's benefit. A sister had to be given hours of time to support her through impending divorce, a brother had to be listened to through the woes of impending redundancy. A neighbour eased in her loneliness with a chat about greenfly on the roses. A housebound relative had ill-fitting shoes to be returned to a shop. A friend's child had to be babysat while the mother took herself to the doctor. Another friend wanted comfort about an erring child.

The list is, of course, as long as life itself and the things it lists encompass life itself, a part of that intangible network which keeps the human community afloat and into which, at one time or another, all of us will fall. When zoologists study animals, they study a particular species' network, the social pattern and behaviour that define them as a species and enable them to survive. When anthropologists study primitive people what they care about, what they write about, is the tribal network, the particular tribal ways of coping with grief, happiness, reproduction, bonding, aggression and the rituals that mark them, assuage them and preserve them.

In other words, when we look at the fox, the bee, the Eskimo or the Kikuyu, we see quite clearly the social relationships and we recognize their overriding importance in the scheme of things. But when we look at our own society, we appear to be exclusively concerned with the hardware of living—monetary policies, foreign policies, legislation, mergers, gold standards, earnings and outgoings —and blind to that network which is just below the surface of every outside activity; so essential to human happiness and even to human existence that it is counted as a reflex happening, like breathing. And yet that whole network is most carefully and lovingly woven, erected, repaired, serviced and staffed by the unpaid women at home.

If it were not for them (and women who have paid jobs and still service the net because they are women) I verily believe that civilized life as we know it would simply collapse. All across the country, community festivals and jamborees would cease for lack of organization, jumble sales and fêtes and sales of work would vanish. No flowers would brighten churches, no gold or silver glitter on the altars. No children would have costumes for school plays or dancing classes. No errands would be run for the old or handicapped, no doors opened to the gas or electricity men, no coffee trolleys wheeled for those in hospital, no gossip exchanged between neighbours, no love exchanged between friends. If women did not do it, who would celebrate a single milestone, arrange a single party, make memorable a day in a child's life? Who would maintain and nurture our tribal life?

Thank heavens there's a man in my road who has taken up one strand of that net before the last woman drops it.

15 June 1978

243

Shedding Divine Light

I ask this question of yourself and readers in a spirit of objective enquiry, being myself an adherent to no organized faith, philosophy, political party, cult, religion or country club. What exactly is the difference between what religious people call a 'cult' and their own particular 'religion'? Why, for instance, did the Home Office recently object to the entry into this country of the leader of the Unification Church (whose followers are, I believe, called 'Moonies') when they would welcome, say, the Patriarch of the Greek Orthodox Church or the Grand Mufti of Jerusalem? Anyone who answers that they rest their case on the 'revealed' word of a particular God will get me nowhere—cultists and religionists both believe that.

THERE ARE, I IMAGINE, very few people in Europe or America who believe, for instance, that God has taken up residence in a particular tree. Such an idea is reserved for various obscure African tribes and is interesting to the West only anthropologically, as a useful study for those anxious to take Ph.Ds in Primitive Religions. But last week in Brussels, the city that calls itself the Capital of Europe, I observed plump Belgian housewives kissing a tree. This tree had been carved to represent a man called Jesus, whom they worship.

So I am as much in need of an answer as my correspondent. To an outsider, the contradictions inherent in what certain believers claim to be a 'real' religion and what they reject as 'cults' are most confusing. Indeed, to the logical and inquiring mind, most statements made by believers are confusing. The overseas division of the Methodist Church has, for example, just warned in a new report that certain all-black churches have 'a ghetto mentality' and add that any 'monochrome' congregation, black or white, is a denial of the catholicity of the Christian Church.

Now, leaving aside the cheekiness of saying this at all when black people have only just been allowed, after several nasty little skirmishes, to join the heretofore entirely white churches of President Carter's own State of Georgia in the most powerful Christian country in the world, what makes these Methodist missionaries feel that 'a ghetto mentality ' is somehow confined to the colour of a congregation's skin? Since ghetto means, in essence, a segregated group, surely anyone who holds that a particular god is the true and only god and must be worshipped in a particular way already has a ghetto mentality.

Do not the Northern Irish, Catholic or Protestant, have ghetto mentalities that have caused more pain and suffering than any black church upon the face of this earth? Do not the Arabs believe that all those who are not Muslim are infidels? Have not the Jews built up a country upon a ghetto mentality, however understandable? Is not the Lebanon being rent asunder by believers who have a ghetto mentality?

But back to the original question. There are some people in this country who pray to Selene, a moon goddess, for miracles. In Nepal, they believe that gifts to a little girl designated a goddess will bring about miracles too. In Africa, gifts to animals, carved poles, birds or stones are expected to produce the same. Jews, Catholics, Protestants, Muslims and, for aught I know, Confucians, would call all these beliefs misguided or even wrong and yet all of them pray to their gods for miracles of one sort or another.

The Catholics, in particular, (a most respectable religion) believe in the miraculous powers of all sorts of things from old bones and drops of blood to the waters of places like Lourdes. Why are these beliefs considered intrinsically superior and acceptable, whereas the totems of Africa are thought anything from heretical to barbaric? Why was a head-hunter of Borneo, who thought a taste of enemy flesh gave access to the strengths of that enemy, regarded as so much more primitive (not to say evil) than a Christian's symbolic eating and drinking of the blood and flesh of Christ?

Is it just that Christians today deal in symbols whereas the head-hunters insisted on sticking to the real thing?

A body calling itself the Deo Gloria Trust had a conference last week to debate 'means whereby the public may be alerted, cults exposed and their victims restored to sanity'. These victims are, among others, the Moonies (followers of Korean Mr Moon), the Divine Light Mission and the Children of God. The Trust, a Christian gathering, says it is concerned by some of the dubious recruiting methods and disciplinary structures of the more arcane cults and objects to the cults that have one man at the top with all the financial and political power.

Myself, I couldn't agree more. I too am concerned about dubious recruiting methods, disciplinary structures and too much centralization of money and power. But I can't, for the life of me, worry more about Mr Moon or the Divine Lighters or, for that matter, the Mormons, Hare Krishna, or Scientologists than I do about the Christian churches. Mr Moon, Divine Lighters and Scientologists recruit adults. The Christian churches recruit new-born babies who can neither read, write, talk or interpret language.

As far as I can ascertain, the disciplinary structures of the 'cults' that so upset the Christian churches require obedience to a leader, time spent in praying, chanting, etc. and various prohibitions concerning food, drink, interaction with those of other faiths and sexual activity. Very nasty, too. But how, I wonder, do these cults differ from the disciplinary measures of, say, the Catholic Church, which has also prohibitions against food at certain times, sex with certain people in certain ways, and the mixing (through segregated schools and segregated marriages) of those of different faiths? As do the Jews, the Muslims, the Mormons and other faiths too numerous to name.

Nor am I among the chosen who can distinguish the difference in the centralization and power of a Maharishi or a Mr Moon and, say, the vast resources, and financial dealings of the Vatican, headed by a Mr Pope. Who can and does tell his followers what to eat, drink and do about sex, up to and including who a person shall marry, what religion their children should be, how many children they should have and an absolute refusal to allow a married couple to part (unless they are rich or titled).

If anyone can enlighten me as to the 'true' versus the 'false' religions, I should be much obliged.

22 June 1978

First Lady

The election presents me with a dilemma—as a Socialist I have waited 40 years to see a woman as Prime Minister. Is it not ironic that the Conservatives should be the party to produce such a leader?

Unless encouragement is given now to an able, clever, middle-class woman, is the opportunity for the top job to be delayed for more decades?

What am I to do? Should all my political hopes and beliefs be put aside and my little cross go towards the important step of women's progress?

I HAVE ALWAYS FELT a shiver of sympathetic dread for those persons throughout history who have heard God's Voice bidding them do acutely uncomfortable and often thoroughly self-destructive things in His Name. Poor Abraham, commanded to sacrifice his son. Poor Jesus, ordered to his crucifixion. Poor Joan of Arc, programmed for the bonfire. There, I have always thought, but for the grace of Godlessness, go I. But now I, too, have heard the Voice. Last Tuesday morning, in the middle of making chicken liver pate, the Goddess said unto me 'woe to the unbeliever who does not vote for my daughter, Mrs Maggie Thatcher'.

Ever since then, like my correspondent, I have been wriggling like a worm on a hook, trying to escape from this fate, and my house has been clamorous with argument and invective. Men and women, entering upon my kitchen table, have been sucked into the debate and ended up howling at each other—sometimes divided by sex and sometimes not. I do not know, yet, whether I can bring myself to carry out the Goddess's command and I turn to you, perspicacious and liberal readers of both sexes, to judge the arguments and adjudicate thereon. The only obvious qualification for joining the fight is that your sympathies are broadly socialist and that you too, would normally vote Labour.

Here, then, is a rough and brief summary of the opposing camps.

One. The sex of a Prime Minister is totally irrelevant. In an election, people should vote for policies or, sometimes, for the immediate candidate whose honesty, dedication and grasp of local issues are likely to make them effective Members of Parliament for the constituency. If one has never voted Conservative before, this is the worst time to do it, since the Tories have never been so right-wing or, as *Time* Magazine puts it, 'rigorously conservative'. The debate escalates to extremes for illustration: if Hitler had been Frau Hitler, would you have voted for her? Could you have shelved anti-Semitism and looming militarism on the grounds that *der führer* had breasts?

Do you realize that by voting purely on sex you wold be denying other women Labour candidates their place in the sun? Do you know that more women, anyway, vote Conservative and that women have traditionally had more power, at lawn-roots level, in the Tory Party than in any left-wing party from Labour through to Trots?

Are you aware that the woman you would vote for is not a woman in any feminist sense? As two women *Guardian* writers summed it up, Mrs Thatcher is a woman but not a sister. Her policies, as judged by many socialists, are hardly likely to help women and certainly not the poorer immigrant women who will probably be deprived of the possibility of importing their children to this country and their right to give English nationality to their foreign husbands.

Do you understand that Mrs Thatcher's policies may well adversely affect, by welfare cuts, the poorest in our society and the poorest are usually female? Surely you cannot be so obsessively feminist as to put your cause above the inevitable changes that will immediately affect ordinary peoples' lives for the next five years? And, believe us, get nothing out of those changes yourselves, as women? How can you be a traitor to such huge and general issues by pandering to one so small—Mrs Thatcher's gender?

Two. The whole history of the women's movement has been a battle against male pragmatism. Any time that women began to think of their own interests, others (men *and* women) have argued that those interests were irrelevant to the *real* issues, that they were being raised in the wrong place at the wrong time. Women are conditioned to put their own needs last if, indeed, they recognize their own needs at all. During the fight for black emancipation in America, women who demanded women's emancipation were accused of diversionary activities. Women who fight for women's jobs during mass male unemployment are seen as selfish and see themselves as selfish.

The extreme left (for instance, the Workers' Revolutionary Party) vaunt the glories of the Iranian Revolution and bitterly attack Iranian women marching for their rights under Islam. Because they do not wish to wear the *Chador*, because they object to anti-feminist laws, because they want equality, the WRP denounce them as bourgeois counter-revolutionary CIA-funded Shah-lovers, intent on undermining the courageous sacrifices of the Iranian masses. At any given point in history, what women wanted for themselves has always been either ignored as unimportant or attacked as pure bloody-mindedness.

All right, but what in heaven's name are these feminine needs that Margaret Thatcher is likely to implement? Nothing uniquely aimed at women, that is for sure. But she is bound to do one thing if she is elected, whether she will or not, and that is for the benefit of all our daughters. Over the past ten years, publishers have printed a cascade of books about the early conditioning of little girls' lives and those books have, on the whole, been well received and their arguments acknowledged as correct. Girls—who begin so smart, who outdistance their brothers so easily—mysteriously fade at about age fifteen and turn, like Cinderella's carriage, to pretty pumpkins waiting for a Prince to reactivate them. Why? Because, as all the experts agree, they have no image upon which to model themselves, no active figureheads at whom they may point.

Now, after thousands of years, we in Europe are on the brink of giving them one indisputable model—a female Prime

Minister—and we are told that is unimportant compared to her policies. But policies are here today, gone tomorrow. Among twenty people in my own random street poll, no one could name a single political policy espoused by Disraeli, Gladstone or Baldwin. No one even knew what political party they belonged to. But everyone knew that each was a man and each was a Prime Minister. So would it be with Margaret Thatcher: policies forgotten, sex remembered forever. Unseating some Labour women candidates for five years might be the one thing necessary to make easier the election of all women candidates in a future election.

Nor is the influence of a woman Prime Minister confined to this country. The press of foreign journalists around Mrs Thatcher has directly to do with her sex and will directly influence other governments and other ordinary men and women, whether they be French, Arabian, or the male chauvinists of our own majorities and minorities. Once the great obstacle of gender is breached, gender can never again be an issue, in politics or anywhere else.

Confronting a male Tory who wished to abstain from voting on the grounds of her sex, Mrs Thatcher was forced to invoke Queen Elizabeth I as proof that a woman could rule. Four hundred years is a long way to have to go back. And wouldn't it be nice to see, at last, little *girls* being photographed outside Number Ten?

26 April 1979

Führer Amin

IN 1937 THE FIRST faint rumours of Nazi brutalities against the Jews wafted into this country. Few people heard, fewer people took any notice. Eight years on, the full horror was revealed as the gates of the concentration camps swung open. My mother, like thousands of ordinary people, put on her hat and, clutching her shopping basket, went to see the ghastly record on film. She came home pale and sickened. Suddenly, the unbelievable was true—Hitler had attempted, among other atrocities, the deliberate genocide of a race. But at least we now knew the full extent of evil and could make sure that it never happened again.

Thirty-four years later, the first faint rumours of Amin's brutalities began to leak out of Uganda. Eight years on, the full horror is revealed as the gates of the prisons swing open. I, like thousands of ordinary people, sit in front of my television screen and see another holocaust. This time, the details are appallingly familiar. Arrests in the night, people disappearing off the face of the earth, torture, beatings, atrocities, massacres, mass graves, obscene rituals (then, human skin made into lampshades, now, severed heads kept in drawers). Between iron bars, the kleig lights flood hideous cells, stained and stinking, where anonymous men suffered and died. Only one difference this time. Most of us, watching, knew what was going on most of that eight years. The prison gates showed us nothing that refugees, reports, books and newspaper articles had not already revealed and spared us nothing of the usual countdown to genocide, including the dictator's statutory visit to the Pope.

And all that knowledge made not a whit of difference to the end result. No machinery set up, during the intervening years from Hitler to Amin, was any more capable of translating the writing on the wall into preventive action. A Grecian inevitability reigned. They say that those who do not understand history are condemned to repeat it. They do not say that those who do understand history are also condemned to repeat it.

The frustration, the sheer helplessness of ordinary people forced to watch extraordinary events, is increasing daily, thanks to television. That helplessness becomes more dreadful in exact ratio to greater knowledge of those events. There is an argument abroad at the moment that news reports of wars and massacres are over-sanitized and, as such, useless. What is needed, say some media men, are reports that relentlessly focus on the blood and guts, the full catastrophe of human suffering and human wickedness, in as much colour and detail as possible. The theory is that we, the armchair audience, will then be shocked right out of our armchairs into. . .well, into what is not clear, unfortunately. The theory is fine but the end result? There is no end result.

Myself, I have come to dread such programmes as *World In Action Special*. Once again, intrepid reporters drag me through horrors, an implicit reproach in their every revelation. Look, they say, here are a man's bones, a man's hair, a man's blood. Look, here is the cell where corpses were piled to the ceiling. Look, look, here is the very spot were prisoners were forced to club each other to death. I look, but there is no point in looking. There is no point in the reporters looking. It is all a fearful voyeurism. I knew all this was happening while it was happening. Most of us did. We would have stopped it happening if we could, but we couldn't. We could do absolutely nothing.

What did Britain do to stop mass killings in Uganda? Three years ago we closed the British Embassy in Kampala. Two years ago we attempted a freeze of all trade goods of a 'potentially military nature'. Days before Amin's defeat we finally stopped pouring whisky down his thugs' throats, whisky flown over on the Stanstead shuttle. In the meantime, we giggled when our comedians blacked up and pretended to be President-for-Life Idi Amin. He laughed all the way to the Public Safety Unit.

Much worse, what could Britain have done? Not a lot,

actually. Even if we had been loud in moral condemnation, which we were not; even if we had made a formal approach to the United Nations, which we did not; even if we had insisted on an absolute trade embargo, which we did not: we would still have been ineffective against majority interests and majority votes. In spite of the United Nations, in spite of The Hague, in spite of the possibilities of international trade embargoes, in spite of being only 20 years from the end of the twentieth century and in sight of being able to prevent death from disease and even from age, we on this planet still have no method whereby we can effectively stop one nation or tribe or group from exterminating another.

Bokassa, self-styled Emperor of the tiny Central African Empire, kept on his throne by monies from France, could personally take part in the murder of school children and be punished only by the President of France refusing to shake his hand. The President of Nicaragua is currently attempting to eliminate the poor that are always with him. Given time he may succeed and thereby solve a whole lot of problems. Given time, tens of thousands of refugees from Vietnam will perish in the South China Sea. What advances time brings!

I do not believe that most people are indifferent to others' sufferings. What I do believe is that ordinary, healthy people must get through each day in reasonable spirits and with some efficiency, and so they cannot allow themselves to think of death. Our own lives are locked in a losing battle with death and our fragile happiness entirely dependent on the fact that no one dear to us actually died today. How can we possible afford to contemplate horrors unless—and only unless—we can do something about them? All else is masochism; useless masochism at that.

Even assuming that some of us have the dedication to begin, like Sisyphus, to push the heavy boulder of public indignation uphill, so complex and time consuming is the task—organizing demonstrations, lobbying Parliament and the United Nations, writing books, setting up the Save the Something fund—that any dictator with a will to murder can have liquidated all his enemies, buried the bodies, and cleaned up the evidence long before the creaking and ponderous machinery has begun its first turn. Indeed, so it is.

Sometimes it seems that the only international morality and preventive influence, such as it is, emanates solely from the building off the Strand that houses Amnesty International. In other words, 30 years after one holocaust and just out of another, the only hope we, the people, have of preventing the worst world horrors, shaming our governments out of their defensive bureaucracy and profiteers out of their indifference to life, is to support, however and wherever we can, that English-based organization that operates on nothing more than the strength of our indignation. That is not a lot, but it is all we have. What else can we do?

21 June 1979

Blue in the Faith

OVER THE PAST 20 YEARS there has been a significant change in our attitude to the police. Before 1960 many people thought our boys in blue were upright and gentle giants who found lost children, fought unarmed against desperadoes, and told you the time. Superhumans. Today many people defend the police by saying 'Well, they're only human, aren't they?' as they watch these humans accused of planting evidence, taking bribes, beating up suspects and freaking out at public demonstrations.

But there is, it seems to me, a vital division among these aspects of being 'only human'. A case can be made for all policemen occupied with habitual law-breakers, whether they be porn merchants or professional villains. As the lady said after seeing *Law and Order*, 'set a thief to catch a thief', and she meant this as a compliment. She was implicitly condoning bent practices used by police against that vague group called The Underworld and there is some justice in that, however rough. But to include police behaviour *vis à vis* the public in the same 'they're only human' bracket seems an increasingly dangerous tendency. To blur this distinction is to treat the police not as super but as subhuman because we are expecting less of them than we expect (or is expected) of ourselves.

Faced with unruly picket lines, public marches and demonstrations, some policemen freak out, laying about them with fists and truncheons, sometimes causing severe injuries and worse. 'You can't blame them,' say supporters, 'they're human, too.' But being only human would hardly constitute a defence for any member of the public who caused such injuries. 'I freaked out' is no excuse. Last year a man in Kent injured a burglar who broke into his house, and was found guilt of grievous bodily harm. Apparently we are coming to believe that not only is there one law for the public and another for its custodians but that there *should* be. Yet they are trained to cope with ugly situations and we are not. They choose their involvement and we do not.

Obviously, the police force faces many real difficulties. They are under-manned, were, until recently, underpaid and therefore could not be choosey about their intake. But surely they could test and deploy that intake better. In America (and, for that matter, at one London department store) psychological tests are applied even to liftmen because propelling a cage up and down eight hours a day, month after month, can cause certain types of people to lose their marbles. Is it too much to ask that policemen are sorted through to make sure they are at least highly unlikely to react brutally, through fear or stress? Anyone who has been present at a large demonstration will know just how edgy policemen are, how frighteningly likely to freak out, even knowing they are surrounded by comrades and have far greater powers than those they confront. Those men who keep their cool are dragged, willy nilly, into violence not of their making and are then tarred with the same brush as their uncool brethren.

Nor does the police Establishment help the average man-on-the-beat win public sympathy. Their spokesmen and superiors often seem intent on alienating even the staunchest supporters. Last month, Metropolitan Police Commissioner Sir David McNee announced 'if you keep off the streets of London and behave yourselves, you won't have the SPG to worry about'—not a statement exactly guaranteed to inspire confidence.

I do not wish to feel that I must stay home in order to avoid being bashed over the head by the arm of the law. The Special Patrol Group were loudly defended as 'completely satisfactory' *immediately* after a man had been clubbed to death in Southall and four eye-witnesses had identified his assailant as an SPG man. Over and over again, for many years now, well-wishers have been pointing out to the police one perfectly logical and reasonable fact that applies to all other situations in life—if you want people to believe that justice is being done, complaints against the police must be dealt with by an independent body. Do they listen? They do not. We are simply told by Sir David that 'if any officer abuses his power, he will be dealt with'.

What are we supposed to feel, told so? Touch our caps and say very kind of you, your sirship? Dismiss those intimations of natural justice common even to three-year-olds? Accept the word of McNee as Catholics accept Papal edicts? On what grounds are we expected to show more pure faith in the police than it is dreamed we should display for any other public servant, up to and including our MPs, whom we do at least elect?

Soldiers in Northern Ireland are under continual stress and in constant fear of their lives. Many of them have seen their comrades killed. They are always in confrontation with the public. Yet if one of them is accused of shooting a member of that public, the police are called in to research the circumstances and deliver the facts to the Director of Public Prosecutions. Even under those rules there are frequent accusations of cover-ups but two such soldiers are presently on trial in the Belfast Crown Court on a charge of murdering a 16-year-old boy. Policemen in England are not under continual stress or in constant fear of their lives. Very few indeed have seen a comrade killed. They are not always in confrontation with the public. Nevertheless, if one of them kills a member of that public, there is no outside body to collect evidence for the DPP.

Blair Peach was a dedicated and talented young teacher and champion of underdogs, black or white. His friends say he was shy, gentle and courageous. What could his worst enemies accuse him of? That he was a 'troublemaker', which, in Sir David McNee's terms, means he would not stay off London streets and he would keep going where trouble might be. For that, his penalty was a fractured skull and death. For that, his family had to fly over from New Zealand and must fly back again now, still ignorant of his killer after ten weeks of internal police inquiry.

Now the National Council for Civil Liberties have started their own independent inquiry. What choice did they have? What choice did the police give them? The Home Office say they are going to review the Public Order Act but they did that last year. They say they are going to investigate the Special Patrol Group but since Sir David has expressed complete satisfaction with it, who can have confidence in that?

I sometimes think that if some foreign power were employing undercover minutemen with the express purpose of discrediting the police in the eyes of the public, they could do no better job than the police do all by themselves. Are they thick as jam butties or simply made arrogant by the closed ranks of the Home Office, that most secretive and tight-lipped organization this side of the Kremlin? Now Mr William Whitelaw has taken up the mantle of the Home Secretary, the mantle that requires him to defend his force at all times, against all common sense. Could you?

5 July 1979

Little Britain

LATELY, DUE TO THE CHANGE of government, the fact of a female Prime Minister and the vague moral imperative of democracy, I have been trying very hard to understand Conservatives, upper and lower case. They are, after all, human, I say to myself. If you prick them, do they not bleed? And they are, you must admit, frightfully patriotic. As they keep on saying, they want to put the Great back into Britain.

Aye, but there's the rub, there's where I and, perhaps, a number of other people cannot help but part company with them. Though I am perfectly content to be British, I have no desire at all to be Great British. Indeed, if it isn't too contradictory, I happen to think that not being Great British is greater than being Great British. Do you notice that saying Great frequently enough turns the word to ashes in your mouth?

Conservatives have short and highly selective memories. They also believe in fairy tales. They think, for instance, that there were good old days when all Britons loved God, King and Country, chose noble statesmen instead of ignoble politicians, possessed Hearts of Oak, and showed a united front which enabled them to win wars, rule the seas and run the world. That, of course, was Great Britain.

Now, at least once a month in some newspaper or magazine somewhere upon this still-sceptred isle someone laments our current state, wailing of 'the sour society', 'the politics of envy', our divisiveness, our lack of purpose, our laziness, our inability to produce statesmen, and our general loss of faith in God, the Monarchy, and Great Britain. Worst of all, according to them, we share no common bond, as we did in the War. In other words, Britons are falling apart and this may mean the end of civilization as we know it.

In fact, it could mean the beginning of civilization as we've never known it if you assume, as I do, that no country can be defined as truly civilized until it is actively democratic. The main reason for the calm, prosperity and unity of the good old days was that all those people who were not calm, prosperous, or unified had no education, no leisure, no money, no power, no vote, and therefore no voice. Whatever their mutterings, whatever the polar regions of their discontent, they went unheard and so could be said not to exist. Only one point of view defined the Greatness of Britain; democracy was confined to the panoply of Parliament and an occasional member of the deserving poor was trotted out to pull his forelock, say 'God bless 'ee, squire,' and quash all doubts.

Real democracy, the extra-Parliamentary kind, is much noisier. When almost everyone has a voice and uses it, the resulting clamour can be quite distressing. One point of view is so soothing, so quiet, so full of wholeness, compared to a myriad disparate views that clash hideously upon tender ear drums, that spill out on to the streets, that fill public halls with speechifying, that insist on being heard. Coarse voices that question everything, that refuse to see that the proper place for the poor man is at the rich man's gates, that things are bright and beautiful, that God's in his heaven and all's right with the world. Just imagine the distress of the Ancient Greek when the hoi polloi emerged from the Oracle's cave and said, "'Ere, Mum, that weren't no Goddess, that were the Senator's lass with a snake round 'er neck.'

And when the blindfold falls from hitherto bound eyes, what happens here or in Spain, in Iran, or in Uganda? Divisiveness happens, of course. Ten nations instead of one. A hundred opinions instead of one. Class against class, cause against cause, solution against solution. The dreaded levelling-down takes place—why can't we all live like the Shah or Samoza or Princess Anne instead of dragging them down? Hideous envy sets in—such a mean emotion, don't you think? Perfectly all right to arouse it with your mansions and millions but rotten bad taste to feel it. Really, when you come to think about it, a good War or a really tough dictatorship is so much more ordered, so much quieter, than all this bickering. You see, if people haven't had any freedom, when they get it they don't immediately know what to do with it. So boring of them.

Conservatives, young or old, English or foreign, do seem to feel that dictatorships (friendly) and Wars, in general, are good things.

Perhaps the deadly danger did unite us, but what is usually carefully overlooked as another possible ingredient of the War's uniting power is the fact that war-time society created a more truly egalitarian society than anything we have seen since. Everyone had an equal share of food, clothes, furniture, and petrol. Empty houses were automatically requisitioned for homeless families. People from, as they say, all walks of life worked side by side for the same pay in the fire or ambulance service, even the munitions factories. Rich people in the country took in poor people from the towns and they all ate good brown bread together. Perhaps if we'd kept all that going when peace broke out, the politics of envy might never have arisen.

Nevertheless, I persist in my view that Britain is greater now than it was when it ruled an Empire. What's more, I believe that by a kind of cosmic accident, we have all the ingredients of character necessary to usher in a better future, as long as we do not listen to the siren voices of a false nostalgia. We are, for a start, blessed with a national temperament that veers towards laziness, a useful asset when faced with the micro-chip. We are basically home loving and, in the future, we may all spend far more time at home. Many of us are less interested in money than in having the time to garden, attend football matches, meet our friends—anyone who has had a British shopkeeper shut the door in their faces dead on five o'clock can bear witness to that. We are on the whole uncompetitive, unaggressive and phlegmatic. We take kindly to the natural justice of minor regimentation, like queues, and we actually quite enjoy the idea of the simple life, rationing, shortages, and cuts in living standards, as long as everyone shares them.

All just the right traits for a tiny off-shore island race, if only they'd stop trying to make us Great and let us be small and beautiful.   *19 July 1979*

Power and Peanuts

ONE OF THE BASIC SIMILARITIES among most Utopian writers is that they almost always envisage a society without leaders. In the more ancient versions, *vide* Plato, there may be a ruling clique of Wise Men but modern idylls dispense with leaders altogether. It is true that, in doing so, authors tend to stay well clear of the boring bits like who empties the dustbins but the intellectual interest lies in the very fact of that common denominator—the future seen as devoid of any Top Person, or group of Top People, there to tell others what to do.

The stories are set well ahead on undiscovered planets or in our own country *circa* 2500 AD, glimpsed through a time warp. But even today, we are, perhaps, already in transition to that future and though all transitional states are extremely uncomfortable and noisome with Cassandras predicting imminent doom, they are also full of hopeful possibilities and many individuals whose attitudes and actions, consciously or unconsciously, reflect what may come about rather than what has been.

Take, for instance, the unlikely figure of Jimmy Carter. Here is the man who has what is often called the most powerful job in the world. A leader of leaders. During most of his tenure as President of the United States, Mr Carter has constantly been accused of what is seen as the worst failure possible in his situation (far worse than Nixonian dirty tricks) —a lack of leadership. Contrite, he says he has finally heard the voices of those who said 'Mr President, you haven't been leading our nation' and is going to change his lifestyle. He has hired someone to coach him in assertiveness, teach him how to move his arms and clench his fists to show forcefulness. He is now intent on being what they all want him to be, a proper leader.

I find the effort at transformation grim. It is easy to criticize the unreconstructed Jimmy Carter for many things. It is possible that he is a weak and vacillating man, unable to make up his mind, unable to see the wood for the trees. But it is also just possible that he is a kind of sombre incarnation of the future—the first American leader ever seriously to convey to his electorate (whether he would or not) that the time has passed when one man—albeit American, President, White, Southern and God-fearing—can actually be expected to lead his people in the all-embracing way that they want to be, insist on being, led.

Could it be that the underlying reason for Carter's present unpopularity lies exactly in his erstwhile inability to pretend to omnipotence when such a pretence (or its reality, Nixonian megalomania) is still so much in demand, so heavily a hangover from history? One can quite see, after all, how extremely uncomfortable, exhausting and generally irritating it must be to have elected such a leader.

All very nice, on the surface, his fireside chats to keep you briefed, his informal visits to your home, his soliciting of your opinions, just as long as you could be sure that such democratic goings-on were the usual façade, the street theatre of all leaders. But imagine the chill if you begin to think he might be serious, he might actually be expecting you to wrestle with moral and political problems, might actually require your help. You went to the polls, you voted him in, you're on the way home to get on with your life and you hear him calling you back, asking you to share some of the burden of responsibility you have just been making sure he should bear alone. The nerve of it. No wonder you turn around and tell him he's no leader and, if he's not careful, you'll exchange him for a better actor.

One of the reasons that the very idea of leadership has been popular enough to endure throughout the life-span of the human race is that leaders, however repressive, cruel or corrupt, do implicitly guarantee to give the rest of us a precious freedom from responsibility. A democracy that requires anything more is simply another word for hard work and who, willingly, would take that on?

It may be that Jimmy Carter's major sin is his possibly unconscious recognition that, as the planet shrinks, the problems that manifest themselves are so general, so basic and so interdependent that they cannot be solved, as once problems were, by one man or one Government's initiative. He is, unforgivably, admitting—if only by his behaviour—that there is nothing important he can do without the people and that a people's democracy is about to become an empirical necessity. He is the first world leader to recognize this because he is the most powerful leader of the most powerful country and therefore the only one forced to disabuse himself of the illusion that power itself is a solution. This Emperor, perhaps, has glimpsed a truth, before his people and brought their fury upon his head for saying in public, 'I have no clothes.'

Italy, as it happens, has been without a Government for six months and the Italians are being told that they are 'ungovernable'. This ungovernability has, of course, partly to do with their multi-party system, which in itself reflects a multiplicity of views. America, with a two-party system, has no such excuse and yet Carter's personal pollster Pat Caddell reports that Americans feel it doesn't matter who is President because the country is spinning out of control. The old world and the new, for different reasons, both becoming ungovernable. The predictable conclusions are dire but they could, more optimistically, be interpreted as ingredients of inevitable change, first tiny and perilous steps away from a reliance upon leadership and towards a recognition that what needs to be done can only be done by the people.

Jimmy Carter says, 'I need the help of the American people' and, clearly, he not only needs it but is quite powerless without it. Increasingly, the necessities of the future must rest upon a wider and wider acceptance by everyone (as in the Utopian dreams) of personal responsibility. The energy crisis, as one instance, cannot be solved by any leader's decree—it can only be mitigated by widespread restraint and solved by new discoveries or a grassroots change in patterns of living.

Where once a country's problems were self-contained and the consequences of leadership, good or bad, confined within national or sectarian borders, every major problem today from inflation to unemployment depends far more for its solution upon the general public than on any single act by any single leader.

If my analysis has any truth to it, it could take years of replacing failed leaders with new leaders, also doomed to failure; years of the slow disillusionment with leaders that has already set in, before we accept the facts—leaders are failing because leaders are no longer relevant. The Utopian future has begun and whether it turns into a dream or a nightmare depends only on us.

2 August 1979

The Wrong Debate

*I wonder whether you would be willing to come and speak at
the Oxford Union next term. On Friday, November 2, we are
debating the motion 'That female emancipation has gone too
far' and so far Jill Knight, MP, has agreed to help propose it
and Maureen Colquhoun, MP, has agreed to oppose it. I
wonder if you would like to join Maureen Colquhoun on the
opposition side.*

The President,
Oxford Union Society.

AS I READ THIS MISSIVE, the corner of one eye begins to twitch
convulsively, an agonizing pain shoots up from the left
ventricle, my psyche is suffused with an imminent sense of
doom and a light foam manifests itself upon my cupid lips. I
appear to have all the symptoms of acute cardiac arrest and
am forced to lie down in a dark place for some minutes before
life ebbs back to my fast-withering limbs.

Dear Mr President. Could I suggest, with all due respect,
that you might be attempting too much too soon, back there
in your time warp among the dreaming spires? Before you
move on to an issue so quintessentially eighteenth century as
women's emancipation, should you not first cover the more
pressing questions of the day? Such as 'This House believes
that 200 angels can dance on the end of a pin' or 'This House
has no confidence in the Roundheads' or even the admittedly
rather daring motion 'Is there honey still for tea?'. I feel sure
all these subjects are more suited to the calibre of your
members and can be guaranteed to provide a jolly evening for
all concerned.

No, seriously though, let us picture the scene. There they

267

all are in the Hall of the Union up there beside the Isis, the *crème de la crème de la jeunesse*, our hope in years to come, their little fingers already grasping at the reins of government, their dewy eyes focused upon the corridors of power, the groves of academe and the halls of fame, fine upstanding lads and lassies with, we are told, the best minds of their generation. And what, ladies and gentlemen, does the conglomerate of all these finely-honed neurones come up with for debate? 'That the emancipation of women has gone too far.' Magic.

I beg your pardon? It's a sort of joke, you say? Lighthearted. Fun. Of course! Silly me, I should have known. I mean, it's about *women*, isn't it? Mothers-in-law, rolling pins, boobs, battered wives, gold diggers, dumb blondes, and such. Sorry, chaps. Well, all I can say is *mea culpa* and gosh, aren't we all lucky that Oxford, at least, can still lay claim to female students with a sense of humour, happy to sit with bright smiles upon their charming faces while others debate the limits to their freedom. Chuckling at the repartee, twinkling at the little reminders that they are, when all's said and done, in a special category, rather like very spoiled children who think they can have it all their own way until Daddy comes along and raps them over their pretty knuckles to remind them of their place—and let's not forget that their place, very recently, was not even *in* the Oxford Union.

I'm sure I speak for most of us when I say that we should be jolly grateful that there are some sports left among the second sex and that not all females have degenerated into strident and dreary dykes. We must be grateful, too, that there are still grown-up women—and Members of the Mother of Parliaments to boot—who think the subject controversial, for or against.

What? I could take women's emancipation seriously if I wished? I'd have perfect liberty to say what I wanted, it's up to me? D'you mean, Mr President, you're offering me and another whole woman a chance to say for the six millionth time what thousands of women have been saying for generations? That we can freely rabbit on about how women aren't yet getting paid much more than half men's wages and aren't yet visible in top executive positions of any kind, not to mention Parliament itself, not even to touch upon any of our Top of the Pop religions? Gee wilikers, Mr P., no wonder Oxford is the eye of the liberal intellectual hurricane in this little world of ours.

There is, of course, one motion I guarantee the Oxford Union has never debated and that really is one of the crucial questions of the twentieth century: 'That male emancipation has gone too far.' How about running that up the Martyrs' Memorial to see how it flutters?

Emancipation is freedom from legal, social, intellectual, political, or moral restraint, it says in my *Concise Oxford* (where else?) *Dictionary*. Right. Mr President, my Lords, Ladies and Gentlemen I wish to propose this motion though, unfortunately, I only have twenty minutes in which to do so and some six million years of examples to draw from. I put it to you that nothing is more glaringly obvious to the most prune-like mind than that when freedom from all legal, social, political, intellectual, and moral restraint is under discussion, the one thing you have to *cherche* is *l'homme*.

It has evidently escaped your attention that there are still, upon this planet, emancipated members of the male sex who designate themselves Kings, Emperors, Shah of Shahs, and Presidents in Perpetuity who claim Divine Right to torture and kill countless of their subjects in one way or another with the help of other males called the police or the military and the aid of foreign males in reputedly democratic or shamelessly totalitarian governments. If you want to trace the sources of starvation in the part of the world called Third, you must look to profoundly emancipated agri-businessmen who turn poor countries into battery hens to fill their own mouths and pockets.

Emancipated men are, at this very moment, laying waste whole landscapes and polluting whole seas, tearing down whole forests, decimating whole tribes, eradicating whole plant and animal species, poisoning whole populations with anything from nuclear wastes and carcinogens to opium crops and factory effluvia, for profit. Socially emancipated men are spending three million pounds per minute on arms throughout the world, intellectually emancipated men are using more than half the world's research funds on weapon research. Granted, there are a minority of men fighting the excesses of their sex's emancipation but these men, because they practise moral restraint, are unemancipated.

I therefore submit, Mr President, that male emancipation has, indeed, gone too far. But soft! What light through yonder window breaks? It is the east and a curious mushroom-shaped cloud. I rest my case.

20 September 1979

A Man too Proud to Kneel

ZEBEDEE WOODING, a 54-year-old Brooklyn man, was one of six customers in a Bedford-Stuyvesant restaurant when three youths, aged 17 to 20 burst in and announced a stick-up. Two of them brandished handguns. James Pettiford, 57, owner of the restaurant, said today the youths ordered the patrons to kneel.

'They were going through the customers' pockets. They got to Red—I never knew his real name—and he just refused. He said, "I don't kneel for anyone." Then, without a word, one of the bandits shot him in the chest.'

That story was front-page news in the *New York Post* headlined 'Gunman Kills The Man Too Proud To Kneel'. Herb Goldberg, author of a book called *The New Male—From Self-Destruction To Self-Care,* quoted it on a New York television programme as a classic example of the way in which old-style macho-men destroy themselves. A few days later, another man, male organizer of a resources centre, also quoted it on Philadelphia television, commenting that the incident illustrated an extreme of the destructive male conditioning that plagued many of the men who came to his centre for help. The new males—in America at least—are on the anti-warpath and where else have the old males to turn but in their graves?

Goodness knows, I feel for the new males. All my life I, like many other women, have been driven into fury by the lemming-like propensity in men to sacrifice themselves for some abstract and often extremely dubious cause; for a religion better called bigotry, a crusade better called racism, a patriotism better called ego. The cry 'For King and Country' has, over the centuries, wreaked more havoc than it ever settled and decimated the foolish lemmings who believed the propaganda put out by their leaders, safe in the background.

Once, in France, I stood in a First World War graveyard, where·the white crosses stretched across the grass to the skyline like neat petit point stitched on green velvet, and wondered whether the world would be in the slightest different if all those graves turned back into the young men, brothers and sons, fathers and husbands, who had mindlessly followed idiots and, so doing, laid waste their own lives and the lives of those who loved them.

Zebedee Wooding had, I imagine, been conditioned much as they had in their time, bemused by an image of courage for its own sake that has been labelled virile and he-man by those for whom it was a great convenience. Being an American male he must, too, have been burdened by all the weight of the Wild West, awed by a thousand celluloid Westworlds featuring all the symbols of masculinity epitomized by John Wayne and Gary Cooper, America's high noon men who did what men must do, in Hollywood at least. Most of us·thrilled with them and most of us exchanged the cinemas for the grey pavements outside, leaving their ethos inside. Zebedee Wooding didn't and Zebedee Wooding is dead.

And yet what shall we do when all the Zebedees have died? Is it entirely ludicrous, absolutely wasteful that a man should refuse to kneel for three hoodlums? On the face of it, such a refusal is exactly the kind of *beau geste* that gets no one anywhere but dead. Better by far, you could argue, that he had done what he was told and lived, thus sparing his family awful anguish. If you veer towards the romantic, you can write a scenario in which Zebedee, still alive, hunts down the hoodlums and delivers them to justice—a far more useful model than dying on a luncheonette floor.

But there are, insistently, other arguments. Suppose all six of the restaurant's clientele had refused to kneel on command? It is possible that even three armed men might have been taken aback, might have been weakened in their resolve, might have run. Perhaps they carried guns because they had learnt just how easily guns intimidate people. Perhaps one of those bandits has already passed up another crime because he was forced to realize that even a gun does not necessarily ensure passivity and most men, unless they are psychopaths, are not prepared always to kill for their own ends.

Besides, these days, who can guarantee that a refusal like Zebedee's is any more surely a death sentence than immediate compliance? Men and women have frequently been killed though they acted in complete obedience to threats. Killed in cold blood crawling, lying down, tied up, powerless and passive in every way. Old men too weak to offer resistance are killed. Old and crippled women are killed. Children are killed. Cowards die alongside the brave.

We can never underestimate the power of a gesture, a power of infinite possibilities in influencing human lives. Gestures make myths and myths make mankind. Today we are all profoundly aware—perhaps because many of us have rejected the idea of an after-life—that we have one short life and death is the end of everything for us. Paradoxically, that fact makes life at the same time more precious than it has ever been and its voluntary surrender a more impressive act. Once, we could romanticize it, revel in its glory, while imagining our hero or heroine safe in heaven, reaping a just reward. Now we know they moulder in the earth and now, for the first time, death really is the supreme sacrifice.

Recently, I read a science-fiction story about a future in which medicine had reached such triumphs of transplant and repair that no one ever died except through an accident of overwhelming dimensions. In that future, people were obsessively safety-conscious. No risks were taken, no person ventured out without taking extremes of preventative and defensive measures. Why? Because the longer life could last, the more years one sacrificed at death, the more 'untimely' death became.

The author might have continued to depict other repercussions. It is possible in such a society (and we are not so far away from it ourselves) that tyranny and crime would flourish because those who wish to impose on others can the more easily do it by threatening that uniquely precious thing, life itself. In the past, when life was cheap and heaven certain, to gamble that life demanded courage but nowhere near the courage the same act demands today.

I would not do what Zebedee Wooding did and I pray

secretly that no one I love would, either. But I also know that we are doomed to pay a high price for the increasing importance we place on remaining alive. Already, too many people know too many other people will not oppose their slightest wish, faced with a gun or a knife or any violent threat. Was Zebedee brave or stupid, proud or pig-headed, heroic or foolhardy? I don't know the answer but I do know that if we all together acted as he did, the worst of hoodlumism would vanish overnight.

11 October 1979

Second-hand Relationships

I HAVE A DISTINCT IMPRESSION that the anthropologists' version of that famous quote from Alexander Pope's essay runs: 'The proper study of mankind is *black* man, or if not actually black, at least poor and a long way off.' Certainly, compared to the volumes written on the habits, kinship ties and family structures of Africans, Polynesians, South American Indians and exotic nomads of various sorts, the books that examine Westerners are remarkably thin on the ground, dealing either with working class communities or treating particular nations as if they were characters in a sit. com.—another way of saying, smugly, aren't we the bee's knees?

Perhaps, as the Third World begins to heave itself out from under the Western yoke in the next decade, we will be forced to see ourselves rather more as others see us and experts on human collective behaviour may at last apply their expertise to us.

In the meantime, may I contribute my own small monograph on observations I have made recently on the odd habit and associated rituals of what could be called 'second-hand relationships', common to most of the Western people I know. The phrase attempts to summarize all those relationships—and they are legion—that are conducted at a careful remove from their subjects, either through someone else or as a part of a group, but never directly between two people, which is the first-hand relationship.

The second-hand relationship often starts right in the home, between the closest of kith and kin and its most frequent practitioners are men. For instance, there are many fathers who maintain only second-hand relationships with their children. They share the same house, they see each other daily in all stages of array and disarray, in all moods, in crises and calms, in sickness and in health but neither father nor child (and by child I mean younger individual) ever manage to be alone together as two separate entities who regard each other closely and attentively and exchange personal thoughts, hopes, fears and preoccupations with each other.

Lectures from the father about school reports or hopeful appeals from the child about increased pocket money do not count. Nor do those halting communications midwife'd by the mother who insists on acting as some sort of UN interpreter, jollying along the one, explaining the other and generally getting in the way, though often, it must be admitted, by popular demand.

Then there is the couple, that bastion of civilization as we know it and one of the worst institutional culprits in forcing second-hand relationships on themselves and others. There are couples who have known other couples most of their mutual coupled lives and yet are quite severely embarrassed when two of the usual four are accidentally left together. Neither are able to talk in any relaxed or open way, both are constrained to keep up the roles they normally play as a foursome (she cute, he macho, she vague, he organized) while uneasily waiting to be rescued by the missing two.

And if one of a couple has a friend, it is as if it were written in letters of fire somewhere 'it is forbidden for the other party ever to approach that friend directly, the one unto the other'. Thus husband's friend remains ritually second-hand to the wife and wife's friend ditto; the ordained second-handedness condemning the two to banalities (nice weather we're having) or, at most, to a jocular flirtatiousness (you look younger every day, I swear. What have you been getting up to?).

Some might explain these constraints as sexual and give examples of such second-hand relationships that have burst their boundaries and flowered into first-hand relationships, in bed. This can happen, of course, but in my view many an ill-considered affair stems purely from the inability to relax and be humanly friendly. The resulting unease is mistaken for sexual tension and, whoops, the two are in each other's arms without the slightest real desire to be there.

'It didn't *mean* anything,' they wail later to their angry spouses and they are right. All it did mean is that they could both manage sex, with all its accompanying complications and regrets, a lot more easily than either could manage to say to the other the equivalent of 'who are you?'.

There are times when I think that almost all male relationships are second-hand, conducted at one remove through their womenfolk. Look around at any gathering, whether it be friends at a dinner party or family at Christmas, and work out who is responsible, not only for the gathering but for those present at it. Ten to one it's a woman. She is the friend of the other women and that accounts for their husbands. She is the link between relatives, his and hers, and that accounts for them. The only exception to the general rule is a business dinner, his business, and that often happens because the men concerned feel they ought to have a closer relationship with colleagues or boss but don't know how to have it without women present to cement things.

There are other taboos. The hierarchy of age is often considered a proper excuse for withdrawing into second-hand relationships. Who expects a parent to talk directly, with any sort of intimacy, to her children's friends? Why, the very thought is vaguely indecent.

When teenagers are present and the child of the house is not, the adult either moves uneasily about clashing pots or hastily turns on the television or, driven, grinds out awful clichés—how's school, haven't you grown, how's your mother—and even these are useful introductions to a proper conversation if they're employed as such and not as ends in themselves. The reluctance to attempt a first-hand relationship is often so great that the adult cannot bring him/herself even to look directly at the young girl or boy concerned.

But if the effort is made in an appropriately serious and diffident way, without using the bolt-hole of a predictable authority, the rewards are great. Veils fall away, masks drop, two human beings in much the same boat, however conventionally distanced by years and by roles, catch a glimpse of each other's reality and, thereafter, are strengthened in an odd way.

Second-hand relationships are the logical outcome of any

insistence on using a role instead of using yourself. I am me, you are you. We are also parents, children, bosses, employees, wives, husbands, mothers-in-law, step-fathers, customers, officials, old, young, teachers, pupils, VIPs, vicars, congregation, MPs, voters, neighbours, baby-sitters, professionals, shop-keepers, aunts and uncles, punks, newly-weds, studs, sex objects.

All these are roles that can be pulled on to disguise what too many of us are at such pains to conceal: that we are vulnerable, unsure, alone, anxious, nervous, childish, ignorant, ridiculous, tired, unimportant. In other words, that we are members of the same human race with the same problems and joys, no matter how different and apparently invincible are our outer trappings.

The rewards of refusing to play a role are first-hand relationships that admit weaknesses and so gain strength. The penalties of playing are second-hand relationships that merely confirm imprisoning roles and, in the end, condemn the inveterate role-player to solitary confinement, cut off from the rest of life.

24 January 1980

What Every Fragment Knows

IT IS AN ODD AND INTERESTING fact that when people say 'I am not political' they usually mean they vote to the Right and this is particularly true of women. Before the last election, I attended a far Left women's meeting where there were activists from the women's movement, Irish women's groups, Communists and Socialist Workers. The women concluded that to many women, conditioned to passivity, Tories were the natural leaders, the ones who said, 'Don't you bother your pretty little heads, we'll do what has to be done,' and the Left, with its emphasis on participation, frightened women who were unused to anyone expecting anything of them but the services of a housekeeper. How, then, to persuade women to the Left?

Beyond the Fragments, by Sheila Rowbotham, Lynne Segal and Hilary Wainwright, addresses itself in part to this question, widened to include all those working-class people who voted Conservative in the last election. 'When the reactionary rhetoric of Tory "freedom" can invoke such a groundswell of working-class support,' says Hilary Wainwright, 'Socialists need to ask...about our inability to translate the awareness of a vanguard of Socialist activists into any lasting change in mass consciousness.' And the question is answered, in part, by a scrutiny of the way in which the women's movement has so successfully involved women and the failure of Socialists to do the same, because they have not recognized that the personal is political and that the way people lead their private lives is crucial to political involvement.

Toryism is intricately enmeshed with what its adherents consider natural emotions. Anyone who has watched the last night of the Proms will know what I mean: the tug of belonging, the crowd euphoria, the identification with a glorious colonial past, with our country right or wrong. Competition, ambition, pride (racial and national), are all ranged against the outsider (racial or national) and the threatening future.

Socialism, on the other hand, posits a way of living that does not yet exist and so cannot yet produce rewards. We are expected to plan for a socialist future and live as if it were already here, yet most of us are conditioned by capitalism and so often find the constant mental and physical effort required not only exhausting but made the more so by having, often, to be practised within socialist frameworks clearly patterned on capitalist ideas of priorities and hierarchies.

It is this framework that the three authors challenge. They pose three fundamental theses. One, that since the Sixties many people have come to a socialist viewpoint through grassroots groups (the 'fragments') concerned with immediate and personal injustices—anything from housing to women's rights. Two, that these groups slowly come to realize that underlying social structures should link them all together in a common fight. And, three, that the major and minor professional Left must change its organization and be prepared to learn from the 'fragments' before a broad socialist movement has any chance either of appealing to such groups or being elected by voters *en masse*.

At the moment, Left-wing parties are unwilling to do much more than note 'special interest' grievances and find it hard to accept that, say, the women's movement has actually lived experiences that are not only invaluable to broader socialism but ought to become an integral part of its whole approach. The great mentors—Marx, Lenin, Trotsky, Engels—were many things but none would have claimed omniscience and are not, as Sheila Rowbotham endearingly puts it, 'the bee's knees in every subject'.

Those who are professional politicians or revolutionaries tend to become locked into theory and thus deny to others one of the essentials for a mass movement: the members' ability to participate actively in forming a new society. Indeed, by setting themselves apart as the vanguard, they confirm others in the very helplessness they pretend to deplore.

One of the great triumphs of the women's movement is the insistence, felt in the guts, that there can be no gap between the hopes, fears, wrongs, and rights of private life and the ideology of politics. No use having endless meetings about injustice when the meetings themselves are so organized and even timed that those unto whom injustice is being done either cannot attend or dare not speak when they do attend.

No use party men making egalitarian resolutions and oppressing their own wives in their own homes. No use, either, splitting off love, friendship, sexual relationships, childcare, women, blacks, gays and the gut-experience of oppression from an abstract ideology overwhelmingly concerned with workers' control and exploitation.

'I really do feel,' says Ms Rowbotham, 'a closeness and love towards women I have known within women's group situations which is quite different from the experience of socialist branch meetings.' And she adds, 'A sure sign of a leader of a Leninist political group is a tendency to look past your eyes and over your head when he talks to you'—because they are on the lookout for a good contact, meaning a shop steward. Her plea is for the human face of socialism.

The professional politico adhering to his interpreted line and, beneath him, all those with special problems, is a recipe for sterility. 'The form in which you choose to organize,' says Ms Rowbotham, 'is not "neutral", it implies certain consequences,' and she describes how women's initial lack of confidence moulded the very structure of the women's movement from its inception. The organization grew out of human needs and existed to answer them.

Women, for instance, fell away from the 1830s Chartist movement because their work at home made it impossible for them to attend meetings as they became more ordered and set. Ms Rowbotham quotes Adriano Sofri, founder of the Italian *Lotta Continua*, who, in the face of criticisms from women and workers, acknowledged that democracy involved not only formally contesting those theories of organization that confined politics to the professionals but also meant examining his own inner sense of being such a professional and that this was 'not a conflict over political lines but a conflict over what politics was all about'.

This is the crux of the future of socialism. The Sixties produced the black movement, women and gay people who wanted change now and realized that their oppression was not simply the classic Left 'class or economic exploitation' but included the personal experience of being subordinated and meant they themselves knew *better* than the professionals what they needed.

Nor could their oppression be hived off from the main political line or grafted on in the form of polite amendments because it questioned the whole body politic. For instance, an abortion campaign raised the issues of personal control over the body, the control men have over women and from thence, the nature of laws, parliament, medical service, childcare facilities, state-determined population policies, investments in contraception and so on, ever outwards into the whole nature of the state and the individual.

This is exactly why such self-help groups give, on the one hand, such injections of vitality into the labour movement and also why, at a certain point, it becomes necessary for them to join a more widely-based movement, a political party. The tragic irony is that just at this point the organized Left fails them, refusing to absorb their lived experience, pushing them out to the fringes, denying their insights in the name of a pure Marxism or Leninism, forcing the separation of the personal from the political and then bewailing the falling-away of the faithful.

What is so heartening and courageous about *Beyond the Fragments* is that three women are willing to stick their necks out and discuss what is, for many politicians (read men) the undiscussable—that is to say, the human feelings that motivate so much of what we do. Many men find this approach so threatening that they either try desperately to dismiss it theoretically, as a deviation of some kind (bourgeois individualism, middle classism, etc.) or they accuse its perpetrators of being frivolous.

Women, within and without the women's movement, have always understood the underbelly of power and known the personal links between individual experience and political stances. Any woman, certainly within the women's movement, is fully aware that it is on the personal level that the truth

282

behind fine words reveals itself and we have given each other the confidence to speak out about what is so easily dismissed as trivial. Political and industrial jargon is too often used to make people feel inferior, ignorant, powerless. Godheads like Lenin and Marx are invoked to put you in your place and the ordinary person fights back in the only way possible—by dropping out.

It is in admitting the relevance of emotion and of the whole way in which people lead their lives and perceive themselves that the women's movement has made a vital step. As Hilary Wainwright sums up: 'It has effectively challenged the self-subordination, the acceptance of a secondary role, which underpins most forms of ·oppression and exploitation...unless such a self-subordination is rejected in the minds of men, of the unemployed, of blacks, gays and all other groups to which socialists aim to give a lead, there will never be much chance of confronting the existing State with a democratic Socialist alternative.'

29 January 1980

True Romance

THERE THEY WERE, gathered round the kitchen table, their shining heads together. Three little maids of four-and-ten, penning Valentines to the lads of their fancy. The Olympic Games may be in jeopardy and Afghanistan at war but roses are red, violets are blue, romance is sweet and so are you. Aaaah.

Curiosity, sadly, killed this cat's illusions. I edged round the table to see what they were writing. Verses, certainly. Illustrated verses, what's more. *Coloured* illustrated verses as meticulously hand-lettered as illuminated manuscripts, each capital letter a little gem of intertwined roses in reds and blues and greens. Beyond that I fear I cannot go, in the pages of a family newspaper.

The three little maids were engraving physiological descriptions of various male adolescents' appurtenances too awful to reveal, except to say that the Happy Hooker herself would have flinched at inflicting such humiliating details of inadequacy upon the most gruesome adult client, never mind upon wretched, acne-ridden, half-sprouted teenage males wracked with all the doubts and fears of their age. Each adjective vied with the next in listing the hopelessness of all possible equipment, mental and physical, I squirmed in deepest sympathy.

'You can't do this,' I said. 'Apart from the fact that these poison pen Valentines reveal the three of you as having minds the like of which would make your average Soho porn merchant blush, you simply cannot push such appalling missives through anybody's post boxes. I hereby forbid it.'

Three flower faces lifted themselves towards me, three sets of orthodontia gleamed. 'Good, in'it?' they said, with modest pride. 'Look,' I said. 'I know the boys on the receiving end of these. One of them is, as you well know, my son. If you send them, I think I'll sue you in his name. I think I'll have you locked up for libel and put away for a life sentence in Borstal. Do you realize, you horrid little womanoids, that boys are sensitive about themselves, just as sensitive as you? That they worry about whether they're normal or not, that they lie in bed fretting over their bodies. That they, too, have feelings?'

Just then, a distant thunder announced the descent of young males down the stairs. The boots of my son and friends appeared round the door, to be followed several seconds later by the rest of them. I attempted to insert my person between the newcomers and the paper obscenities and failed. They were picked up and read.

A minute or so later (reading levels being what they are) my son was stamping about the room, hitting his thighs, doubled up with what passes for laughter in teenage males—a fearsome cacophony of hoots and growls and phlegm-racked coughing noises. His friends by this time, were laid out on the floor, heaving and groaning and beating themselves. The girls regarded this general collapse with small smug smiles. 'Good, in'it?' they said.

After that, things deteriorated. My son, his cheeks aglow with the pleasure of such flattery, kept reading out loud particularly dreadful excerpts denigrating his own physique, much as a war hero might gloat over his mention in dispatches. One friend, green with envy, argued that each insult directed at my son applied equally to him, was actually meant for him.

'Go on,' he kept saying, ''at's never you. 'At's me.' Ignored, forgotten, I went about my legitimate business, regarding them all, these teenage monsters, with wonderment and loathing. Clearly, not one of them had a sensitive cell in their great milk-sodden, protein-logged bodies.

Flashback. Me at 14, loonily in love with one Douglas, blond and blue-eyed limb of the local grammar, recipient of my Valentine card, replete with hearts and tender sentiments, posted with a beating bosom and sealed with careful capitals HOLLAND: Hoping Our Love Lasts And Never Dies. Best friend Moira and I practising filmic embraces, the kind where you go full turn around and then swoop down, like Nureyev and Fontaine in *Swan Lake.*

Boys were romantic and distant creatures then, as different from one's brother peering at spots in the bathroom mirror as willing imagination could take them. Love was a moon in June, sex was a thudding heart and a single kiss. Bodily encumbrances, real or imagined, were nowhere. Nice, we were. Nice, romantic gels, of the kind Barbara Cartland would recognize and Mrs Mary award the Whitehouse Seal of Approval.

Disapproval vented, sobering thoughts intervened. Where, in fact, had romance got me except into the Divorce Courts? If you start from the heights, the hearts and roses, the some-day-my-Prince-will-come and the hand-in-hand-into-the-sunset, reality is too rude a shock to bear.

Who ever sees Casanova in his socks, Don Juan with a runny nose, any matinée idol with a hangover? Those girls at my kitchen table start from the opposite end of the spectrum, from the muddy browns and blacks instead of the shell-pinks. They know the worst, which is to say the least romantic, before they have a hint of the best. Their knowledge of the crummier shores of sex is comprehensive, so their bonus will be the warm and normal. Beady-eyed, they focus on all that can go wrong, so all that can go right is a blessing.

I regard them with a kind of awe not unmixed with envy. From these birds' eye views, there is nowhere to go but up. With steady stomachs, they face the worst the male sex can hand out and come up not only smiling but shrieking with glee. And when I say 'the worst', I mean violence too.

Last week my son informed me that there was a ruck due shortly at his school. 'But I'll be all right,' he said soothingly. 'I know the leader, she's a friend of mine.' 'She?' I said, thus manifesting all my own inner sexist discrimination. It turned out the 'she' had so far, on her own, laid out all the hardest boys at the school and was generally admired and feared, not as a girl but as a 'hard one', a non-gender-identified fighter, a sexual missile who gave, with her two fists and her feet, better than she got.

I was floored just hearing about her, sunk in awe and

admiration. Will this female bomber lose out? Have these girls missed something sweetly innocent, the dawn glow of romance?

Indisputably they have, and a good thing too. Romance, applied to females, was only ever a polite word for such useless and damaging things as ignorance, vanity and the short life-span of a butterfly. Applied to men, it was the sugar coating for the bitter pill of domination, the chivalry that pretended to compensate for the boring inertia of perching on a pedestal.

The three little maids sitting at my kitchen table know nothing of oppression and perhaps it is because of this that their Valentines have no sting. Equality is not romantic but then, it has no sour and repressed edges that injure, either.

14 February 1980

The Acceptable Face of Terrorism

ABOVE THE HOUSE a chopper buzzed and circled, a robot mosquito too big to swat. 'My mother,' said the housewife, frowning up through a bent Venetian blind, 'was a real Christian woman, the kind that never wanted to upset anyone. But I remember a peeler coming to the door and she wouldn't let him in. She told him stay there, son, if you don't mind, because the likes of you bring bad luck on the house. And she sprinkled him with holy water.'

'When I was fourteen,' said another housewife, 'me and Eileen and Tom were coming home one night and Eileen knocked over these milk bottles. A peeler came up and shouted at us and we ran round the corner and Tom yelled "Up the Rebels" and we were lifted for that, taken down to the barracks.'

The stories are endless and the very words used—peeler, barracks—show that long before this decade of trouble, Ulster Catholics saw the police as an alien occupying force. At the end of the Sixties that always strained relationship snapped. Now the police are considered a straightforward arm of the military. Brits in black uniforms. 'Last time they were up here after some man about social security, they all came rushing up in their cars, spilled out and flattened themselves over there and here and behind there with their guns, just like the Brits. We never see them without the Brits, they must be trained by them too.'

So today the people of the Catholic ghettos feel they have no recourse to official law and order, even for everyday motoring problems. 'If someone crashed into my car here,' said one man, 'we'd just have to sort it out for ourselves, we'd neither of us report it.' Women nodded agreement. Nothing, they said, would persuade them to call the police,

288

not even if they were raped. Especially not if they were raped. Thus they live in Ulster: whole communities as effectively lawless as America's Wild West or the Deep South after the Civil War, China post-liberation or Sicily after countless invasions.

Yet despite colonization, war, liberation or invasion, crimes and disputes continue and must be dealt with by some group in some way if total chaos is to be averted. In the American West, the people appointed sheriffs; in the Deep South the Ku-Klux-Klan took over. In China, Communist cadres set up People's Courts and struggle meetings; in Sicily the Mafia was born—the word itself means 'place of refuge'. And in the Catholic areas of Northern Ireland, the Irish Republican Army and its sympathizers do the job. This is a message from one of their posters, headed 'Crackdown on Criminals' and signed by the Belfast Brigade of the IRA:

'In the weeks of September the IRA on request from you, the local Republican population, cracked down on Thieves, Vandals, Sex Offenders and Muggers within the areas. The Summary Justice meted out was, because of the war situation, harsh punishment, and in that one Month, the crime-rate sharply declined. Our Political Opponents and other Bodies in the areas condemned us, despite the fact that you, the Local People, were aware that known Criminals were being punished. These Criminals in the past were punishing you, by breaking into working-class homes and stealing, mugging Old-age Pensioners and sexually assaulting young people. We have canvassed opinion and are happy that you realize the necessity for this short-term though imperfect Policy of dealing with criminals. Our enemies have called for the reintroduction of the hated RUC, as if that would solve things. Areas like the Shankill and Newtownards Rd, where they do patrol, have a crime rate five times ours: so clearly they are not the answer. Crimes reported to us by the People, and demanding action, will be dealt with. First offenders will be given an initial warning. Ideas from you for a less arbitrary method of adjudication (People's Courts etc.) will be studied.'

That message, or words to its effect, must have been duplicated thousands of times across time and the world.

This time, it applies to a part of the British Isles. At the moment, Sinn Fein—the political arm of the IRA—operates five Belfast advice centres open six days a week and four smaller centres open only at night. To their shabby, barricaded doors come the people of the area with their complaints: an old woman has water coming through the ceiling, a wife isn't getting her family allowance, kids setting bonfires are frightening an elderly couple, a woman has had her handbag stolen, another woman wails of her battering husband.

Sinn Fein also run creches for working women, three Peoples' Co-operatives for cheaper food, transport for prisoners' families, and the People's Taxis—eight passengers crushed into old London taxis for 10p each. They spearhead ring road protests, tenants' associations, demolition demands, and environmental enquiries. They organize children's bands and children's holidays in the South and when new groups need help to organize, they teach them anything necessary from how to run off stencils to the writing of press statements. And they are, for better or for worse, the law.

In any country, in peace-time, criminal statistics are tricky figures, capable of being interpreted in many different ways. In Northern Ireland, an outstandingly law-abiding community until the end of the Sixties, any attempt to separate 'ordinary' crime from that connected with the troubles is well-nigh impossible. Of the 55 women currently serving sentences, 51 have committed apparently 'ordinary' crimes. Yet 32 are presently involved in demanding political status and the Northern Ireland Office reckons the nineteen left have all had something to do with the troubles.

Male connections are even more inextricable. Of 1,859 convicted during 1978, only 48 are imprisoned for offences unlikely to be anything but 'ordinary' (sex offenders, drugs). The rest, whether guilty of dangerous driving, burglary, riotous behaviour or malicious damage, could well have done what they did for the cause. Even the destruction of telephone boxes, a common vandal's crime in London, could, in Ulster, be done to prevent informers telephoning out.

The police, sealed off in the outside world, cannot pin down motives with any certainty. British law denies the existence of political crime on the grounds that, in a democracy, wrongs should be righted by the vote and not by violence. The men and women in Ulster prisons demand political status because, among many other grievances, they resent being treated as common criminals when they are arrested as uncommon criminals, under the Emergency Provisions Act. Confusion reigns.

But on the inside, in the areas, it is easier to mark out the motives for crime, easier to distinguish the ordinary from the political. Partly because of this, anger is endemic—they *know* who does what and why, or doesn't do it. Because they know, back doors are still left trustingly open, car doors remain unlocked. Nevertheless, ordinary crimes are committed and problems arise. Who copes? Your man, the Godfather, the paramilitary, the IRA.

'This woman down the road, her boys are getting drinks at the local pub, under age. So she went to your man. The pub got two warnings and then it was blown up.' 'This woman, her husband kept beating her up, wouldn't give her any money. She went to your man and he got a good lacing.' A man rapes a girl and gets a concrete block dropped on his feet. Another mugs an old lady and gets kneecapped (these days more generally a flesh wound in buttocks or calves). Your man visits lads making trouble and they don't make trouble again.

Am I saying, then that the IRA and its cohorts are some kind of gun-toting social workers? Do I pretend that men who maim and kill children with random bombs are actually Clark Kents, always ready to strip in to Supermen and zoom off to avenge the weak? The myth of the vigilante, the Robin Hood, the Jesse James, is ancient and seductive and, in everyday life, grim; a lot nearer to the real Mafia than the surreal Superman. The heart may leap up to hear of one crime avenged and sink with horror to hear of another, far murkier, execution.

Whatever you get, you pay for and the price of unofficial justice is high. Underage drinking may be stopped in one place only to be encouraged at another, run by the paramilitary. Random juvenile vandalism may be prevented but the same lads may then be recruited for far more destructive and lethal jobs. Battered women may be protected one day and battered by their protectors another, for stepping out of line. The paramilitary look after their own on the understanding that their own will look after them.

This arrangement is, at best, rough justice but what other options are there when, for whatever reason, official justice has been rejected? If all the normal barriers have broken down, they must be rebuilt in some form, however rough, and at least in close communities, forced in upon themselves and clearly identifiable, a great deal is known about each individual member, a fact that offers short-cuts to decisions on guilt that, in London, would require a vast organization to establish. Even then, mistakes are made. Even then, some would say, justice is often rough enough.

The community role of the IRA is the acceptable face of terrorism and there always is one. Guerrillas turn monstrous faces to the world, murderers' masks, the blank visages of psychopaths. But the faces turned inward, towards their own people, are different and unless we recognize the human beings beneath the masks we shall never understand how they gain and keep support and so never resolve the war.

19 February 1980

The First World Chauvinist and the Third World Woman

IF I WERE A THIRD WORLDER with any inkling of the dealings between my half of the planet and the West, I would by now be reduced to arranging my fingers in the sign that wards off the evil eye whenever a First Worlder hove in sight, under whatever toupee. Whether we come in the guise of explorers, missionaries, colonial servants or governors, agribusinessmen, multinational executives or members of charity organizations, we have been, are and may always be, individually and collectively, the Wicked Witches of the West whose spells bring death and disaster, whose demonic brooms leave swathes of destruction wherever they sweep.

Some of us arrived to exploit, some of us meant and mean nothing but good, yet our motives, taken as a whole, have been irrelevant because we ourselves are ignorant of what we do and are blind to the infinite variety and subtleties of the societies into which we blunder. On our backs we bring our own unconscious luggage, all the assumptions, attitudes and customs that make up our civilization. But in our arrogance, in our belief that what we are is best, we are unaware of these encumbrances and so we dump them, all unknowingly, upon quite other attitudes and customs, distorting and deforming and obliterating them in the process. Thus, like an upsidedown King Midas, everything we touch turns to dross.

Barbara Rogers, in her book *The Domestication of Women*, reveals this endemic Western blindness. I hasten to add, for fear of alienating readers, that Ms Rogers does not attempt to stir the emotions through harrowing emphasis on swollen bellies or other descriptions of physical suffering. She sticks to the facts, to the links between cause and effect, to the outline of policies that, however well meant, wreck what they set out to cure. Ms Rogers is concerned only with the

293

international aid agencies and the way in which their programmes have affected what one can only, in the end, be called their victims—women.

Ms Rogers's overall message is that ever since the first colonial servant set foot in the Third World, Western emissaries have brought their own particular brand of female oppression with them. Since it was men who colonized, men who administrated and, right up to the present, men who select those who receive aid, women in the countries they colonized, administrated and now subsidize, not only continued to suffer but suffered the more as both Western bureaucrat and Third World men conspired to ignore them and walk roughshod over the rights they once had. To the men of the old British Colonial Service, women were domestic creatures. Whether they were worshipped for their sweet fragility or despised for their supposed inferiority made little difference, since one idea was paramount. Women's place was in the home, women's work was the care of the household, the mothering of children, the servicing of husbands.

Deep in the cerebral tissue of Western man is cut the Western pattern that seems to them God-ordained—marriage is monogamous, the husband is head of the household and breadwinner, woman is his dependant. Solely through his endeavours and his worldly goods is she endowed and her contribution is the production of children and the more or less skilled management of his largesse. To this day, the largely male-staffed aid agencies assume that if poverty exists and funds are available, to the man shall go the funds and the woman (if the funds extend that far) shall go to classes in Home Economics.

Undaunted, blinkers carefully in place, we proceed to distribute our monies with one more-or-less acknowledged aim in view—to reform 'primitive' attitudes to coincide with our own, ignoring any indications that these attitudes may, at times, be ahead of our own, as Ms Rogers makes dazzlingly clear.

To begin with, most aid programmes and even the research that goes into the backbone of those programmes, rest on the unquestioning assumption that a male is the head of the household, chief producer of the family's food, owner of the family or tribal land and, often, the only sex polled for statistics on anything from literacy to prevalence of disease. *Cherchez l'homme*, goes the message, and only when you've got him may you then dole out the goods, whether in hard cash grants for redevelopment projects, agricultural technology, agricultural know-how, medicine, education or land reform.

So-called primitive societies, however, do not conveniently conform to the requirements of these surveys or the red tape of grant allocations, though the history of colonization right up to the present day aid insists, against all signs visible and invisible, that they do and twists them till they do.

In many parts of Africa and Latin America, for instance, heads of households are women, either because of tribal custom and polygamy or because of male emigration to towns or abroad. Yet Western men, anxious to fill in the proper forms, frequently ignore the facts and enter a man's name, thus making him the sole recipient of monies.

Another Western dogma is that land must be owned by men and so men are diligently sought who will give credence to this dogma, sometimes in ignorance of what they are actually being asked.

The facts, though unwritten and undeeded, are often otherwise. Land may be owned outright by women through the matrilineal line, but matrilineality, being unknown or unsettling to Western men, is brushed aside. Land may also 'belong' to a man but be given in lifetime possession to wives, widows, and other women relatives for the production of family food and this, too, is frequently ignored.

Indeed, in many parts of the Third World, it is women who are solely responsible for growing the food that feeds the family but as this function does not fit in with Western ideas of the male breadwinner they receive few benefits. Quite often, men are corralled into classes on agricultural techniques while the women, who actually do the work, are left out.

Many Third World surveys count only male working hours, called *man*-units, and women's working hours remain uncharted because it is assumed she is concerned only with housework and child-tending, like the Western image of womenfolk.

Thus, in the name of aid, many women have literally been robbed of their traditional land rights in order to funnel monies towards male education and male-run cash crops. Where such agencies do consider women, it is at the level of Western-type home economics classes that teach women better nutrition, often an unmitigated disaster since the adviser may shift the women towards expensive imported foods and away from the locally grown food that, unknown to Westerners, supplies the necessary vitamins quite satisfactorily.

Ms Rogers cites such ineptitudes as teaching the use of disposable nappies in localities where not only are there no nappies, disposable or otherwise, but it is the males who traditionally care for the children.

Ms Rogers's examples are many, varied and appalling and her suggestions for late remedy—the staffing of agencies with non-Establishment-linked women of the country—so obvious and highly unlikely to happen in time to prevent further deprivations.

Recently West German Chancellor Willy Brandt presented his views for the urgent reshaping of relationships between the West and the developing countries. He describes his call to action as 'a crucial commitment to the future of mankind...We believe this to be the greatest challenge to mankind for the remainder of this century.'

But under 'mankind', will anyone read 'womankind'?

21 February 1980

Saturday Night Fever

IT MUST HAVE BEEN nice in the long ago when invitation cards were read in high excitement over the breakfast silver. Oh la, Mamma, Robert and I are bidden to attend Lady Evangeline's birthday ball this day a month cum Michaelmas. Pray let us send for the seamstress upon the instant. Plenty of time, then, for the trimming of fichus and the refurbishing of breeches, plenty of evenings for strict parental injunctions as to dancing partners and the finer points of the curtsey. No necessity at all for worry, since everyone who was anyone knew everyone and, anyway, Mammas would be there as chaperones, gossiping over their fans. Things weren't too bad in my time, for that matter. Boogie records, fruit cup and a bit of smooch in the sitting-room while the parents lurked upstairs or came in shortly after midnight, full of *fausse bonhomie.*

But today? Unless you live in a stately home on Jennifer's Diary list or a derelict squat on the local cop shop's list, forget it. Teenage parties, fondly imagined by uninitiated parents to be the cosy way of introducing lass to lad, are seen by large numbers of those lasses and lads as convenient short cuts to four desirable ends: a. drink, b. sex, c. dope, and d. mayhem, though not necessarily in that order.

In a moment of innocence, I offered my son the freedom of the house for a birthday frolic, only to see his face whiten with shock. 'A party? What, here? At home? No *thanks,'* he said and gave the short dry laugh of the Grim Reaper. Once that refusal might have mean the boy was ashamed of his surroundings. Now, as I came to realize, it was proof of his tenderest affection for us, for his home and for his own neck. Parties, he informed me, as one who instructs the mentally retarded, were for going to, not for having.

'But you're invited to so many. I thought you'd want to invite people back.'

'Invited?' he said.

'Yes, invited. Asked, requested, importuned, petitioned. Invited.'

'Oh. Ah. Well. Yes. To *some* I am,' he said, looking shifty. 'Could you get me a razor?'

'A razor?' I said.

'Yes, a razor. A blade, a Gillette, a Wilkinson's, a . . .'

But I digress. Slowly it dawned upon me that being a party-goer, at least in London, at least in 1980, had nothing in the wide world to do either with knowing the family who gave the party or even the teenager for whom the party was given. The workings are otherwise. On Fridays, about 4 p.m., family front doors across the city open. The returning scholars (for it is they) first make themselves a snack (ten slices of bread, a half-pound of Cheddar and two tins of Sainsbury's sliced peaches) and, thus fortified, begin the serious business of the weekend upon the telephone.

'Mike? Anything doing? Oh yeah? Great. Where? What's she look like? Camden? Ben'll know. Look, I'll ring Ben and I'll ring you back but you keep ringing and ring me back if I don't ring you. Right? Right.'

'Ben? What's happening? Oh come on, mate. Yeah? Great. You get me in, I'll get you in up Archway, Saturday. No I won't. O.K. See you.'

'Mike? It's on, come over. Dan? Vince? Janet? O.K. but don't tell anyone else, right? Right.'

So it goes and if, perchance, it doesn't, if no one that Friday knows of a party or isn't letting on, plan two goes into action. Toilettes accomplished (Vaseline on hair, Clearasil on spots, a stroke of the magic razor over hairless chins, for luck) they pound off into the twilight zones, to the district listening posts, the underground stations. Once there, at Hampstead, at Golders Green, at any likely tube, they hang about like flocks of gaudy vultures, eyeing each new clump of kids, mingling, exchanging notes.

One of the distinctive features of comprehensive schools, as opposed to old-style boarding schools, is that the daytime

298

inmates know every kid within their neighbourhood and each kid has another circle of friends and contacts in a different school and the friends have friends have friends that extend yea unto the furthest corners of the metropolis, thus creating a network of possible parties that stretches both sides of the river and back via Kentish Town.

So a group moves deliberately off from the underground and others follow, bidden or unbidden, and the motley crew eventually arrive at a designated front door. This is crunch time because very much depends on who opens that door. It may be the teenage host with muscle, in which case the uninvited will be turned away, to drift back to the underground or, depending on their sort, heave bricks through the window. It may be a teenage hostess, in which case blandishment may work or, at worst, storm trooper tactics. Parties being what they are, the door-opener is often the latest arrival, who either lets everybody in anyway, without question, or happens to be the soul-mate of one of the outsiders. Thus everyone in the group will be through the portals in a flash and threaded invisibly into the crowd within before you can say Sid Vicious.

And there they all are, a mixed and mixed-up bag. Little girls in black leather jackets and tight tight jeans, teetering sideways on steeple heels, mouths the colour of a heart attack. Gangly great yobs with hair like sunbursts or shaven an inch past the scalp. A few, over there, are pogo-ing up and down to the sound. Some are wholly dedicated to pouring beer down their throats. A few, in a dark and aromatic corner, are exchanging flakes of a brown substance and laughing a lot and up and down the stairs go both sexes, in search of dim beds or the family jewels.

As the evening wears on, various events are more or less likely to take place. A girl will have hysterics and gain herself a lot of attention. Five boys will get drunk, one will lock himself in the loo and the others, perforce, will relieve themselves of pain upon the best Afghan. Some will continue to behave in a reasonable way. Others will crush cigarettes out on antique table tops, climb on to roofs, collide into greenhouses, knock down ornaments and fall into furniture. By this time, the children of the house are either taking part in these activities or having panic attacks at the thought of Dad's face.

The worst that can happen is the crashing of the party by groups intent solely on looting. Under cover of the general cacophony this lot, who probably know no one there, nick everything they can safely lay their hands on, even to the organized extent of forming a firemen's line and emptying a handy cabinet of all its contents—silver, cutlery, plates, vases.

So, at one party given some months ago, the list of the evening's damage ran as follows: one plate-glass window worth £500; 20 pairs of socks, one drawer full of jumpers, a tape recorder, a colour television pitched from a verandah, ten steaks from the freezer, innumerable broken glassware and a pond of dead goldfish, drowned in beer. The police, called too late, could do nothing. Next morning, parents all over the area were telephoned with varying accusations: they said they saw your son heave the brick, they said the others said they saw your son take the telly, they said your daughter knows the lot that splintered the table. Denials, recriminations, outrage filled the air.

No one knew anything. No one could judge anything. No one could even make any prejudiced guesses. The skinhead seen lurking in the bushes turns out to be a TV celebrity's son. The whey-faced punk last glimpsed by the freezer is the local doctor's issue. The two lads who tidy up in the small hours come from the local boys' home. The parents question their children, the children react with outraged indignation, the parents, weak with relief, press no further and keep their fingers crossed until delinquent adolescence is passed. Parties, in other words, are not good scenes.

So does that mean the end of them, once children have gone beyond the stage of jellies and jam tarts and pin-the-tail-on-the-donkey? For the timid, the neat and the indifferent, probably yes. But for the stouter-hearted, ways can still be devised, things can still be wangled to make surer that less goes wrong, particularly if the teenagers concerned are worldly-wise and know who's who, as well as what's what. Rooms above local pubs can be hired for the evening, with all the advantages of beer-soaked cachet and men on the premises in case of trouble.

300

Parties in a home well cleared of nickable goods (or well-locked doors) can be policed by a couple of local bruisers, hand-picked for muscle and ferocious appearance—Dads, no matter how massive, are merely embarrassing. There are, it is rumoured, some few staggeringly trendy parents who manage to share a party with their teenagers, booze and joints and all, but this, I feel, is terminal togetherness—either they are too young for their age or their children too old.

17 April 1980

That's How They do Things Over There

ONE OF THE MAJOR TOURIST OCCUPATIONS—a pleasure that often takes precedence over anything that Nature has to offer, or Michelangelo for that matter—is shopping. And as all of us will know who have ever read a tourist guide, as opposed to Mungo Park or Sir Richard Burton, shopping involves bargaining and bargaining begins at Calais. Mary and Roger will tell you as much and Mary and Roger have been around.

'Oh, you *have* to bargain. I mean, that's the way they do things over there, don't they, Roger? They'll give you a price and then you offer a quarter of what they ask and you go on from there. We've spent whole days just bargaining, haven't we, Roger?'

Roger taps his nose, narrows his eyes, winks, nods, confirms Mary's exhortation and adds the details so vital to the innocent neophyte. When you name your first price, the shopkeeper will look stunned, desolate, as amazed as if he'd never heard of bargaining in all his life before. He will roll his eyes to heaven and implore you to think of his wretched wife and eight starving children. He will invoke the name of his dead grandmother for your shame and pity. But you must walk away, pretending a total disinterest and he will let you go, oh quite a way, sometimes, and then come running after you to start the whole business over again on a descending scale. And eventually, if you are a traveller as sophisticated and as adept as Mary and Roger, you will get what you wanted at—guess what—one sixteenth of what the same would cost you in England if you could find it. The Holy Grail of tourism. The bargain. And wagging their fingers earnestly, shouting last instructions, Mary and Roger turn and dive, yet again, into the crowded bazaars or souks

302

or flea markets, clutching their handbags and their wallets, their faces alight with the glow of Jehad.

The world clearly divides into two sorts of people, the Marys and Rogers who see bargaining as a duty and the others, irresponsibles like me, for whom the very idea causes a light sweat to bedew the brow. Many are the countries I have trekked through without buying so much as an ashtray because I cannot bring myself to start this ambiguous and time-consuming process. So bad am I, in fact, that even in this country I will not enter, say, a junk shop if there are no prices displayed, for fear that what I hoped would be £10 turns out to be £100.

I am aware, of course, that Mary and Roger are accurate enough in their assessment of foreign ways. I know enough about certain stallholders in this country to realize that they spot suckers a mile away and raise their prices accordingly. Nevertheless, when it comes to bargaining in the poorer parts of the world, something about such received tourist wisdom smells faintly but distinctly rotten. To begin with, the half of the asking price that Mary and Roger would have you offer is half of the fraction you would pay at home. The game, then, is to whittle down this fraction into a fraction of a fraction. For example, a dress that would cost £15 in England (and cheap at that price) is initially offered for £3 and must be squabbled over for 10 minutes, with all the statutory coming and going, until it is finally bought for £1.50. I must do this because otherwise, God forbid, I am being rooked, ripped-off, taken for a ride. I, who earn more in a week than many of the people of that country earn in a year. *Quelle catastrophe.*

A few weeks ago, I stood on a dusty streetcorner in Delhi and—all that bargaining lore ringing in my ears—offered half what a seller was asking for a painting on cloth. Eventually, I paid her three-quarters of what she wanted. As money changed hands, a large and be-jewelled white woman passed by. 'How much?' she asked. I told her. 'I paid *half* of that for *two*,' she said scornfully and bustled on, virtue trembling in every fold of flesh. The virtue of having extracted from the workshops of the poorest people in the world two cloth paintings that cost, by her standards, nothing.

Ah now, hold on a minute, Mary and Roger are here to tell you that by paying nothing, you are *spoiling* these people. Besides, do you not realize that your money never gets to those who actually *make* the merchandise? The woman you bought from looked poor enough, you say? Possibly so, but how naïve of you to think that paying her will enrich the even poorer. Better, apparently, by far, to screw the lot of them than risk, even for a moment, your two-pence-halfpenny falling into the wrong hands.

Nor, of course, must you dare to commit the most irresponsible sin of all—giving to beggars. Only the greenest of the green do that. All that happens, as you part with less than a farthing, is that other beggars materialize from under your feet and pester the life out of you for your stupidity. Wave their bandaged stumps at you and otherwise discommode you. And, as with shopkeepers, these beggars are not the *real* beggars. Mary and Roger imply that these are imposters, con men. That under their rags and their deformed flesh are wads of notes that Getty would have envied, riches that enable them, at night, to rip off their rags and bed down in palaces.

Do you know, say Mary and Roger, drawing closer to impart their nuggets, do you *know* that some of these beggars maim their own children to make you give? Not, as you might stupidly think, because they are driven to such horrors by a murderous poverty. No, no. They are actually tycoons who *like* chopping off children's hands for a farthing from you. Nice work if they can get it. And, obviously, it is your job, you Western tourist—nay, verily, your duty—to end such fearful practices by refusing to give even those coins too small to reproduce in your own currency.

Mary and Roger invite me to imagine, hidden from sight in the unimaginable recesses of a tattered city, the poor who are *too proud* to beg, and the people who exist on a pittance of the pittance you pay, in your profligate way, to the seller. Their invisible nobility, their true poverty, is conjured up to justify Mary and Roger's refusal to give a sou to the cringing, whining front men, the underserving poor. You don't want the wrong people to profit, do you? The fact that, curiously, you never meet the right people, is beside the point. Clench your fists, close your purse, shout at them all to go away and rot. Otherwise, a fearful fate will befall you. The stall-holders scratching a living from the recycled goods of the world, the leprous beggars who dare approach you in the streets *will not respect you.* And how can a Western tourist staying at the Grand Hotel possibly be expected to endure such a fate?

8 May 1980

How to Make Friends

'MEN,' THE WOMEN TOLD each other when I was a girl, 'only want one thing.' Well, a lot about the relationship between the sexes has improved since those simple-minded days and girls are no longer branded good or bad, depending on whether they will or won't give a man what he wants. Nor do men today only want one thing. Indeed, listening to three 20-year-old college girls talking about men last week, I found myself thinking that the one decision of yesteryear appeared positively restful compared with the complexities of sexual mores today.

None of the girls were virgins. Their preoccupation bore no resemblance to the one aired so often in the magazines of my day: Dear Agony Auntie, my boyfriend wants me to go the whole way, should I? Dear Worried Blue Eyes, no, dear, he won't respect you. They had no Rubicon of sex to cross, they had already gone the whole way with boyfriends and the question of respect had never arisen—the relationship lasted or it didn't and that was all. But what did concern them was the impossibility of having men friends, without sex.

'What happens,' said the first girl, 'is you meet a man at a party, at college. You get talking, the conversation is interesting, he's interesting, you like him, he likes you. Then he asks if you can meet again and your heart sinks. You already know, either because you've got a sexual partner or just because you know, that you aren't going to sleep with him. But you also know that, inevitably, he's going to make a pass at you, inevitably you're going to say no and inevitably he'll drift away. Often, now, I say no to another meeting, simply because I can't face the whole boring scenario one more time.'

'I know,' said the second girl, 'and it's all such a waste. I got talking to this man the other day. He was obviously really lonely and a nice bloke. I'd have been happy to see him again, have a drink, the odd lunch, the odd movie. But I've got John, I sleep with him and I don't want to sleep with anyone else at the moment. What was I supposed to do? Say to him, embarrassingly, look, I'd like to be a friend but no sex, right? And maybe offend him because he wasn't thinking of sex anyway? Or leave it, go out with him and know in my bones that we'll have to face the same scene later? It's really awful to feel so constricted. You want to offer friendship but you fear that's not what's wanted. How many times do you risk it before you cut yourself off for good from the idea of men as friends?'

'I met this man,' said the third girl, 'and I told him almost immediately that there was no question of sex, that I had a boyfriend, and he seemed to understand. Over the next four months, we really had fun together. I liked him a lot, we argued, we discussed everything under the sun, I thought we were really friends. Then, he met a girl who did sleep with him. Fair enough. But he vanished. Apparently, everything we'd had together meant nothing to him compared to having sex. I was really hurt.'

'It makes you wonder about sex itself,' said the first girl. 'I don't have a particular boyfriend and I will sleep with different men, if I want to, but that doesn't mean I want to sleep with every man I'd like as a friend. You miss a lot, though, feeling like that. One girl I know automatically sleeps with every man she quite likes, not for sex but to keep them as friends. And she has a great time. There was one man, for instance, she went across Europe with him on holiday, in his car, paying her own way and enjoyed every minute, she said. She didn't much want to sleep with him but she knew it wouldn't work unless she did. I know that because he asked me first, and I'd *love* to have gone, for the fun and because he's a good companion. It was no good, though, because I couldn't sleep with him. He didn't ask, I just knew it was taken for granted.'

The girls went on talking. Perhaps, they said, casual sex between friendly people was the best thing. Perhaps their view, that sex was special, only came down to some sort of conditioning or a temperamental quirk of a sort—some did, some didn't and the lucky ones did. They all agreed that those lucky ones didn't sleep with men for gain. They didn't want diamond rings or dinner at the Ritz or rich husbands or champagne and gifts. They just wanted male companionship and if the hassle was sex, then they got it over with, right away.

Those girls—and the word promiscuous never came up nor was, I imagine, even thought—had another advantage. When they stopped sleeping with one man, for whatever reason, they usually kept that man as a friend, even if he had sex with another girl. It was a bond between them and the bond lasted. Perhaps they would all be better off to accept that sex was just one of the ingredients of friendship between men and women, no more and no less.

Listening to them, I wondered myself. Obviously, these nice intelligent girls were talking about nice and intelligent men. Obviously, too, relationships between them were gentler and easier in general, *particularly* when sex was involved. The problem was almost the opposite of the one that had obsessed my girlhood—men no longer wanted one thing, they wanted (and were prepared to give) everything. Companionship, shared interests, fun, equality, support, kindness and sex. But sex was essential; without it, a girl was shut out, deprived of the rest on offer.

What it comes down to is a very ancient question. Must the sexes continue to be divided by the sexual act? Are we all more or less forced to categorise the opposite sex as Sex and so reserve friendship solely for our own sex? Is old age the only way to end sex and begin friendship? Here we are, after all, with thousands of young people who will only reach middle-age in the first decade of a new century and still, it seems, the 1940 Agony Auntie's problem—shall I go all the way?—is the great gap between men and women.

It may be that all those generations of focusing on Sex as Sin, plus one generation of selling Sex as Virtue, has still missed the happy medium—sex as sex, as normal a part of a whole relationship as talking and listening, comforting and laughing, sharing ideas or sharing a meal. Seen any other way, seen as 'special', it seems doomed to divide.

22 May 1980

Holding On

I despair of the West at times. We seem to be impotent in the face of any violent and unreasonable tyrant, bankrupt of any ideas about how to cope with irrational dictators. America can do nothing about the Iranian hostages and neither we, the Greeks nor the Italians can stop Colonel Gaddafi's campaign to liquidate his opponents by the simple means of shooting them down in our countries, on our streets. What is wrong with our rulers, what has happened to democracy that it is so apparently powerless when confronted with any sort of oligarchy?

THIS LETTER is just one among many such that have been filling my postbag since the beginning of this year, all of them expressing the same doubts and fears, the same loss of confidence in the effectiveness of democracy in a world that sometimes seems hell-bent on creating the sort of local crises that carry, within them, the looming threat of wider conflict, even nuclear war. Readers write about their anxieties for their children's future and about their reluctance to have children in what they see as an increasingly unstable world. Some readers are so pessimistic that they fear nuclear war will finish off a large proportion of the human race by the end of the Eighties.

All I can contribute to these worries is my own personal view. Leaving aside any specific conflict-by-conflict analysis, whether in Iran, Afghanistan, Israel, Libya, Saudi Arabia, Pakistan, or the Lebanon—analyses I am in no way competent to carry out in any case—I am left with no more than a general philosophy that focuses mainly on the point about the impotence of democracy when faced with any challenge from dictatorships.

309

Many commentators today seem to believe that if democracy cannot immediately cope with the irrational behaviour of tyrants and demagogues, it is then revealed as a flawed or even useless system. You can feel their impatience with the slow processes of Parliament and law, you can practically see their trigger fingers itching, you can sense their frustration in the words they use—'impotent', 'paralysed', 'incompetent,' 'weak'. Unconciously, perhaps, they assume that if democracy is all it's cracked up to be, it must instantly be able to bop all its enemies on the head and lay them low, as proof of its superiority.

Unfortunately, the test of democracy lies elsewhere and to expect it to prove itself simply in terms of muscle-power is to confuse its purpose, if not to mistake it completely. There are inherent and probably endemic weaknesses in any democratic system. It is, in many vital ways, ill-fitted to cope with tyranny and I, personally, can see no way in which it can become better-fitted without losing its essential ingredients.

If you are a reasonable, rational and law-abiding individual who implicitly accepts certain limits of behaviour beyond which you are neither used nor prepared to go, you will have a hard job to preserve your rights, your liberty or even your life against another individual who recognizes none of these limits. In everyday domestic life, within a democracy, those people who are not prepared to lie, cheat or use violence to gain their ends are quite likely to be done down by others who ignore such ethics.

One of the basic injustices of life is that a conscience, an awareness of a code of behaviour and a refusal to discard that code is no guarantee of victory, success or survival. A sane man, faced with a homicidal maniac, may well be killed. A woman, faced with a rapist, may be unable to defend herself through lack of physical strength but she may also be rendered unable because she cannot summon up enough violence to kick him where it hurts *before* she is in no position to kick at all.

In other words, any deeply held belief in an ethical code that outlaws violence and is used to respecting other people's rights rests on the hope of reciprocity and if that is lacking, it renders both individuals and countries what many call impotent. The paradox is that only by discarding the principles that make for democracy can a country regain potency against the undemocratic.

If you, believing deeply in non-violence, in reason and in law, are confronted by me, axe in hand, with no such scruples, you have only two choices. Either you give up your beliefs and fight for survival or hold on to those beliefs and risk death. And if, giving up the beliefs, you win the battle and live, you may almost immediately feel that having betrayed your deepest principles, the ones upon which your life was based, then merely surviving is in some way worthless.

In the same way, democracy is inherently vulnerable when faced with tyranny. Democracy does not prepare itself to confront undemocratic methods and those who love peace find it almost impossible to prepare for war, in spite of the cliché that would have us do just that. Apart from any other argument, preparing for war today, in the hope of preserving peace, is so costly and so psychologically threatening as to seriously deprive that peace of any quality and may even, directly, add to the chances of war.

I myself am resigned to the view that if we, the human race, cannot manage to live in peace and if democracy is somehow fated to succumb to tyranny, then I would rather be defeated than give up those principles. In a way, I am even proud that democracy is impotent when faced with tyranny, reason powerless against unreason and pacifism useless against aggression. To many of us, being human has to be synonymous with an ethic and an ability to choose one's behaviour, even if that behaviour makes survival unlikely, otherwise 'being human' is meaningless. Democracy must be judged upon its ability to give a nation's people a say in the way they wish to lead their lives and not upon whether it is as good as other systems at imposing violence or winning battles. Perhaps one man's idea of weakness is only another man's idea of strength.

29 May 1980

311

Doing the Continental

EUROPE. YURUP. A curious sound, that. More a cowboy's cattle call than anything originally, mythically, Greek. Labelled European myself, I have differing reactions, depending on where I am and who does the labelling. In America I feel European but if Americans in Britain address me as such I look involuntarily about me to see whom they mean. And if the French, the Germans, the Dutch, or the Italians include me in I am faintly embarrassed, as if I were letting them assume some close family kinship that only I know does not, in fact, exist.

It is all very complicated and made no simpler by tourism. We, wishing to visit, must cross water at some expense and so cannot help seeing ourselves as 'the English, going to Europe'. What's more, most of us go on holiday, which is to say we pick the most backward parts of that continent in which to disport ourselves. In Italy, we choose Florence, Venice, Pisa, not Milan nor Turin. In Holland we bypass Eindhoven and Rotterdam for Amsterdam and Gouda. In France, we head in the opposite direction from Lille or Clermont-Ferrand, and to Germany...well, to Germany we hardly go at all. Coalmines, steel works, car factories and agribusiness do not march hand in hand with touristic delights and so we, like the holidaying Americans, are caught in a European time-warp.

Recently, in the *Chicago Sun-Times*, a cartoon summed up this anachronistic view. Depicted: a grinning boyish Carter-figure holding an umbrella labelled NATO over another sheltering person. And who could this person be, in his black jacket, his pin-striped trousers, his homburg hat and his mean, pinched features, slyly stabbing the Carter-figure in the ribs with his rolled umbrella? Why, a European is who. The nasty, cringing, medieval lot. Yet the fact is that if the

Americans—and ourselves—occasionally glimpsed the real-life centres of Europe, they would think they were back home and we...well, we wouldn't.

To drive from Ostend, circling Brussels and Liège and zooming ever onwards on the E5, over the German border into the Rhineland, is an eye-opener to all but seasoned Eurocrats. Vast highways ablaze with lights whistle with racing and disciplined cars that, stopping for a moment to tank up, can pay in anything from francs to sterling. Farmland stretches as far as the eye can see, with never a blade of grass unclipped or a straw out of place. More street-wise data flashes up for drivers than anything we or the Americans provide: automatic computed road-signs inform you of exactly what speed you must keep to hit every green light and at borders, marked only by brighter lights, a flash of passports at the windscreen and you're revving and away again.

In the towns, not a single discarded cigarette pack, not a bus ticket blowing in a gutter signals messy human life. All around, dwarfing the old church, the one ancient monument, soar glassy office buildings, gigantic intercontinental hotels, huge water towers and gasometers and sci-fi chimneys and the enormous shopping precincts are crammed full of goodies. Fountains flow, music blares, people bustle, spotless trains rush into spotless stations, everything works.

Within my English bosom, conflicts rage. How prosperous, clean, efficient it all is and how deeply un-English. Is that a good thing or a bad, something to be desired or disliked, envied or rejected? How much of my divided reaction is jealousy, how much a kind of warning? An American abroad, in this part of Europe, would fall back amazed. This shining, gleaming, hand-manicured and modern machine, the Old Country? Never. Whereas I see Europe as England's future, and it works. But do I want it?

Settling for a few days into the hubbub, Europeans approached me and talked of the EEC. Their faces were puzzled, reproachful. Why were we being so difficult? Did we not want...all of this? One man, peering anxiously at me, asked how we thought we could survive if we left the Community. I argued Commonwealth links, access on better terms to EEC food mountains. He frowned and muttered worriedly. I caught the words militarily unstable island...the Russians...Wedgie-Benn.

A German MP attacked on the domestic front. Surely the English housewife could see the advantages? Surely she wanted six grades of eggs and identical graded Golden Delicious? I gulped and said I admit that some of us could. Perhaps being a housewife in England was not quite the life's career it obviously was in Europe? Even so, said the German, knitting her brows, grading means value for money. How is that not *better*? Foxed, I lapsed for a sullen moment and rose again. Because, I said, we don't want more decisions. I think we may think they're not that important. The German fell back, foxed in her turn. Not important? Six grades of eggs, all carefully priced not *important?* Sadly, she surveyed me, an obstinate lump upon her velvet sofa. You know, she said kindly and patiently, you *are* Europeans. And we are all so disappointed in your lack of European spirit. So very disappointed.

Next day, I sat on the sofa of an English EEC executive in Brussels. The Germans say they are disappointed in us, I said. Do you think they are right? A dull flush mantled the cheeks of this cool, urbane and polyglot Anglo-Saxon. He stiffened. Disappointed, are they? he said. Well, *I* was disappointed in *them* when they entered Poland. I was *very* disappointed when they marched into Holland and France. Disappointed, indeed. Huh.

His cover broken, he assured me that though he was no Thatcher man himself, he had a long memory. He remembered Monsieur de Gaulle saying Non. Non, non, non. He could not help, therefore, feeling a certain thrill when Madame Thatcher appeared, perfectly coiffed, and told those gentlemen No. No, no, no. Do them good, he thought, secretly.

Nevertheless, I said. There is Europe, all efficiency and modernity and apparent prosperity and there is us, all crumbling stately homes and litter and inflation. Was there something deeply wrong, were we a cul-de-sac off-shore island? Could we, in fact, manage at all if we ever left the EEC? Manage? he said. Look at Iceland. No help from

314

anyone, no alliances, no nothing and the most truly and deeply democratic country in the world. If we had to, of *course* we could manage. But don't they live on fish alone? I said. So what, he said.

Personally, I don't feel European. Personally, I am anti-Common Market. But those four days made me pause, made me uneasy. Was I hopelessly out of touch and out of date? Were we all? A memory rose up, ridiculous and, somehow, disturbing. The huge central square in Cologne, clean as a whistle, its steps polished, its paving marred by nary a curl of dust, its underground lavatories sparkling, its over ground cafés irreproachably hygienic. And out of the general bustle, an English girl appears, looks around and turns to her English friend.

'Can one drink the water, d'you think?' she says.

5 June 1980

Postscript

If you have read this far, you may be a little confused about my personal life. I frequently am, myself. The story so far:

I was born in Egypt in 1936, a twig on the largest English family tree in the Middle East. I grew up in England, went to twelve different schools, including an amazing Swiss school, where they finished me. I lived in Canada for ten years, disguised as an Hungarian Countess, and had ten jobs, including pushing fat women in and out of rubber girdles while dressed up as a reindeer for the Christmas sales.

When I was seventeen, I fell in love with the local vicar, joined the Young Conservatives and roared around to hunt balls with a load of Hooray Henrys in MGs with the roof down. Later, I put away childish things. I am now an atheist and politically rather to the left of Lenin, except on Tuesdays, when I am a fascist.

I have had three husbands—well, not all exactly husbands—and I have three children—well, not all exactly children. I started in journalism writing about mastitis in pigs for an oil company's house organ and eventually joined the *Guardian* in 1968, where I have lived happily every since, doing the odd broadcast, television programme, book and freelance article for the money.

I now live quietly—or noisily, as the case may be—in London with writer Alan Brien and on high days and holidays we discover, to our astonishment, that we have eight children between us, though only two are in permanent residence. I dye my hair red to cover the grey bits and because you never know what might happen next. Anyway, as my step-daughter Jane always says, it's all good for a giggle up the flats.

Index

317

319

320